ABRAHAM LINCOLN AND

WHITE AMERICA

Abraham Lincoln AND White America

Brian R. Dirck

University Press of Kansas

Published by the University Press of Kansas (Lawrence, Kansas
66045), which was organized by the Kansas Board of Regents and is
operated and funded by Emporia State University, Fort Hays State
University, Kansas State University, Pittsburg State University, the
University of Kansas, and Wichita State University

Library of Congress Cataloging-in-Publication Data

Dirck, Brian R., 1965–
Abraham Lincoln and white America / by Brian R. Dirck.
p. cm.
Includes bibliographical references and index.
ISBN 978-0-7006-1827-9 (cloth : acid-free paper)
1. Lincoln, Abraham, 1809–1865—Relations with
African Americans. 2. African Americans—History—To 1863.
3. African Americans—History—1863–1877. 4. Lincoln, Abraham,
1809–1865—Political and social views. 5. Slaves—Emancipation—
United States. 6. United States—Politics and government—
1861–1865. I. Title.
E457.2.D565 2012
973.7092—dc23
2012001796

British Library Cataloguing-in-Publication Data is available.

Printed in the United States of America

10 9 8 7 6 5 4 3 2 1

The paper used in this publication is recycled and contains 30
percent postconsumer waste. It is acid free and meets the minimum
requirements of the American National Standard for Permanence of
Paper for Printed Library Materials Z39.48-1992.

FOR JULIE

Contents

Preface

Most people like Abraham Lincoln. He has his critics, to be sure, and any mature evaluation of his character must include recognition of his entirely human shortcomings, mistakes, and oddities. But on the whole, it is fair to say that the vast majority of Americans, indeed a fair number of people around the world, find Lincoln to be an appealing man—a good guy. He got things right most of the time, and even when he didn't, we generally believe he had his heart in the right place.

This is one reason why people avoid asking hard questions about him. Americans would much rather talk about his triumphs: his rags-to-riches life story, his crusade against slavery in the 1850s, his presidential leadership, and his eventual triumph as savior of the Union and as the Great Emancipator. These are good stories that reflect well upon a good person, and it is easy for Americans to celebrate these stories, over and over again. This is completely understandable. Americans are no more or no less given to lionizing their heroes than any other people.

But it is the sometimes unenviable task of professional historians to probe deeper and darker truths and to ask uncomfortable and even ugly questions about even the best of the men and women of America's past. And there is no darker, uglier area of American history than racism. With all its painful afflictions, racism has shaped America since Europeans first arrived, and it continues to do so today. Would that it were not so. All

Americans of goodwill wish racial prejudice had never stained a nation that otherwise stands for so much that is honorable and just.

But wishful thinking about America's past is at best a distortion and at worst an invitation to perpetuate past mistakes in the present and future. This is no less true when we examine the life and times of our greatest American heroes. If we ignore Abraham Lincoln's mistakes and limitations, we create a blind spot in our historical consciousness not only about a vitally important individual but also about the operations of American history as a whole.

In pursuing this inquiry into Abraham Lincoln and race—specifically, his views concerning whiteness and white racial identity—I found that Lincoln very definitely functioned under a set of limitations where race was concerned. He was in many ways a product of the predominant white culture of his time, and he was far less willing or able to transcend the limitations of that culture than I would have wished. In many respects, he was a typical nineteenth-century American white man, with all the problems and shortcomings this entailed.

Yet at the end of the day, he was still a likable man. He did not, it is true, fundamentally question the underpinnings of white supremacy, along the lines of radical abolitionists such as Theodore Dwight Weld or William Lloyd Garrison. He could have done more to confront white bigotry. And he might well have been capable of transcending the limitations of his whiteness to a greater extent than he did. He was far from perfect, and there were troubling moments in his life during which he seemed to cater to white America's worst instincts.

But after all was said and done, I found that Lincoln's approach to these matters was better than that displayed by most whites of his day. He was a flawed, eminently human, and yet still fundamentally admirable American white man. And perhaps this is where we as Americans should aim when we seek a mature perspective on Abraham Lincoln: critically informed admiration, of the sort that allows us to both celebrate his considerable accomplishments and simultaneously recognize his limitations. This is the only truly honest approach possible.

■
Acknowledgments

I decided long ago that I would make it a point to thank my mentor and friend, the late professor Phillip Paludan, in any book of history that I write. Phil's untimely passing in August 2007 left a hole in many people's lives that is impossible to fill. For my own part, I greatly miss Phil's wisdom, wit, and vast knowledge of the Civil War era. But I draw some comfort in the thought that I was able to benefit from his advice and guidance, and I hope my scholarship reflects well on his tutelage.

Fred Woodward, my editor at the University Press of Kansas, persevered through what was a difficult writing process. I'm afraid I tested his nearly inexhaustible patience on more than one occasion—a fact which causes me no small distress, since he is not only a first-rate editor but also a very nice man. Fred should receive a great deal of credit for anything of value to be found in this book.

More generally, the staff at the University Press of Kansas performed their various editing and publishing tasks to their usual superb standards. Sara Henderson White, Kelly Chrisman Jacques, and Susan Schott ably shepherded the manuscript through the illustration, copyediting, and marketing processes. Gerald Prokopowicz, professor of history at East Carolina University—and a very fine Lincoln and Civil War scholar—acted as peer reviewer for this manuscript, and gave me absolutely indispensable advice and encouragement. They have all saved me from numerous gaffes. Any remaining mistakes are, of course, my responsibility alone.

During the research stages of this project, I was (as always) aided immeasurably by the staff at Anderson University's Nicholson Library. Jan Brewer and Barbara Hoover have always been ready and willing to help. Jill Branscum of the Interlibrary Loan Department brought her expertise to the task of locating the sort of off-beat and obscure materials that delight us historians (but probably drive librarians to distraction).

Having served as a faculty member at Anderson University for over decade, I have come increasingly to appreciate how blessed I am to be part of such a fine institution. I am particularly grateful for the sabbatical leave granted to me in the fall of 2009 to pursue the research and writing of this book. My fellow members of the faculty of the department of history and political science—professors Dan Allen, Michael Frank, David Murphy, Jaye Rogers, and Joel Shrock—are not only fine colleagues but good friends. Blake Janutolo, dean of the College of Science the Humanities, has always been a source of unflagging support and friendship, as have Dr. Marie Morris, vice president of Academic Affairs, and Dr. James Edwards, the university's president. Taken together, my friends and colleagues at Anderson University—and my students—have created a most amiable and positive academic community.

I have likewise benefited from the friendship and support of Doug Nelson and Paula Maris-Roberts, former members of the Anderson University faculty and my boon companions for many a fine Friday afternoon lunch. Jim Leiker, professor of history at Johnson County (Kansas) Community College, read an early draft of this book and gave me invaluable advice. Kristine M. McCusker, professor of history at Middle Tennessee State University has (as always) been a tremendous source of inspiration and friendship.

My mother and father have always been loving and supportive in my career and my life generally. I could have never aspired to the proper pursuit of a college degree, let alone my academic career, without their steadfast love and support.

My mother and father-in-law, Annette and Larry Hutchison, have also been tremendously supportive; they are the most generous people I've ever met. My children and stepchildren—Nathan and Rachel Dirck, Brad, Chris, and Evan Patrick—have been at various times tolerant of the distractions caused by my writing, or (more often) interested observers of the process. They contribute more to the enrichment of my life than they could ever realize. I must also find room to express my gratitude to our cat, Ella. She has been (especially during the daily writing routine of my sabbatical) an endless practitioner of the various feline shenanigans that at times drove me to distraction, chiefly her curious desire to lay across my laptop keyboard at the most inopportune moments.

Finally, I have chosen to dedicate this book to my wife Julie. I often joke that she let herself in for far more trouble than she realized when she married a Lincoln scholar: my endless ramblings about my research and writing, occasional ventures into the fascinating but admittedly sometimes peculiar world of Lincoln aficionados, and tolerance of my traveling and absences while speaking at this or that conference or book panel. I have told her less often than I should just how grateful I am for this and her many other virtues, too numerous to mention. Perhaps placing her name at this book's forefront might begin to make amends.

ABRAHAM LINCOLN AND

WHITE AMERICA

Introduction

Frederick Douglass once called Abraham Lincoln a white man's president, during a speech he delivered in 1876 at the dedication of the Freedmen's Monument in Washington, D.C. His exact words, spoken before a predominantly white crowd, were, "[Lincoln] was preeminently the white man's President, entirely devoted to the welfare of white men."[1]

These were controversial words. But then, the monument itself was controversial. Begun by African Americans (an ex-slave named Charlotte Scott started the project by donating $5 to construct a statue honoring Lincoln) but quickly co-opted by Lincoln's many white admirers, it offered a swirl of the heavily symbolic visual images popular among sculptors during the era, drawn from the nation's recent history, antiquity, or the sometimes shifting whims of the monument's design committee: the Emancipation Proclamation, a whipping post in the background, a profile of George Washington, a shield with an American flag design. The controversy arose from the demeanor of the statue's central figures—Lincoln helping a struggling black man from his knees, having broken his chains through the device of emancipation. To some, this depiction was as it should be, honoring the author of the Emancipation Proclamation. But to others, it was patronizing and demeaning, giving Lincoln too much credit and black people too little for the role they played in bringing about their own liberation.[2]

Douglass's precise purpose in tagging Lincoln as a white man's president in his speech is not entirely clear. At first glance, the label does not seem to have been a compliment. Douglass followed with the tart observation that to Lincoln, black Americans were merely "stepchildren." The president was "entirely devoted to the welfare of white men," he argued, and "he was ready and willing at any time during the first years of his administration to deny, postpone, and sacrifice the rights of humanity in the colored people to promote the welfare of the white people of this country."[3]

Lincoln detractors such as Lerone Bennett make much of Douglass's words as proof positive of Lincoln's fundamentally racist character, but others offer a more balanced assessment. Lincoln scholar Michael Burlingame, for example, points out that in other speeches, Douglass was far more charitable toward Lincoln. And historian Lucas Morel sees the 1876 speech as a shrewd species of racial politics, as Douglass sought to reassure a white audience in those racially charged times that they should support Reconstruction policies as a matter of white self-interest and as a way to honor Lincoln's legacy. A number of scholars suggest that Douglass wanted not so much to demean Lincoln as to elevate the freedmen in the (white) public eye.[4]

That such an extensive and nuanced scholarly conversation could grow around one passage in one speech illustrates the capacity for controversy in nearly all matters related to Abraham Lincoln. But if we clear away all the swirling words, arguments, and ideas, there remains one rather obvious but often overlooked truth in Douglass's speech: Lincoln indeed was a white man's president, in the simple fact that he himself was a white man and a product of nineteenth-century America's white culture. Whiteness defined him, his presidency, and his era.

Oddly enough, historians have rarely explored just what this meant. Lerone Bennett is almost the only scholar who has even tried to explicitly examine Lincoln's relationship with white racism, and his analysis is sadly limited. Bennett's controversial 2000 anti-Lincoln polemic, *Forced into Glory: Abraham Lincoln's White Dream*, though valuable in its provocative call to reexamine Lincoln's racial legacy, is utterly lacking in nuance or sophistication concerning either Lincoln or whiteness. Bennett's arguments are severely limited by their laserlike narrowness. He wants only to prove that Abraham Lincoln hated black people and sought to protect white supremacy. He does not exhibit much interest in trying to figure out exactly what *white* meant in Lincoln's time or what it may have meant to Lincoln himself.[5]

For all the many words that have been written concerning Abraham Lincoln's attitude toward African Americans, almost no one has asked what would seem to be a natural corollary question: how did Lincoln understand white Americans and whiteness? This question has not often been asked because the very concept of analyzing and explaining white as a racial identity, with its own rules and history, is relatively new. What has been termed *whiteness studies* in American history is the product of pioneering work by David R. Roediger, Matthew Frye Jacobson, Noel Ignatiev, and (most recently) Nell Irvin Painter. Most of this scholarship has appeared only since the early 1990s.[6]

A key premise of the new literature on whiteness is central to my approach to Lincoln: that it is impossible to understand the intricate and insidious ways race functions in American society without looking at whiteness as a distinct racial category. To suggest (as has usually been the case) that only nonwhite people are people of color, whereas whites are normatively neutral and colorless by definition, perpetuates the thinking that has made white supremacy so powerful and pernicious a presence in America's history.[7]

Uncovering Lincoln's ideas about whiteness is not easy. Like most other whites in his day, Lincoln rarely thought of himself as possessing a racial color, and he was not given to analyzing what it meant to be white in his America or the nature of race in general. As historian James Oakes rightly observes, "Most of Lincoln's brief utterances on race have lent themselves to extravagantly different interpretations."[8] Any investigation of Lincoln and race will involve caution and qualification. And any investigation of Lincoln and whiteness will involve careful analysis of what he thought about blackness and other racial categories, for it is often only by analyzing what Lincoln thought about blacks that we can draw inferences concerning his ideas about whites.

However difficult getting at Lincoln's ideas about whiteness may be, those ideas were terribly important—perhaps as important as Lincoln's ideas concerning blackness and other nonwhite people. When he formulated political arguments and policies related to African Americans, Lincoln inevitably affected and was affected by issues and problems related to whites and how they perceived both themselves and the nation. And on a more personal level, Abraham Lincoln was himself a white man. He carried within himself the multiple assumptions, prejudices, and limitations of white racial identity that pervaded the culture of his times. He was taught from birth, in a myriad of ways great and small, that as a white American, he belonged to the master race, the top tier of America's racial pyramid. Few people questioned this order of things. Surprisingly few white people were self-aware enough, racially speaking, to perceive how America's pervasive white racist ideology shaped their lives and their destinies. Lincoln swam in this white culture as a fish swims in water.

As obvious as this may seem, it is not a common way of viewing Lincoln. His popular legacy as the Great Emancipator confers upon him a kind of racial neutrality in the popular memory. In our mythology, he is simply a good man and a good American, his skin color be damned, who rose above the muck that is America's sad racial legacy and conferred freedom on millions of slaves in the name of color-blind principles of justice, liberty, and equality. Those principles, we believe, should transcend black and white. Lincoln, we believe, should transcend black and white.

But he does not. He cannot. Abraham Lincoln was not color-blind. Nor was he some sort of translucent racial anomaly, a man with no skin color of consequence. Whiteness shaped him, transformed him, and in some ways severely proscribed what he would or could do in the name of American racial equality.

He has long defied simple answers because he was not a simple man, and he did not live in simple times. Readers looking for a straightforward, linear story arc concerning Lincoln and whiteness will be disappointed. In some respects, he was quite critical of the various ways in which white supremacy operated in his era; in others ways, he was not. He could be extremely critical of whiteness, but he could also take great pains to forgo such criticism. He could sometimes see past the limitations imposed by his white skin. At other times, those limitations severely constrained him.

We will see that there was a broad progression, a growing impatience in Lincoln toward white bigotry, especially during the latter part of the Civil War. This progression roughly paralleled his increased wartime willingness to embrace a black presence in American life and to support a measure of black racial equality. But though of course closely related, the dynamics of Lincoln's white and black racial progress were different. When Douglass observed that Lincoln was the white man's president, he did not pose that as a serious analytical category. But to better understand not just the Lincoln presidency but also the man himself, that is exactly what we should do.

ONE

■

Seven Negroes

Abraham Lincoln's first recorded, face-to-face encounter with people who were not white occurred on a river flatboat, sometime in 1828.[1] He was in all likelihood terrified.

He was nineteen that winter and still working for his father, Thomas, on the family's Indiana farm. He didn't earn much in the way of actual cash, and most (if not all) of what he did earn went into Thomas's pockets. It was a common arrangement among farming families of the day but one that chafed Lincoln, who was fast becoming "ambitious to make his way in the world."[2]

To that end, he hired himself out, sometime in the late fall or early winter of 1828, as a crewman on a flatboat loaded with "hoop poles" (used in the construction of barrels), bacon, and other odds and ends on a river trip from Rockport, Indiana, down the Ohio and Mississippi rivers to New Orleans, Louisiana. His employer was James Gentry, a man of means (the town of Gentryville was named after him) who later purchased the land that encompassed the Lincoln family farm. He was "*the* rich man in our very poor neighborhood," according to Lincoln.[3]

Lincoln's companion on the trip was Allen Gentry, James's son. Gentry was a bit younger than Lincoln, and he had his wild side; he would meet his end years later when in a drunken stupor on a steamboat, he fell overboard and drowned.[4] Between the two of them, Gentry and Lincoln split the various tasks of manning a fully loaded flatboat, either guiding the craft by means of the long steering oar from the stern or plying a sweeping pole to clear driftwood, brush tangles, and other obstacles from the boat's path. The pay was $8 per month, plus the price of passage home once the cargo and raft were sold (flatboats were too unwieldy to transport back upriver).[5]

A typical Ohio River flatboat—variously nicknamed an "Orleans boat," a "Kentucky flat," or a "broadhorn"—was simple and unadorned, basically "a covered shed . . . with a bottom sufficiently strong to contain it." It was constructed near the riverbank from materials easily at hand, such as poplar, gum, or green oak wood, and sealed by driving hemp into the cracks between the boards; the hemp was soaked in "tow" or "oakum," a form of caulking made from tree sap. More elaborate boats were available from professional builders (usually living near river towns), but most farmers made do with their own carpentry skills, since their creations were designed to do little more than float in a straight line with the current while keeping cargo and occupants reasonably safe and dry.[6]

And there were a lot of them. Flatboats crowded the Ohio River and its tributaries throughout the first decades of the nineteenth century. One historian estimated that nine-tenths of Indiana's surplus corn, bacon, hogs, hoop poles, and the like was carried on flatboats downriver for sale, with yearly voyages numbering in the thousands. "I have often passed fifty of them in one day, rowing with their long sweeps or floating leisurely on the current," noted the author of a traveler's guidebook, adding that "this form of navigation is slow, compared with the steamboat, but it is cheap."[7]

Those flatboats were more than just the sum of their wood and oakum parts. There was a thriving flatboating culture along the banks of the Ohio River. Families banded together to form cooperatives, sharing a voyage's risks and profits. Their annual spring flatboat launch (the vessels were nearly always launched in spring, when the poplars used in constructing the gunwales had seasoned properly) was a social event, giving rise to frolics or barn dances near the local river landing; "sometimes half the population of the village was present to tender their wishes for a prosperous trip."[8]

Some men made flatboating a career. "They are a distinct class of beings, livers on the water," noted one observer, "strong, hardy, rough and uncouth." Another described them as an "adventurous, muscular set of men, inured to constant peril and privation."[9] Flatboaters could attain the status of cult heroes, among them Mike Fink, the "legend of the Ohio," a

Bunyanesque giant who was said to be the match in drinking, brawling, and general mayhem of any man on the river.[10]

Lincoln and Gentry weren't flatboaters in the Mike Fink sense, given that their sojourn on the river was temporary. But they were part of a little ritual of their own, whereby young men from isolated farms grew up a little by manning flatboats through the Ohio and Mississippi river regions and seeing something of the world. Lincoln's father hired out for several such trips himself in his younger days, ferrying loads of pork and similar items to markets along the river. Thomas once was compelled to walk all the way back home from New Orleans (making his son's deal for the price of homebound passage probably seem all the sweeter). "The instance of a young man of enterprise and standing, as a merchant, trader, or even farmer, who has not made at least one trip to New Orleans is uncommon," claimed one Indiana man.[11]

This thriving flatboat culture was many things, but underlying it all was one subtle characteristic: it was white. Those enterprising young Hoosier men who made their way to New Orleans and back were white, and the professional flatboatmen were likewise white.[12] Mike Fink, the quintessential flatboatman of history and legend, not only was a white man, but also threw his whiteness into sharp relief by besting whatever nonwhite people he happened upon during his exploits, in ways that white storytellers and wags of the day found highly amusing. According to one tale, Fink at some point saw a black man

> who had the singularly projecting heel, peculiar to some races of Africans. . . . [Whereupon Fink] raised his rifle to his shoulder and fired, carrying away the offensive projection. The negro fell, crying murder, believing himself to be mortally wounded. Mike was apprehended for this trick at St. Louis, and found guilty. But we do not hear of the infliction of any punishment. . . . Mike's only defense was, that the fellow could not wear a genteel boot, and he wanted to fix it so that he could.[13]

Lincoln and Gentry would have been well within their comfort zones, at least racially speaking, as they push-poled their cargo out onto the Ohio River that spring, taking their place among dozens of other boats manned by similar-looking and similar-acting young men. The Indiana counties on the Ohio's right bank were predominantly white, as was the entire state.

Black people were rare. According to the 1810 census, there were only a little over 600 blacks living in the entire Indiana Territory (as opposed to over 23,000 whites). Only 5 African Americans lived in the county surrounding Pigeon Creek ten years later when the Lincolns established their farm. It is hardly surprising, then, that there is no reliable record of an encounter between Lincoln and any nonwhite person while he lived in Indiana.[14]

The state was inhospitable to blacks. In the early days of the territory's existence, a number of Hoosiers, many with Southern roots, tried to persuade Congress to overturn the antislavery provisions of the Northwest Ordinance and allow slavery's introduction into their midst. Failing that, they made Indiana one of the most racially restrictive states in the country, passing legislation that imposed a variety of restrictions on black people crossing its borders. In 1805, the state's legislature created laws declaring that African Americans could not lawfully refuse to enter even lengthy and highly discriminatory indenture contracts with white masters, and in 1806, it imposed harsh punishment such as whipping on slaves who traveled without proper paperwork, participated in large assemblies, or uttered "seditious speeches."[15]

As they floated down the Ohio, Lincoln and Gentry saw on their left the slaveholding land of Kentucky. The dynamic of race there was, of course, substantially different than in Indiana, since there was a palpable difference between owning human beings, on the one hand, and not doing so, on the other. But the differences weren't all that great. If Indiana had its Black Laws, then Kentucky had its slave code. Nonwhites, including Indians and mixed-race Kentuckians, lived under severe and humiliating legal restrictions. For instance, Kentucky law in Lincoln's time provided that "any negro, mulatto, or Indian, bond or free," who "shall at any time lift his hand, in opposition to any white person, shall receive thirty lashes on his or her bare back, well laid on."[16]

Despite Kentucky's much larger African American population, as compared to Indiana's, Lincoln seems not to have come into much contact with black Kentuckians. The family farm at Knob Creek in Kentucky was located near the Natchez Road, and it is possible that as a small child, Lincoln sometimes saw Native Americans as well as black men and women as they traveled by his front door, in chains perhaps, as part of a slave coffle or labor force. A fairly large number of African Americans lived in the Knob Creek area—around 17 percent of the local population, according to one estimate.[17] Still, there is no reliable extant record of Lincoln interacting with any nonwhites while living in Kentucky. At least one neighbor thought it unlikely that he saw many black people at all, telling an interviewer, "I doubt whether the Negro cut much figure here."[18]

White in Kentucky, white in Indiana, white on a flatboat slicing its way between the two—things were pretty much the same all the way around. Here was one way, perhaps the most prevalent way, in which whiteness was defined in Abraham Lincoln's world, as a ubiquitous sameness, a homogeneity so pervasive that often whites themselves were not aware of it as such. This sameness was created, at least in Lincoln's part of the world, by a combination of circumstances: by demographics; by cultural affinity; and if need be by laws, rules, and regulations that kept nonwhites bounded off and away from polite white society. What exactly was "white" in 1828?

It was skin color, of course. But matters were not nearly so simple. White was difficult to pin down, more so than black or red or any other ethnicity, because white was not seen by most white Americans—the people who by and large defined "American"—as an ethnicity. Nonwhite people had ethnicity; *they* were "colored." Whites were "normal," to the point that their whiteness faded into the background. White was everywhere, and therefore, it was nowhere.

If pressed to answer, an American in 1828 would likely have responded that white was a race of some sort—or, rather, races. People of that day did not commonly believe in one homogeneous white race but rather in a collection of subgroups filed under the broad heading of white. Just what separated one category of the white race from another was hard to say. Some intellectuals tried, with limited success, to delineate the precise lines between types of white people. An atlas published two years before Lincoln's flatboat trip, for example, identified two broad families of the white race: one included "the Hebrews, the Druscs and other inhabitants of Mount Libanus . . . [and] the sun-burnt hordes of Northern Africa," and the other encompassed Europeans, Americans, "the Caucasian tribes of Usbeca," and a variety of other eastern European "tribes."[19]

Few ordinary Americans had ever heard of Druscs or Mount Libanus. For most people, whiteness was more about vague associations—the ineffable and often ill-defined links between white and that which was beautiful, desirable, and successful. White was strong like Mike Fink or industrious and enterprising like all those young men making their way down the Ohio River to New Orleans. White was the beauty of a milky-marble Greek statue, of the fair hue of ladies and gentlemen of quality, or of an angel's robes. White was the presumed color of Jesus.[20]

White was also the presumed color of American democracy and citizenship. The Founding Fathers—and most Americans who came after them—associated the liberty and individualism of American citizenship with whiteness. *White* was a common qualifier for the various national and local laws regulating naturalization. "I use the word citizen as not embracing the colored population," stated a delegate to Pennsylvania's 1837 state constitutional convention.[21]

The very words that came from people's mouths or were printed on paper buttressed this valued sense of whiteness. Noah Webster's *Dictionary of the English Language,* published the same year Lincoln took his flatboat trip down the Mississippi, defined *white* as "being in the color of pure snow," as "pure; clean; free from spot; as white robed innocence . . . unblemished," and—following the Bible—as "purified from sin; sanctified." The Bible equated whiteness with a wide variety of positive attributes. It was the color of the manna from heaven that saved Moses and the chosen people (Exodus 16:31), and one of the Psalms declared, "Cleanse me with hyssop, and I will be clean; wash me, and I will be whiter than snow" (Psalm 57:7). Ecclesiastes enjoined godly people to "always be clothed in white, and always anoint your head with oil" (Ecclesiastes 9:7). And the book of Daniel described God as wearing clothing that "was as white as snow" (Daniel 7:9).[22]

In Indiana, Lincoln acquired a copy of James Barclay's popular dictionary of the English language, which would have told him that white was equated with that which was "pure," "unspotted," and "innocent." Thomas Dilworth's *New Guide to the English Tongue* (commonly called *Dilworth's Spelling Book*), which Lincoln carried with him to the various little "ABC" schools he attended off and on as a boy, contained a passage titled "On Youth" about the fragility of purity, admonishing that "White Lilies hang their Heads, and soon decay; and whiter Snow in Minutes melts away." *Pilgrim's Progress,* another book the young Lincoln read, associated white with heaven. "You are going now, said they, to the Paradise of God," read one passage, "and when you come there, you shall have white robes given you, and your walk and talk shall be every day with the King, even all the days of Eternity." *Robinson Crusoe,* also among Lincoln's books, described two native islander women as "well-favored, agreeable persons" who, "had they been perfect white, would have passed for very handsome women, even in London itself."[23]

Slight and understated inferences these were, background details in a life and time when people such as Lincoln were not encouraged to think of whiteness as an ethnicity at all. But they were real enough. Language mirrors thought and vice versa, and there is no reason to think that Abraham Lincoln was immune to this sort of thinking, no evidence setting him apart from the overwhelming majority of his neighbors in Kentucky and Indiana who spoke, thought, and acted as if white entailed all that was good, pure, and superior. Being told on occasion that this or that person was white and then reading and hearing white described as the color of purity, innocence, beauty . . . Lincoln surely made the connections.

The corollary was the opposite of white: those people who were defined in various ways as the nonwhite Other. A community defines itself by setting boundaries, beyond which lie those who do not belong and who are not part of "us." Some devote so much time and energy to this negative act of self-definition that community members understand who they are largely by articulating who they are not.

White America did just that in Lincoln's day. Whites often were not all that aware of their whiteness, and typically, they held no intellectually coherent definition of the word *white* in their heads. But they knew and could usually describe in vivid and sharply distinct terms exactly what a *nigger,* an *Indian savage,* or a *Paddy* was (in an era when most Americans thought of the Irish as a nonwhite and separate race). The very use of the term *black* by whites to denote African Americans was itself a glaringly reductionist example of this sort of thinking, given the fact that most black people were actually nothing of the sort, having skin colors in a wide range of hues. Yet that simple, stark category of blackness was quite efficient and tidy in its rendering of those who did not stand within the boundaries of polite white society.

Part of this was simply a matter of hardwiring. Children categorize at an early age, and they do so based primarily on what they see: skin color, eye color, body type, hairstyle, clothing, mannerisms. Children are also predisposed to favor features that remind them the most of themselves, particularly those that are judged worthy and beautiful by the adults around them, such as white skin.[24] They do all of this instinctively—dividing, subdividing, associating, and disassociating one thing and another, one experience and another, one person and another—in constant negotiation with the world around them.[25]

Lincoln would have been no different from the generations of children who have done so before and since. Like any other child, he would have been susceptible to grouping other children and adults according to categories based upon what he saw and what society told him mattered. By the time he reached young manhood, those categories would have been so firmly embedded in his consciousness that he likely never gave them much critical attention. Race was just such a category. Surely for Lincoln—as for nearly any white person around him—race was a readily available and (by the standards of his day) entirely reasonable and viable means by which to understand and make sense of the world. For white people, the fact that race was configured in ways conferring upon them superiority and power simply made racial categorization all the more appealing.

Consider the Indians. They were a separate and distinct "race" according to white Americans, most of whom alternated between lumping all Native Americans under that one imprecise (and inaccurate) Indian category and identifying different tribes as ethnicities unto themselves: Creeks, Fox, Sac, Cherokees, and so forth. Indians as a race were subjected to many of the same indignities, biases, and discriminations that defined other races in America, such as African Americans. But there were differences. Some whites—Thomas Jefferson, for one—believed in a rough original equality between whites and Indians, before whites outstripped Indians in their development of so-called civilized behavior. Some held out hope that the native "savages" of America could someday be assimilated into white American society, a sentiment not often applied to African Americans.[26]

Indians were often fixed by whites with the label *savage*, a term connoting wildness, non-Christian heathenism, brutality, and a harsh disregard for the value of human life. The Savage was an integral part of the sixteenth-century European mind-set that invented concepts of race in the first place, describing the nonwhite peoples then being discovered in Africa and the New World alike.[27] To the average white American living in Lincoln's time, particularly in the West, *savage* had a more immediate, raw meaning when applied to Indians. According to whites, Indians had recently engaged in barbarous acts—and in their own backyards. In his *Traits of Indian Character,* published in 1836, a self-described expert in the "aborigines of North America" named George Turner asked, "What can be attached to the character of the savage [Indian] man, but the brutality of the forest[?] . . .

Abroad, he is worse than the most ferocious feeder upon man. The brute beast of the forest is satisfied with his meal; savage man requires more: he must first torture—and then feast upon his unhappy victim!"[28]

Lincoln was born in a region known for its violent clashes between white settlers and Indians. Kentuckians harbored a dark heritage of conflicts over land rights, white invasions of tribal hunting grounds, bloody reprisals between whites and Indians, and a general brutality that echoed down through the years. In his time, the image of the Indian was still marked by a fresh smattering of savagery and uncivilized behavior, despite the fact that few Native Americans lived in the immediate vicinity of either Hardin County or Pigeon Creek.

But memories lingered. Hardin County was named after Col. John Hardin, who won his fame and fortune by participating in the Indian wars in Kentucky during the 1790s. John's kinsman William Hardin was celebrated for the harsh skills he employed in fighting Indians. "In warfare he acted on the principle that the only effectual way to subdue the red man was to kill him," noted one admiring observer. Hardin's nickname among Kentucky's settlers was "Indian Bill."[29]

Hardin's exploits took place only a few years before Lincoln was born, and stories of bloody encounters between Indians and whites would have still been floating around in his corner of Kentucky. Residents along Indiana's Pigeon Creek possessed even more recent and vivid memories of Indian hostilities. In 1812—four years before the Lincolns arrived—warriors of the Pottawattamie, Miami, Delaware, and other tribes clashed with white settlers in raids ranging all across Indiana Territory. Stories of Indian cannibalism, kidnapping, and terror abounded, and whether true or not, they fastened upon Indiana's Native American populace an unsavory reputation for atrocity and mayhem.[30]

Lincoln grew up with stories about Indian savagery, starting with one of his favorite books—the classic biography of George Washington written by Mason Locke "Parson" Weems, which as a boy Lincoln read thoroughly "by 'spells' as he could snatch from his daily toil."[31] Biographers have long noted the influence of Weems's biography on Lincoln, as seen in his life-long veneration of Washington and the Founders, his overall patriotism, his desire for self-improvement, his sense of republican virtue, and even the way he wrote the Gettysburg Address.[32]

Nestled among the stories Weems related in his biography (most famously his dubious rendering of Washington chopping down a cherry tree and then forthrightly owning up to the deed) were darker influences: passages recalling the lurid exploits of Native Americans during the French and Indian War. Lincoln read that the "whole country west of the Blue Mountains" in Washington's day was "from time immemorial the gloomy haunt of ravening beasts and murderous savages. No voices had ever broken the awful silence of those dreary woods, save the hiss of rattlesnakes, the shrieks of panthers, [and] the yell of Indians." Similarly, he read that during British general William Braddock's defeat, the Indians allied with the French had attacked, "grimly painted, yelling like furies, burst[ing] from their coverts, eager to glut their hellish rage." Elsewhere, Weems wrote that the Indians were "a great public terror," that one of Washington's good friends was burned at the stake by Native Americans at Sandusky, and that the roads "were filled with thousands of distracted parents, with their weeping little ones," fleeing in "dread of the Indians."[33]

Lincoln heard such stories from his own family. His grandfather (also named Abraham) was killed by Indians. The elder Abraham arrived in Kentucky in 1786, and with his sons, Mordecai, Josiah, and Thomas (Lincoln's father), he carved out a homestead in the woods. While clearing a cornfield, the men were suddenly attacked by Indians. Abraham was killed instantly; his son Mordecai grabbed a rifle and shot an Indian who was about to assault Thomas. "Mordecai said the Indian had a silver half moon trinket on his breast," remembered a relative, "that silver being the mark he shot at. He said it was the prettiest mark he held a rifle on."[34]

The story was told and retold, with embellishments. One cousin's recounting had the Indian grabbing Thomas "by the nap[e] of the neck and seat of the breeches and was running Down a lane with him" until Mordecai shot him dead.[35] It was said that Mordecai felt "an intense hatred of the Indians—a feeling from which he never recovered." He "swore eternal vengeance on all Indians an oath which he faithfully kept as he afterwards during times of profound peace with the Indians killed several of them." Another claimed that Mordecai murdered an Indian who had been passing through his neighborhood and boasted of leaving the body in a sinkhole as a grim means of gaining "satisfaction" for his father's death.[36]

All these tales made quite an impression on Lincoln. "The story of [Grandfather Abraham's] death by the Indians, and of Uncle Mordecai, then fourteen years old, killing one of the Indians, is the legend more strongly than all others imprinted upon my mind and memory," he later wrote. That account, along with the Indian bloodlust in Weems's book and other such stories he surely heard occasionally from neighbors, friends, and playmates, would have etched an image of Native American savagery in his mind—an image of brutality that was sharply at odds with the more civilized conduct of whites. Perhaps even his uncle Mordecai's rage seemed more justified than the random killing of his grandfather, couched as Mordecai's behavior was in the language of honorable revenge and "satisfaction."[37]

That said, Lincoln does not seem to have been afflicted by any sort of deep-seated hatred of Native Americans. In fact, his only direct experience with an actual Indian war, the Black Hawk War of 1832, revealed him to be a young man with more compassion and sympathy for Native Americans than many others of his day.

When Black Hawk, a Sac Indian chieftain, and several hundred followers entered Illinois in April 1832 to reclaim lands they believed were fraudulently taken from them through an earlier treaty, the governor of Illinois called out the state militia to repel them and issued a call for volunteers. Along with hundreds of other young white men, Lincoln joined the militia, and he was elected his company's captain.[38]

By all accounts, the men in his company were a wild bunch, hard young frontiersmen who posed a variety of discipline problems with their drinking, fighting, gambling, and overall reluctance to obey orders they did not like. They also harbored the usual prejudices and biases toward Native Americans, exacerbated by the threat of war and violence that Black Hawk and his followers represented.[39]

Their attitude was made abundantly clear when an elderly Indian stumbled into camp, waving a piece of paper stating that he was a "good and true man." Unimpressed, Lincoln's troops began to grumble that the old man was "a damned spy," adding, "We have come out to fight Indians and we intend to do so." Sensing trouble, Lincoln got between his men and the Indian, preventing any violence and saying, "Men this must not be done—he must not be shot and killed by us."[40]

This anecdote is entirely hearsay, a secondhand account recalled many years after the fact by friends who were not above embellishing their tales. We should allow for the usual coating of romantic mythmaking that routinely surrounded Lincoln's life story following his death in 1865—it is entirely possible that his rescue of the old Indian was greatly exaggerated or perhaps even entirely fabricated. Yet the story accords with multiple accounts depicting Lincoln as a compassionate young man. Moreover, it suggests that he was less inclined toward the more vicious aspects of defining nonwhite Others than were many of his white contemporaries.

By the 1820s, Indians had as often as not been superseded by African Americans, with their corresponding "blackness," as white America's foil of choice. *Webster's* defined *black* variously as "destitute of light," "sullen," "atrociously wicked: horrible," "dismal," and "calamitous." *Dilworth's Spelling Book* lamented "the dark discourse" of "some gay idiot" suffering from an "untutored tongue." And in *Pilgrim's Progress,* "a man black of flesh but covered with a very light Robe" led the pilgrims to what they believed was the Celestial City. But they became lost, and when "the white Robe fell off the black man's back," they saw they had been led astray by "a false Apostle, that hath transformed himself into an Angel of Light."[41]

Weems's *Life of George Washington* matched its depictions of Indians with equally negative characterizations of African Americans. In one passage, the author's imagination had a poor Irishman thanking Washington for meeting with him promptly concerning a land sale. "I do thank you a thousand times," the Irishman declared, "for many a great man would have kept me waiting like a black negro." Elsewhere, Weems conjured up age-old images of the black trickster and buffoon. He described a British officer named Sir Peter who when crossing a river queried his black pilot, Cudjo, "'What water have you got there?'" Cudjo replied, "'What water, massa? what water? why salt water, be sure, sir?—sea water always sea water, an't he, massa?'" To which Sir Peter replied, "'You black rascal, I knew it was salt water. I only wanted to know how much water you have there?'" Cudjo then replied, "'How much water here, massa? God bless me, massa! Where I going get quart pot for measure him?'" "This was right down impudence," Weems wrote, "and Cudjo richly deserved a rope's end for it."[42]

Lincoln would have seen a similar passage in *The American Preceptor,* a primer of speeches and writing selections that he read while living in Indiana.[43] The *Preceptor* contained a dialogue "showing the folly and inconsistency of dueling" between a white gentleman named Mr. Fenton and a black man named Nero. Fenton finds Nero loading a pistol and asks if he intends any mischief. "I only going to fight de duel, as dey call em, with Tom," Nero replies. When Fenton asks why, Nero responds, "He call me neger, neger, once, twice, three time, and I no bear him." After Fenton lectures Nero at length concerning the folly of dueling, including its violation

CHAPTER ONE

of Christian precepts and the fact that Tom is the best shot around, Nero thinks better of the matter and exclaims, "O Masser Fenton, take de pistol fore Nero shoot himself. Let de world call Nero neger, neger, neger; what Nero care?"[44]

As the Bible elevated the concept of white to the level of purity and holiness, it likewise subsumed under the concept of black a variety of sins, impurities, and evils. "My skin is black upon me, and my bones are burned with heat," reads Job 30:30, in reference to Job's suffering. Lamentations 4 describes the accursed state of "the precious sons of Zion," whose "visage is blacker than coal" because of their various transgressions. The second book of Peter, chapter 2, promises that for "false teachers," the "mist of darkness is reserved." The Song of Solomon reassures that "I am black" but comely despite that fact.[45]

There was also the so-called Curse of Ham, which many people directly connected with Africans, African Americans, and black skin. Ham was one of Noah's sons, the father of Canaan, who saw Noah lying naked in a drunken stupor within his tent "and told his two brethren [Shem and Japheth]." Shem and Japheth hurriedly covered their father's shame with a cloth and avoided staring at his nudity. When Noah awoke and learned what Ham had done, he cursed Ham and Canaan. "Cursed be Canaan," reads Genesis 9:25, "a servant of servants shall he be unto his brethren."

White Christians in Lincoln's time commonly held that this Curse of Ham and his descendants was the origin of dark-skinned Africans. Although the Bible itself nowhere states that Ham, Canaan, or any of their descendants had dark skin, ancient Jewish scholars connected the name Ham to the Hebrew words for "dark" and "black." Christian scholars and ministers followed their lead, and by Lincoln's time, established Christian wisdom held that Ham and his lineage were the foundation of Egyptian and African tribes and that the dark-skinned peoples who were from those places deserved their degraded status as part of God's just punishment for Ham's sins.[46]

Of course, race was a matter of more than just black or red skin. Dig a bit and one could find in early America all sorts of unsavory notions about Jews, or Chinese ("Celestials," as they were known), or brown-skinned people from Mexico. Who knows exactly what Lincoln picked up from Thomas (who, according to one neighbor, was especially fond of "Indian stories") or what he overheard in a local general store conversation or from other boys poking around the woods in Pigeon Creek? A "nigger" joke here, a crack about "Sambo" or "Cuffy" or "Paddy" there, a lurid Indian tale or two . . . they floated in the air, thick as germs. Lincoln had no known immunity.

But there were other influences as well. He may have absorbed some antislavery sentiments while growing up in Kentucky. Historians have speculated that Thomas Lincoln was not enamored of slavery and that he left Kentucky because of his antislavery beliefs, speculation fueled by Lincoln himself. He claimed in 1860 that when Thomas moved the family to Indiana, "this removal was partly on account of slavery."[47] A number of biographies have suggested that his father's antislavery motives provided an early foundation for the future Great Emancipator's crusade for freedom and equality.[48]

But Thomas's exact motives for moving to Indiana are difficult to pin down. One neighbor who knew the Lincolns in Kentucky felt that slavery played no role in Thomas's thinking. "I have never heard that Slavery was any Cause of his leaving K[entuck]y," he noted, "and think quite likely it was Not." Lincoln's cousin Dennis Hanks agreed: "It is said in the Biographies that Mr. Lincoln left the State of K[entuck]y because and only because Slavery was there. This is untrue. He moved off to better his Condition." Hanks believed that "Slavery did not operate on him."[49]

Hanks's account should be treated with the requisite amount of caution, coming as it did long after Abraham Lincoln's death. Nor is there any reason to think that, for his part, Lincoln was lying about his father's motives. He himself qualified his statement about Thomas's motives with the word *partly*, indicating the truth probably lies somewhere in between; escaping slavery's influence may well have played some role in shoving Thomas and his family across the Ohio River ("to better his condition" included escaping the skewed labor market that slavery created) but likely not in the form of an outright moral crusade.

Some have also argued that Lincoln picked up antislavery ideas at school and at church. During his brief time in school, he studied from a book called *The Kentucky Preceptor*, which contained among its subjects for student debate the question "Which has the most right to complain, the Indian or the Negro?"[50] In church, two of the Baptist ministers who preached at services attended by the Lincoln family in Kentucky, William Downs and David Elkin, were known to be vocal critics of slavery. Downs was described by one critic as "a disorderly preacher" who introduced a "factious spirit" among Kentucky Baptists by constantly agitating against slavery from his pulpit. Elkin was similarly controversial for his antislavery leanings, as well as his generally slovenly demeanor and (later in life) his habitual drunkenness.[51] Some believe that the two ministers exerted a powerful influence on Lincoln's thinking about slavery while he was still a child. "Even before Abraham could read or write, he learned of the wrongs of slavery by listening to these men of God," one historian has claimed.[52]

Lincoln's early reading habits also exposed him to antislavery sentiments. He likely read a poem by Englishman William Cowper (in a literary compilation called *The English Reader,* which he saw while a boy in Indiana) criticizing the British Empire's complicity in the slave system. He also read in *The Kentucky Preceptor* two selections of antislavery sentiment, "The Desperate Negro" and "Liberty and Slavery," both of which offered passionate arguments against the injustice of human bondage.[53]

But even if we allow the most generous possible interpretation—that the young Lincoln was influenced by his books, his family's antislavery ideas, and his church leaders' antislavery principles—all this says little about their beliefs concerning black people themselves or race in general. *Race* is not *slavery,* and it is naive to think that opposition to the latter necessarily involved a more tolerant perspective on the former.

Slavery, in an odd sort of way, was clearer than race. A boy such as Abraham Lincoln could get slavery handed to him in well-defined images by his ministers or possibly by his father: human beings in shackles, families torn asunder on the auction block, field hands abused while working on the land. Americans with antislavery leanings learned how to use dramatic and clear-cut images to shock and cajole their audiences. Later in life, Lincoln became pretty good at this himself.

But race was different. It was a muddled mix of bits and pieces of ideas, perceptions, assumptions, and half-formed images—shards and nuggets buried in the silt of everyday American life. Those shards, when sifted, billowed up ugly clouds of anxiety and fear. Fear was the foundation of race in Lincoln's America: fear of the "savage," fear of the "nigger," fear of Ham's Curse, fear even of the quasi-comical Neros and Cudjos whose moronic behavior and goofy mannerisms provoked laughter among whites that sometimes had a forced nervousness about it.

A young man such as Lincoln could learn to detest slavery, to think it a backward, immoral, and un-Christian institution. He could be told that slaves were the victims of great injustice, that they hardly deserved their fate, and that the world would be far better off if slavery had never existed.

Seven Negroes 19

Yet the powerful cultural undercurrents of the words *black* and *savage,* the baggage attached to all the unfortunate and ugly things said and written about people in America who weren't white—all of that would still operate on him, as it did on all of white America in his time. Such was the gloomy pervasiveness of race in Lincoln's age.

VETERAN FLATBOATERS said they could see the exact place where the Ohio River collided with the mighty Mississippi. It was a matter of color. The Mississippi River, the "father of waters," had a more brownish, muddy hue due to its swift currents that constantly stirred the mud beneath. The flatboaters said you could literally see the line in the water demarcating the two rivers and know precisely the moment when you crossed from the Ohio to the mighty Mississippi.

Lincoln and Gentry's flatboat crossed that line and bobbed out into the Mississippi near Cairo, Illinois, probably sometime in the late summer of 1828. They made the big left turn and headed south—to the Deep South, with slave soil on both sides. Lincoln was now entering completely unfamiliar territory.

They would have stopped often, for there were frequent landings along the river where they could sell their wares or dock at nightfall to cook and sleep.[54] As they did so, their odds of running into people who were not white steadily increased, both onshore and out on the river itself. But *colored* carried a different connotation in this region, particularly as the flatboat floated deeper into Louisiana. No longer was Lincoln plying predominantly white waters, with relatively few blacks and even fewer people of different ethnicities. What he instinctively thought of as white was mixed in Louisiana with Creole and its various combinations of white, black, Indian, and possibly Spanish and French blood. He might also have discovered that *colored* and *Negro* carried different meanings in Louisiana. The two terms were used more or less interchangeably in Kentucky and Illinois, denoting simply a black person. But in Louisiana, *colored* meant any person with a mixture of black and some other ethnicity, whereas *Negro* was used almost exclusively to label a person of pure African descent.[55]

The river itself would also have been peppered with a different sort of racial mixture. Lincoln and Gentry likely crossed paths with crews of African American slaves who manned boats loaded with cotton—nicknamed "cotton boxes" because of their high sideboards—or other staples. Flatboats near slaveholding and slave-trading states also sometimes sported African Americans not as crew but as cargo, either being shipped downriver for sale at some distant slave market or accompanying a white master. Lincoln may have glimpsed his first slave coffle on a passing flatboat, hauling away human beings as if they were so many hoop poles or barrels of pork.[56]

At some point, the two young men entered what was known as the Sugar Coast region of Louisiana. Stretching just north of Baton Rouge and extending along the Mississippi River on both banks to New Orleans and the Gulf of Mexico, the Sugar Coast boasted some of the largest plantations in the entire nation. The plantations were typically situated between the river coast and the swamplands a few miles back, with necessary drainage and flood control provided by complex systems of levees that required constant, diligent maintenance. Lincoln and Gentry would have seen long networks of cross-ditches, interspersed between fields of sugarcane, occasionally mixed with a bit of cotton, corn, wheat, and indigo.[57]

Those levees and ditches were raised, dug, cleaned, and continuously cleared of their brackish (and potentially deadly) water by black hands. Sugar production as a whole was intimately connected with slavery, as it had been for centuries. Black men and women—and often young boys and girls—worked the cane fields in an endless cycle of year-round labor, from weaving cane mats to protect the sugar seeds in the winter, to the backbreaking process of harvesting the cane crop in the summer, to the fall preparation of the following year's seedlings, then back again. If they arrived in the late summer or early fall, Lincoln and Gentry might have seen pillars of smoke rising through the skies and smelled the acrid, sweet stench of "boiling season," when slaves were engaged in the grueling work of boiling down the sugar crop.[58]

Life for a slave on the Sugar Coast was cruel. Black men were sent into the swamps to collect fuel for the sugar-boiling fires, which necessarily exposed them to malaria, yellow fever, and other deadly diseases. Black women were usually used for the "lighter" tasks of tending the boiling fires themselves—hot, sweaty, and exhausting work, especially in the fetid Louisiana climate. Sugar planters and their overseers often drove their labor force mercilessly, especially during the harvest and boiling seasons when the pressures of time and profit were intense—the sugar had to be harvested and processed before cold weather arrived. "The planters generally declared . . . that they were *obliged* to over-work their slaves during the sugar-making season, (from eight to ten weeks) so as to *use them up* in

Seven Negroes

21

seven or eight years," wrote an appalled Northerner upon a trip through the region. Some planters coldly calculated that they could turn a better profit by overworking and "using up" a labor force in a short period of time and replacing the lot, rather than working them more lightly and being obliged to feed and clothe them for a longer period.[59]

Even aside from the high mortality rate among plantation slaves, life was cheap on the Sugar Coast; the area had an ugly reputation. Pirates and brigands had been an ongoing problem since the eighteenth century, and roaming bands of thieves and ne'er-do-wells, of all colors, preyed upon unwary river travelers. "Murder and Plunder are already too common," complained a man living in Rapide Parish. A congressman from the Mississippi side of the river agreed: "It has become the great thoroughfare of crime and vice as well as of wealth and enterprise; villains of every description, outlaws from other States, refugees from justice, thieves, robbers, and banditti of all sorts are continually floating upon its currents."[60]

Lincoln and Gentry slowly made their way south through this land. Lincoln later wrote that the "nature part of the cargo load . . . made it necessary for them to linger and trade along the Sugar coast."[61] Exactly what he meant by this was unclear. Maybe he and Gentry felt that their load of hoop poles would find a ready market among the sugar planters who were constructing hogshead barrels to hold the sugar and molasses they were in the process of harvesting and boiling down. Whatever Lincoln and Gentry's purpose, their lingering in the area meant that their presence would have become well-known to the locals—not all of them friendly.

They passed through Concordia Parish, perhaps stopping in the town of Concordia itself, across the river from Natchez, Mississippi. Then they moved past Point Coupe and Baton Rouge; through Iberville Parish; and, just beyond a slight southwestward dip of the river, through Ascension Parish. New Orleans was not far off—only some 20 or 30 miles away.[62]

A few miles into Ascension Parish, they saw on their left the Houmas plantation, named for the Houmas Indians who had sold the place to white settlers at the end of the eighteenth century. By Lincoln's time, Houmas was owned in absentia by Wade Hampton, Virginia congressman and grandfather of the future Confederate general Wade Hampton III. Today, it is a tourist attraction, marketing its moonlight-and-magnolias ambience as an appropriate setting for weddings and special events of all occasions.[63] But in 1828, it was a no-nonsense sugar-production facility with a substantial labor force of slaves and a simple, altogether unromantic four-room, frame main house (where the more grandiose mansion standing on the site today would eventually be built). A hard little world, this Houmas plantation, with its sugar mill and boiling house, its humid and disease-infested sugar brakes, its endless hours of backbreaking work—for the dark-skinned backs, anyway—its slave quarters, and no doubt its whipping posts.

Lincoln and Gentry apparently floated into the Houmas plantation's general vicinity near the end of the day, and as the sun set, they searched for a place to spend the night. We do not know exactly where they ultimately landed. Some later said it was close to the Houmas plantation proper, but others placed the landing site closer to a plantation owned by a Madame Duchesne—possibly Phillippa Rose Duchesne, a Catholic nun who had established missionary facilities in the area a few years earlier in order to work with the local Creole and Indian populations.[64]

Wherever they landed, they cooked their dinner and bedded down for the evening. Lincoln slept in the flatboat's cabin. Perhaps Gentry did so as well, though if both of them decided to sleep without setting any kind of watch—traveling as they were in a strange and dangerous land—they committed an egregious lapse of judgment and common sense that nearly cost them their lives.

Sometime around midnight, their boat was boarded by seven African American men. They were armed with makeshift clubs, and according to Lincoln, they rushed the flatboat "with the intent to kill and rob" the two young Hoosiers.[65] Hearing a commotion—splashing water, maybe voices, and the loud stomp of feet on the raw oak deck—Gentry yelled to Lincoln inside the cabin. Lincoln scrambled up and staggered sleepily to the cabin's door, probably not entirely certain what was happening. As he emerged, one of the thieves swung a sharpened fence stake at his head. The stake hit Lincoln, who would carry the scar for the rest of his life. But it also glanced off some part of the cabin's upper structure, maybe the roof overhang, deflecting the force of what might otherwise have been a fatal blow.[66]

The next few seconds must have been a confused blur. Lincoln and Gentry ran from whichever part of the boat the thieves boarded. There likely wasn't much light, so neither they nor the thieves could see too clearly, a situation Lincoln and Gentry used to their advantage. As they ducked out of sight—in the cabin, perhaps, or behind cargo piled on the deck—Gentry shouted, "Lincoln, get the guns and shoot!" They had no guns, but the thieves fell for the ruse and beat a hasty retreat back into the night darkness.

Who were the thieves? We can only guess. Possibly they were slaves from the Houmas plantation or some other plantation in the area, on the prowl after dark to augment what little their masters gave them with whatever they could steal along the river. They may have been runaways, eking out a shaky existence in the Louisiana swamplands, dodging slave patrols, and stealing to survive. Or perhaps they were free African Americans, living not so different an existence than runaways, forever marginalized at the fringes of Louisiana society, and likewise making do with whatever they could take.

Lincoln and Gentry didn't know, either. They were understandably rattled, staring out into the Louisiana night and wondering if the gang might regroup for another assault on their boat, potentially with reinforcements. Traveling on the Mississippi River at night was difficult and perilous, the inky blackness of the night sky and the water hiding all sorts of dangers: floating driftwood, snags, sandbars, and other boats. But Lincoln and Gentry's fear of the thieves surpassed their fear of the dark. As Lincoln later wrote, they "'cut cable,' 'weighed anchor' and left."[67]

He recounted this story in an autobiography he gave to Chicago publisher John L. Scripps, who had requested a sketch of Lincoln's life as the basis of a biography he would publish of the Republicans' presidential candidate for the 1860 campaign. Lincoln responded with a 3,200-word document, the most comprehensive autobiography he ever wrote.

Lincoln related the story of the flatboat assault in considerable detail, sandwiched among various anecdotes that seem designed by him to establish his bona fides as a pioneer boy made good (which had become a substantial feature of his political image). He wanted to paint an image of himself as a young man who overcame hardships on America's primitive and hazardous frontier, highlighting his want of education, an incident when he was ten and "was kicked by a horse, and apparently killed for a time," and then the flatboat trip.

In his account, the assailants were identified merely as "seven negroes with intent to kill and rob them." (Lincoln wrote the account in the third person.) There was no apparent malice or latent fear in his language. Yet he did not write "seven men" or "seven thieves." They were "seven negroes," the fact of their blackness apparently adding just a bit more of an edge to the tale—more so, perhaps, than if they had been white or an unidentified neutral color.[68]

T W O

■

White Trash

Lincoln's second recorded encounter with African Americans occurred three years later. He was once again traveling down the Mississippi River to New Orleans, and he was once again a crewman aboard a flatboat. This time, Lincoln's embarkation point was Illinois, where he and his family had lived for a little over a year on a small farm near the town of Decatur.

They moved to Illinois when his father's periodic restlessness resurfaced in Indiana. Thomas Lincoln had done fairly well for himself as small farmers go, having under cultivation 40 acres of land and about $500 worth of cattle, hogs, corn, and other goods. But Thomas received letters from his cousin John Hanks, who had recently moved to Illinois and sent back glowing reports of the riches to be had in that area. And so, Thomas and his family picked up stakes yet again.[1]

Hanks was Abraham Lincoln's second cousin, related to his mother, Nancy. Seven years older than Abraham, he lived with the Lincolns in Indiana, sharing chores, stories, and jokes with Abraham.[2] Cousin John was a rather talkative, gregarious sort, with the wanderer's streak so common among his family and friends. He ambled from Kentucky to Indiana and back again during Lincoln's boyhood years, eventually heading for Illinois permanently, where he lit Thomas Lincoln's imagination with descriptions of the Illinois prairie.[3]

Among the settlers in the Decatur area was a man with the unlikely name of Denton Offutt. Offutt was a curious character, a braggart loud and brash who was full of ideas about how to get rich quick, none of which were particularly well conceived or executed. He was "a gassy, windy, brain rattling man," an "unsteady, noisy, fussy" sort, "wild and un-providential."[4]

But if Denton Offutt wasn't rich, he was at least ambitious, trying to get ahead by shooting as many arrows into the air as possible, hoping one at least would land on target and turn him a profit. He had a half dozen proj-ects going simultaneously, among them a local mill and a general store (where Lincoln would eventually clerk) and later an impromptu veterinary and horse-training service. Offutt claimed to have special knowledge of an-imal physiology and also "to have a secret to whisper in the horse's ear . . . by which the most refractory and vicious horses could be gentled."[5]

He also had his eye on the profits to be made in riverboat traffic. He gathered a collection of the usual flatboating odds and ends—bacon, pork, corn, and a bevy of live hogs—that he thought might be sold at a profit along the Sangamon and Mississippi rivers. Offutt heard good things about John Hanks's boat-handling skills and enlisted him to run a flatboat.

Hanks was game, but he needed help. He turned to Lincoln and his stepbrother, John Johnston, and introduced them both to Offutt. They all struck a deal to take the boat to New Orleans. The original idea was for the men to head down the Mississippi, sell their cargo, winter in New Or-leans earning money by "Cut[ting] Cord Wood," and then return north.[6]

Hanks and Lincoln set out by canoe down the Sangamon River in March as the weather turned warmer, thinking to rendezvous with John-ston at a place called Spring Creek, where Offutt arranged for the delivery of a boat. That deal went awry, however, for there was no boat to be found when Hanks and Lincoln arrived. They went looking for Offutt and found him in a nearby place called Elliot's Tavern (adorned by a sign with a large deer, which "the boys one night shot . . . full of bullet holes [so that] he looked as if he ought to be dead").[7] Offutt was "disappointed" at the news of the wayward boat project, the upshot of which was that Lincoln and his fellow crewmen now became boatbuilders, at a salary of $12 per month.[8]

Building the boat was backbreaking labor. The men cut trees along Spring Creek—or, to be more accurate, they poached the trees, felling them on what Hanks later admitted was federal property—and then "rafted" the timber, using their canoe, down to the embarkation point along the

Sangamon River. They sawed the trees into planks at a local mill and fash-ioned what eventually became a substantial vessel—80 feet long and 18 feet wide. Meantime, they erected a shanty near the work site as a tempo-rary shelter and pressed Lincoln into service as a cook, the culinary results of which can only be imagined.[9]

The crew poled their boat into the Sangamon River sometime early in April. Almost immediately, they ran into trouble. The river wasn't always fully navigable, even for a flatboat, and there were numerous obstructions, both natural and man-made. Near the village of New Salem, the flatboat stuck fast on a mill dam. After a day or so of trying in vain to dislodge the thing, Lincoln found an ingenious solution by boring a hole in one end of the boat—thus allowing water to flood through and weigh it down—and simultaneously lightening the cargo at the other end, tilting the boat up and over the dam.[10]

More troublesome were the hogs. They were carrying a few of the ani-mals onboard when they stuck on the mill dam; those hogs weren't much of a problem. But in New Salem, Offutt purchased thirty more irascible, "large, fat, live" hogs from a local farmer. These new additions absolutely refused to be loaded onto the flatboat. The crew tried to drive them down to the river but couldn't and finally ended up returning them to their pen.[11]

Offutt then conceived "the whim" (Lincoln's words) of sewing their eyes shut, thinking the beasts would be more manageable if they couldn't see where they were going.[12] Lincoln was too queasy to perform this dis-agreeable task himself. "I can't sew the eyes up," he confessed to his com-patriots, though he was able to hold their heads while Offutt did the deed.[13]

Unfortunately, Offutt's horse-whispering genius, such as it was, did not extend to swine. The blinded hogs were even trickier to handle and all the more upset. "In their blind condition they could not be driven out of the lot or field they were in," Lincoln later remembered. In the end, the men were compelled to tie the hogs into carts and wheel them helter-skelter down to the boat.[14]

The entire rig—flatboat, hogs (blind or otherwise), corn, and all—was quite a sight. "We used plank as sails and cloth sometimes [and] people came out and laughed at us," Hanks recalled. They slept on the boat at night and ate their meals onboard as well. In this fashion, they made their way through Illinois and then out onto the broad highway of the Missis-sippi, past Cairo, Memphis, Vicksburg, and Natchez, retracing the journey

Lincoln had made a few years earlier. They probably passed the site along the Sugar Coast where he and Gentry were assaulted by those African American thieves. Nothing of the sort occurred this time, though, and after the incidents with the dam and the hogs, the trip was entirely uneventful. "There is nothing worthy of being known going down the river," Hanks claimed.[15]

As they angled south and a bit east, following the boot-shaped "toe" of Louisiana into the more congested river traffic on the outskirts of New Orleans, they must have been struck by the rapid increase in river traffic. Boats and vessels of all shapes and sizes fed into the lower Mississippi as it approached the Crescent City and the Gulf of Mexico. In 1816, over 1,200 flatboats landed in the city; by the mid-1840s, the number had more than doubled. "Hundreds of long, narrow, black, dirty-looking, crocodile like rafts lie sluggishly without moorings . . . and pour out their contents upon the quay" was how one onlooker described the scene. "Here is a boat stowed with apples, inferior enough in quality, cider, cheese, potatoes, butter, chickens, lard, hay . . . pork, alive, in bulk, in barrels, fresh, salted, smoked, of all sizes and conditions." Lincoln and his crew would have blended right in.[16]

Or at least they would have been entirely unremarkable in terms of their cargo and occupation—theirs was just another flatboat from the Ohio Valley area. But as white men, they were (for once) not necessarily part of the dominant majority. New Orleans was one of the few locales in antebellum America where this was so.

Brown-skinned people were everywhere, constituting nearly half of the city's population. Slavery was of course the predominant context for their lives, hovering over them like a thunderstorm that never went away. Maybe Lincoln saw one of the work crews of African American slaves employed to clear obstacles on the Mississippi River's approaches to the city. Or perhaps he saw enslaved laborers on the city's docks, sweating and grunting under the hot Louisiana sun as they off-loaded cargo. Slaves ran errands for their masters, and they were used as domestics, entertainers, skilled artisans, and laborers of all kinds.[17]

But New Orleans was much more of a racial kaleidoscope than the traditional black-and-white, slave-or-free divide suggests. There was the city's Creole population, "persons of pure white race, without any admixture of Indian or African blood," but with varying degrees of Spanish or French ancestry, cultural background, and customs. The city also hosted a substantial population of free blacks, numbering perhaps 10,000 or so, ranging from persons with pure African blood to mulattoes, "meztisoes," and "quadroons," the latter described by one visitor as a class of persons "with the smallest mixture of African blood."[18]

No one knows how much of this cultural and racial bazaar Lincoln witnessed. Nor do we know the exact length of his stay in New Orleans or which parts of the city he visited. Only two accounts exist concerning this trip, one by Hanks. Relating the tale to an interviewer shortly after Lincoln's death, Hanks offered few details about the New Orleans visit. But he did recall that at some point during their sojourn, they saw firsthand a group of "Negroes Chained—maltreated—whipt [sic] and scourged." The precise circumstances are unknown, but according to Hanks, the sight profoundly affected Lincoln. "His heart bled," Hanks claimed. Lincoln "said nothing much—was silent from feeling [and] was sad." Warming to the subject, Hanks embellished the story. "I can say knowingly that it was on this trip that he formed his opinions of slavery." He believed "it ran its iron in him then and there . . . I have heard him say [so] often and often." The crew also witnessed a slave auction involving a mulatto girl. Lincoln was supposedly moved to say to his companions, "By God, boys, let's get away from this. If ever I get a chance to hit that thing, I'll hit it hard."[19]

The Hanks story is a dramatic moment—melodramatic, actually, conjuring up a grim-faced young Lincoln, his destiny years in the future to "hit it hard," against all odds, from the White House. In his reconstruction, Hanks knew full well that he was channeling the future Great Emancipator by suggesting not only that Lincoln's antislavery, antiracist roots ran deep but also that he, John Hanks, was present at the moment the seed was planted for emancipation, when slavery "ran its iron in him."

But did this actually happen? Lincoln surely saw slaves in the city of New Orleans, not only in 1831 but also during his first visit with Allen Gentry three years earlier. He was likely taken aback by the sight of humans being bought and sold in the streets and the city's auction houses, which were ubiquitous and a fundamental aspect of the city's economy. Other visitors were shocked by the spectacle of a slave auction, and there were slave coffles aplenty in the city's streets. Lincoln himself later wrote that he witnessed some sort of poignant scene involving slaves "every time I touch[ed] the Ohio [River] or any other slave-border."[20]

But as to the precise circumstances of this second flatboat journey, Hanks's account is highly suspect because it does not square with the other

extant account—Abraham Lincoln's 1860 campaign autobiography. According to Lincoln, his cousin left the flatboat long before it arrived at its final destination. Hanks "had not gone to New Orleans," Lincoln wrote,
"but having a family, and being likely to be detained from home longer than
at first expected, had turned back from St. Louis." There is no reason to
doubt Lincoln's memory or veracity in this regard, and Hanks was given to
exaggeration as well as fogginess concerning details. Most Lincoln biographers accordingly treat Hanks's tale with caution or ignore it altogether.[21]

Still, there is a fundamental truth about Lincoln and race contained
within this second flatboat trip. It lies not in Hanks's hackneyed, mythical
encounter between Lincoln and a coffle of slaves in New Orleans. It lies instead in the realm of Lincoln's whiteness, not the slaves' blackness. And if
Lincoln's first flatboat encounter with race illustrated the extent to which
whiteness created its own sense of superiority via the exclusion of nonwhite Others, this second flatboat trip usefully demonstrated how whiteness in Lincoln's day carried its own peculiar internal set of fears and
anxieties.

A FEW YEARS AGO, British writer Jan Morris, after visiting the region of
Lincoln's boyhood and youth, wrote that the place might rightly be characterized as a "white trash homeland." "In my own mind," Morris stated,
the present-day region of Lincoln's roots is "exemplified . . . by hugely bul-
bous young mothers in trousers smoking cigarettes, by the peculiar stale
smell of downmarket hotel rooms, by junk food of awful nutrition, by
trailers parked in messy woodlands, by dubious evangelical preachers and
six-packs of tasteless beer and abandoned cars with grass growing over
them and TV game shows and lugubrious country and western theme mu-
sic thumping out of pickup trucks."[22]

This was an unfair characterization, to be sure, made all the more grat-
ing in that it appeared in what was really a poorly written book about
Abraham Lincoln. Morris can justifiably be criticized for engaging in vast
oversimplification and more than a bit of elitist snobbery where late twen-
tieth-century America is concerned.[23]

But on the subject of Lincoln himself, Morris's assessment was not
unique. Woodrow Wilson once observed that "Abraham Lincoln came of
the most unpromising stock on the continent, the 'poor white trash' of the
South." Famed African American scholar W. E. B. DuBois likewise believed Lincoln's "taste was educated in the gutter. In his taste, education,

and prejudices, he was 'poor white trash,' and yet he became Abraham Lincoln."[24]

Wilson and DuBois—and maybe even Jan Morris—were on to something. The point is not whether Lincoln and his family were in fact white trash.[25] Rather, it is whether Lincoln worried about being perceived as something akin to white trash and how such fears shaped his early adult life.

Modern Americans find something appealing and endearing in the rustic roughness of Lincoln's early life. There is a whiff of that irrepressible American democratic style and rags-to-riches mythology hovering about the young Lincoln as he push-poles his way down the river, ponders and then solves the problem of his stranded boat with the so-stupid-it's-brilliant idea of drilling a hole in the deck, and earns a few dollars the hard way by ferrying a richer man's goods down the Mississippi River. And the details? Lincoln's goofy appearance, Denton Offutt's hickish name and antics, the tavern with its set of shabby deer's antlers, hogs with their eyes sewn shut, people guffawing at the entire spectacle—it is all window dressing for what legend tells us is an all-American tale.

We don't attach anything shameful to these scenes, and it rarely occurs to anyone that they might have something to do with race. Again, since everybody in the story is white, no one is white. But among those laughing onlookers standing on the banks of the Sangamon River and watching a then-anonymous Abraham Lincoln and his equally nondescript compatriots make their way down the river, perhaps at least one thought them a "poor species of white trash."

The label *white trash* had its origins in Lincoln's own time. The term was primarily Southern, at least at first. One theory has it originating among African American slaves in the early 1830s, as an insult describing disreputable whites in their midst. Mary Lincoln's niece Katherine Helm described a Todd family slave named Nelson who voiced his disapproval when young Mary and her sister Elizabeth ran into the streets of Lexington to shake hands with a drunken white man claiming to have known the Todd family hero, Henry Clay. Nelson was "scandalized" and scolded the little girls for "shaking hands with every po' white trash dey meets on de road."[26]

Another theory holds that the term was born in Baltimore in the 1820s, applied to the unskilled white laborers who competed for jobs in the city; there is also a reference to white trash in an 1824 fictional story about life in Washington, D.C.[27] Harriet Beecher Stowe claimed that the phrase had a very specific usage in the slave South, describing "a tribe of keepers of small groggeries, and dealers, by a kind of contraband trade, with the negroes in the stolen produce of plantations." One neighbor of the Lincoln family, George Balch, sneeringly characterized Thomas Lincoln as "an excellent species of white trash."[28]

There were also different versions of *white trash* in Lincoln's time, labels that conveyed the same message without quite the same language. John Russell Bartlett's 1859 edition of *The Dictionary of Americanisms* listed under *poor white folks* the variants *Mean Whites* and *Poor White Trash*. An 1860 study of the South listed *Squatters, Ragtag[s],* and *Bob-tail[s]* as different versions of *poor whites,* depending upon the particular region.[29]

Cracker was another label for poor Southern whites. Its origin is not entirely clear, but references tying the term to poor rural white people can be found as far back as 1836, and they were scattered in journals and books throughout the 1840s and 1850s. In 1857, for example, Frederick Law Olmsted wrote of "'Cracker girls' (poor whites from the country)" being employed in cotton mills, and in 1859, Virginian Edward A. Pollard used *cracker* to describe "the poor, needy, and unsophisticated whites, who form a terribly large proportion of the population of the South." The abolitionist Cassius Clay also used a variant of *cracker* to describe poor whites from Lincoln's home state of Kentucky, writing of "a corn-cracker from Kentucky" whom he placed on a par with "a poor miserable drunken vagabond."[30]

Northerners had their own versions. Some Missourians referred to the poorer people in their midst, especially those who were from the South, as *pukes*. Missouri puke carried much the same baggage as white trash—being described as lazy, "degenerate," and given to uncouth habits such as tobacco-spitting and excessive alcohol consumption. They were "filthy, shiftless, debauched and lawless," according to one observer, and had used the comparative lawlessness of Missouri's frontier to give their worst impulses full rein. "As a class, they were cowardly," it was said, and they were "merciless to the defenseless or helpless, whether man or brute. . . . They were, without doubt, the most desperate and depraved specimens of humanity within the borders of the Republic—the very jackals of the human race."[31]

The Irish came in for their fair share of abuse as well in the days before they had successfully transitioned to white. *Paddy* was as much a loaded epithet as *puke* in some parts of the country, carrying with it assumptions about excessive Irish drinking habits, slovenly lifestyles, and a general inability to ever fully integrate with mainstream Anglo-American culture. The tremendous influx of Irish immigrants during the early decades of the nineteenth century fueled fears of an unwanted Irish and Catholic influence in American politics and culture.[32]

The crisscrossing currents of Irishness, blackness, and whiteness were sometimes dizzying in their oddity. Mary Lincoln's sister recalled the attitude of their African American slave cook, Chaney, toward the Irish servants whom Mary hired as cooks in Springfield: "Old Chaney was grieved that 'Miss Mary didn't have no beaten biscuits at home because the po' white trash Irish didn't even know how to make good co'n bread.'"[33]

White trash, puke, cracker, or some variant thereof became part of the American lexicon roughly during Abraham Lincoln's time. All generally signified a loose grouping of lower-class, light-skinned people who were thought to possess common, pseudoethnic traits.

There was, first and foremost, the association of white trash with poverty, of a sort so extreme that it placed its white victims in the same general neighborhood with African Americans. "Both the negroes and the poor white trash are the serfs" in America, thought one observer. *Poor* (sometimes shorthanded to *po*) was commonly prefixed to *white trash,* and every variant of that term suggested a lack of money and means. "Money, in truth, is almost a perfectly unknown commodity in their midst," observed one supposed expert on white trash Americans, "and nearly all of their trafficking is carried on by means of barter alone."[34]

Such primitivism and poverty meant a great deal in a time when people commonly believed that the poor suffered because of their own inherent moral failings, rather than bad luck or the heartless mechanisms of the economy. In this vein, white trash Americans weren't simply victims of circumstance; they were lazy. They were "no count" and "shiftless," were said to believe that "honest labour is a disgrace," and were wallowing in ignorance. "It gives but a poor description of the 'poor white trash' to say that they cannot read," wrote one correspondent to the *Atlantic Monthly.* Another writer described the poor white "clay-eaters" and "Sand-hill people" of the South as being "commonly as immoral as they are ignorant . . . [and] without schools, and very nearly without any instruction at all."[35]

Their general poverty led to all sorts of low and disgusting habits, it was said. "This wretched class," sniffed one contemporary observer, was "too proud to do such work as is done by slaves, too ignorant and shiftless for anything higher, [and] getting a poor subsistence by thieving and poaching." Another summed matters up neatly: "They are too proud to dig, but they are not ashamed to beg." A third observer, writing of "po' white trash" in 1818, contended that the "most characteristic vice of the class referred to is pilfering" due not just to their straitened economic circumstances but also to their lack of moral judgment.[36]

Being white trash entailed cultural oddities of dress, mannerisms, and style. This was largely a function of the individuals' extreme poverty, but it was also thought that poor whites were afflicted with a basic lack of judgment concerning proper manners and day-to-day social relationships. They were described as crude or sometimes "mean," implying a smallness of mind in their dealings with others. "Of all the pizen critters that I knows on, these-ere mean white trash is the pizenest," one of the characters exclaims in Harriet Beecher Stowe's novel *Dred; A Tale of the Great Dismal Swamp*. "They ain't got no manners and no bringing up." This indictment especially included the consumption of alcohol. Poor whites were (like Missouri's pukes and Irish Paddies) commonly thought to be fond of hard liquor. "The height of their ambition," claimed one person, "is to get an old horse and a pair of wheels, with corn-husk collars and rope reins, by which they may obtain sufficient money to buy a quart of whiskey."[37]

Low-class whites also possessed suspect family trees. White trash carried an odor of hereditary illegitimacy: the familiar old stereotype of lower-class whites' inbreeding, "marrying cousins," and behavior of that sort. "Many of them—owing, no doubt, to their custom of intermarrying—are deformed and apparently idiotic," stated one observer. An English writer believed that the "crackers" and "Sandhillers" were defined by the fact that, among other things, "the females of the class are all but universally unchaste."[38]

Much of this rhetoric shared a common frontier with the rhetoric about deficiencies allegedly present in other racial and ethnic groups. Writers who described white trash behavior in Lincoln's time often did so by way of direct comparison with black people and Indians. "The civilized life of the White Trash is lower than that of the Indians," said one Northerner. Similar themes ran through the racial stereotypes of black people—lack of sexual control, poor breeding and manners—and white trash, to the point that the precise distinctions between the two groups could nearly disappear.[39]

Nearly, but not quite. White trash was not black trash or Indian trash. Appending that term *white* to *poor* and *trash* was a way of racializing poverty, giving to those who were poor a quasi-ethnic identity that compromised their claims to white racial purity by placing them down among the dark-skinned denizens of depravity and ignorance that inhabited the American imagination. There was a common assumption that well-behaved blacks should look down on the poor whites in their midst. A typical passage in an 1857 issue of *Ballou's Monthly Magazine*, for instance, told of a black servant named Jane "who, like most of her class, had a decided aversion to 'poor white trash.'" Novelist Francis Colburn Adams had a character from the South named Mr. Snivel state that "our colored population view these [poor white] people with no very good opinion, when they get down in the world." Another writer's African American slave character exclaimed, "Wouldn't mind so bad gwine to a good [white] family—but I ain't gwine to live with white trash."[40]

Be that as it may, however, white trash folks were just that—white—and therefore set to a different tune than blacks. Trash they may have been, but there was a sense that, being white, they possessed some indefinable something that set them apart and at least potentially above even the "better sort" of African Americans, or, conversely, that they were somehow all the more wretched if they remained as they were, in their degraded, impoverished state. Their lighter skins should have afforded them advantages unavailable to African Americans and other nonwhites—people who, it was often assumed, were fated to be poor, ignorant, and depraved because of nature. A white man or woman should have known better, should have at least had the potential of superiority. Consequently, his or her status as trash (often identified as such by, of all people, African Americans) was even more shocking, lying as it did in the realm of effort, of suitable white ambition or lack thereof.[41]

White trash was an exceedingly slippery category, intersecting race, class, and region in all sorts of odd and unpredictable ways. It was a creation of the South, but it would eventually come into general American usage. It could place poor whites at or below the level of African Americans, and it was both related to and distinct from the racial categories of black and Indian.

The Abraham Lincoln of the early 1830s—winding his way down the Sangamon River and out into the wide Mississippi, guardian of a motley collection of unruly hogs, bacon, corn, and whatever else could be scraped up in barter along the riverbanks—might well have been considered white trash or some variant thereof by other white Americans of his day.

There was the fact of his Southern roots. Originally a Kentuckian, he hailed from the region where the term *white trash* originated. Perhaps Lincoln would have been spared some of the more biting condescension directed at "corn-crackers from Kentucky" by virtue of his having steadily moved away from his Kentucky origins. By the time he reached adulthood, he was living out on the Illinois prairie. Even so, Illinois (and Indiana) carried a strong Southern flavor for many. Quite a few of Lincoln's Hoosier and Illinois neighbors likewise hailed originally from Kentucky and the South.

Lincoln's Southern roots had their shady side. Some people in Kentucky thought that his mother, Nancy Hanks, "was of low character" and "did not bear a very virtuous name."[42] There were also rumors of illegitimacy, suggesting that Lincoln was not the son of Thomas Lincoln but rather the child of another man. One Kentuckian thought Lincoln might have been sired by a man named Abraham Enlow who was "as low a fellow as you could find." Another rumor had Lincoln as the offspring of a man named Brownfield, and still another made him the progeny of an unknown farmer living near Louisville. Members of the Lincoln and Hanks families hotly rejected these rumors, but they persisted. And they were of a piece with that image of poor white illegitimacy and questionable moral behavior.[43]

Those rumors aside, Thomas Lincoln's lifestyle would also have fit the white trash mold. His farms in Kentucky, Indiana, and even Illinois might well have been seen as examples of a "white trash homeland" by other whites of the day. Abraham's future wife's family, the well-to-do Todds of Kentucky, later sniped that the Lincolns "had not yet struggled up from dirt floors." The observation was more than metaphoric. Hoosier neighbors described the Lincolns' Indiana cabin as having "one door north and one south," with "two rooms, a plank partition [and] one window." Their Macon County, Illinois, dwelling was similar, constructed as it was of rough-hewn logs split by Lincoln and his family soon after their arrival in the area.[44] Consider by way of comparison an account of the so-called mean white class, "which includes all who are appropriately called 'poor trash,'" that appeared in an 1864 issue of *Harper's New Monthly Magazine*. The article described their dwellings as "small huts of rough logs, through the crevices of which the wind in winter whistles a most melancholy tune. The one room of these huts is floored with nothing but the ground . . . and it is furnished with a few rickety chairs, a pine log . . . a cracked skillet, a dirty frying-pan, an old-fashioned rifle [and] two or three sleepy dogs." Leaving aside the belittling references to "rickety," "cracked," and "dirty" possessions, this description could easily have been applied to the various Lincoln homesteads.[45]

And what of Lincoln's odd manner of dress, his "blue shin bones," and his threadbare and ill-fitting clothes—an appearance that later generations of Americans, filtering his homespun image through the lens of time and his post–Civil War apotheosis, found so charmingly rustic? During his day, those traits would more likely have received a frown, being proof of his status as a denizen of the poorer white nether regions. The same *Harper's* article described the dress of that "mean white class" as "costume[s] of the most mean and meager description," the men wearing "slouched hats, and linsey trousers, and hunting shirts." Not quite Lincoln's dress, which was described by a New Salem resident who saw him trying to work the flat-boat loose from that mill dam as "a pair of mixed blue jeans pants, hickory shirt and common chip hat," but not much different either.[46]

Lincoln was also quite capable of behavior that lacked "manners." Early on, he acquired a reputation as a jokester and a storyteller, and some of his stories and jokes were on the seamy side. According to an acquaintance, he at times had "an insane love in telling dirty and smutty stories." "Lincoln's mind ran to filthy stories," said another friend.[47] He could also indulge in his share of fighting. Though he had a reputation as a gentle sort and a peacemaker, friends remembered that he was sometimes willing to pitch into brawls when the opportunity arose. Several friends and neighbors recalled that Lincoln was one of numerous spectators of a brawl between his stepbrother and a man named William Grigsby. The two "had a terrible fight," and according to one witness, Grigsby was getting the better of his opponent when Lincoln "burst through, caught Grigsby [and] threw him off some feet," after which he "stood up and swore he was the big buck at the lick."[48]

Later generations would either ignore these stories or make them part of the grand Lincoln frontier image, seeing in the rough, uncouth man still more proof that everyone in America can make good, no matter how humble one's origins. When modern Americans conjure up an image of Lincoln on his flatboat trip in 1832, they see the future savior of the land and emancipator of slaves. This is no doubt what ran through Hanks's mind when he offered up his mythic story of Lincoln's moral outrage against that coffle of slaves.

But other people of that time would have seen a lower-class white boy struggling on the edges of poverty. Had they known something of his

Southern roots, his poor farming background, and his illiterate father's migratory habits, some would have instinctively thought "white trash" or a variant thereof.

That characterization would not have been fair but no more or less so than any of the labels placed upon poor white people in Jacksonian America—or black people or anyone else of color. Thomas Lincoln was a hardworking farmer and carpenter. He and Abraham had a difficult relationship, and there is some evidence to suggest that he could be excessive in punishing his son. But Thomas was not by any reasonable standard lazy, mean, or shiftless. If some thought him an "excellent specimen of poor white trash," others found him "good, clean, social, truthful and honest."[49] He and his family were poor, but they were not dirty or slovenly. Their values weren't compromised or suspect, nor was there any validity to the rumor about Lincoln's questionable parentage or his mother's supposed "low character."[50]

But what was fair and accurate is not really the point. The point, rather, involves perception, in the sense of what other people would have seen in Abraham Lincoln as he came of age on the Illinois frontier. Granted, we do not know for certain just how others saw him. No one in 1832 thought to record their impressions of the young man and his circumstances at the time (a fact that itself suggests something about Lincoln's obscurity and unremarkable blending into his social and cultural background). The only available evidence is the collection of post-1865 reminiscences, a collection tainted by the romanticism that surrounded Lincoln's legacy. His friends, neighbors, and family members understandably portrayed him and his circumstances in the most favorable light—particularly since they were themselves part of those circumstances.

But what if, say, a middle-class businessman from the East had seen Lincoln and the rest of Offutt's crew as they wound their way downriver in 1832? Or perhaps one of the more successful farmers from a settled region of Illinois or even a foreign visitor—a nineteenth-century version of Jan Morris—writing one of the many travel and observation guides so popular at the time? Lincoln's height and generally gawky appearance would have been noted, surely; these were features that made him stick out a bit even among his neighbors. But otherwise, everything about him—his clothes, mannerisms, obvious poverty, maybe even a trace of a Kentucky accent— would have said poor white farm boy with Southern roots. In the cultural milieu of the day, our hypothetical observer would not have found it diffi-

CHAPTER TWO

cult to further transform the poor white farm boy into a "corn-cracker" or something similar.

Had Lincoln remained a semiliterate farmer, he might never have been self-aware enough to resist association with white trash. But his poor relationship with Thomas and his general ambition—a trait that, by the standards of the day, itself separated him from his stereotypically low-white origins—combined to push him outward and (at least according to the sensibilities of his time) upward. There was not, therefore, just society's perception of Lincoln; there was also Lincoln's perception of himself, as he became an adult and began to decide who he was and what he wanted to be.

Whatever his future occupation might be, he knew it would not be in agriculture. The foundation of a poor white life was the endless cycle of hardscrabble farming, plowing a small piece of land that could eke out a few acres' worth of sustenance year in and year out. When he got back from New Orleans and especially when he moved to New Salem, Lincoln would try nearly anything other than farming, finding work as a general store clerk, postman, land surveyor, election official, and river pilot. Occasionally, he was compelled by necessity to do some plowing, rail-splitting, and other farm labor—but he only took these jobs if he had no choice.

Lincoln's family was all about farming, and as he came of age, he tried to shed them as much as possible too. He was dedicated enough to his family that he remained with them during their sojourn to Illinois, helping drive the oxen, build the cabin, and fence the fields. But he struck out on his own as soon as he thought he could properly do so.

Historians and biographers attribute Lincoln's hasty departure from his family as a sign of alienation from his father. True enough. But Lincoln also wanted to shed Thomas's lifestyle. Escaping the white trash label required escaping rural poverty, first and foremost. And escaping poverty propelled him away from his family. The two things went hand in hand.

Some sense of this can be gleaned from a letter Lincoln wrote to his father and his stepbrother in 1848. By this point, Lincoln had discarded the last vestiges of a poor white lifestyle. His days of log cabins, blinded hogs, and split rails were gone. But his family continued to languish in financial difficulties, and in 1848, he gave Thomas $20 to avoid foreclosure on the family farm. In lending him the money, Lincoln felt compelled to lecture his father on the matter, in a tone that strongly implied both his distaste for how his father was still living his life and more than a little condescension concerning Thomas's financial mismanagement and general ignorance.

There is even a touch of doubt concerning Thomas's word or at least his competence. "I very cheerfully send you the twenty dollars, which sum you say is necessary to save your land from sale," Lincoln wrote. "It is singular that you should have forgotten a judgment against you; and it is more singular that the plaintiff should have let you forget it so long, particularly as I suppose you have always had property enough to satisfy a judgment of that amount. Before you pay it, it would be well to be sure you have not paid it; or, at least, that you can not prove you have paid it."[51]

Along with the money and this brief note, Lincoln enclosed a longer and more scolding passage to his stepbrother, who was also importuning him for a loan—$80, a considerable sum in those days. Lincoln gave full vent to his dissatisfaction with his family's values and work ethic. "At the various times when I have helped you a little, you have said to me, 'We can get along very well now,' but in a short time I find you in the same difficulty again," he wrote. "I doubt whether since I saw you, you have done a good whole day's work in any one day. . . . This habit of uselessly wasting time, is the whole difficulty." Lincoln worried that his stepbrother might take it into his head to wander off to the California goldfields or the lead mines in St. Louis, and he encouraged him to instead remain in Illinois and do solid farmwork. "You say if I furnish you the money you will deed me the land, and, if you don't pay the money back, you will deliver possession," Lincoln stated. "Nonsense! If you can't now live with the land, how will you then live without it?"[52]

Laziness, ignorance, a shiftless approach to labor and finances—there is a flash of white trash here, with Lincoln not a victim but a perpetrator of that image. Only a flash, though. Annoyed as he was with his stepbrother and father, Lincoln likely would not have been so harsh in his judgments. There is no record of him having used the term *white trash* or any of its variations to describe anybody. Still, one wonders if Lincoln—having by this point attained a degree of respectability—did not accept to some degree his society's assumptions concerning the behavior of the poor white folks whom he had now left behind.

The process of leaving them behind had begun at about the same time he began the flatboat trip for Offutt, and it involved more than his choice of occupation. He was also pushing away from his poor rural roots intellectually. Lincoln's reading habits expanded greatly during this period, carrying him beyond the relatively limited world of the Bible, John Bunyan, and Parson Weems. He had always been an avid reader—"Abe read all the books he could lay his hands on," recalled his stepmother—and this set him apart when he was a boy.[53] By the time he was ready to strike out on his own in Illinois, his reading habits had become truly liberal, even a bit eclectic. Soon after the Offutt flatboat journey, he settled in New Salem, and there, people saw him reading "books on science and comments on law" as well as local and national newspapers. Eventually, his repertoire expanded to include books on mathematics, "Natural Philosophy, Astronomy and Chemistry."[54]

He also started to shed his homespun clothes, at least as far as was possible given his straitened financial circumstances. He was careful to remain at least "tolerably" neat and clean, according to his stepmother, when he was a boy. "Fashion cut no figure with him," she declared.[55] But this seemed to change as he entered manhood. Not long after the flatboat trip, he was seen in New Salem wearing "a suit of grey jeans clothes and a stove pipe hat," an ensemble that was "a very fashionable style in those days."[56]

One also wonders if Lincoln's growing aversion to alcohol might have been rooted in an attempt to avoid that poor white trash image of drunkenness. Exactly when and under what circumstances he chose to forgo alcohol is unclear. Some of Lincoln's Hoosier neighbors remembered that he was a "temperate drinker" who "took his dram" while living in Indiana.[57] But by the time he arrived in Illinois or soon thereafter, he seems to have completely given up alcohol.[58] He never said exactly why, other than to claim that alcohol left him feeling "flabby and undone." Whatever the reason, his teetotal approach to drinking—along with tobacco—was a rejection, wittingly or not, of a staple of white trash stereotyping.[59]

Abandon alcohol and avoid slovenliness, shun farmwork in favor of just about any another pursuit, adopt a life of expansive reading and eventually the bookish professions of the law and politics: here was a recipe for a nearly complete reversal of the usual image of white trash America carried in the heads of many people during Lincoln's day. He may not have consciously aimed for that outcome, and there were doubtless multiple reasons for the decisions he made with his life as he grew into a man. Nor was the process linear. Well into his twenties, Lincoln was sometimes seen as a rube. "His dress was of the most ludicrous character" when he arrived in New Salem, in the opinion of one of the town's citizens. "His long arms protruded through the sleeves of a coat which scarcely reached beyond the elbow in one direction, or below the waist in the other." He described himself as a "floating piece of driftwood" at this point in his life, and more than one person in New Salem and later in Springfield took him for a peculiarly tall species of backwoods hick.[60]

But he ardently wanted to be more than that. It was, at bottom, all about ambition, and ambition was the key trait that set Lincoln apart from his humble beginnings, that pushed him out and up from the rural white world of his origins, that separated him from the white trash life that was supposed to be his lot. His law partner later observed that his ambition was a "little engine that knew no rest," and this was true long before Lincoln became an attorney. "He was ambitious and determined and when he attempted to excel by man or boy his whole soul and his energies were bent on doing it," remembered his cousin Dennis Hanks.[61]

There were multiple sources for that ambition.[62] On a psychological level, it likely stemmed from his troubled relationship with Thomas. On an intellectual level, his reading habits surely sparked a desire to see and experience something of the world outside Indiana and Kentucky, to go seek a fortune commensurate with that of childhood heroes such as George Washington. And though ambitious, he was not entirely ignorant of the possible costs and dangers stemming from his "little engine." Later in life, he would warn of the consequences inherent in an overweening ambition. "Many great and good men sufficiently qualified for any task they should undertake, may ever be found, whose ambition would aspire to nothing beyond a seat in Congress, a gubernatorial or a presidential chair," he told the Springfield Young Men's Lyceum in 1838.

> Think you these places would satisfy an Alexander, a Caesar, or a Napoleon? Never! . . . Is it unreasonable then to expect, that some man possessed of the loftiest genius, coupled with ambition sufficient to push it to its utmost stretch, will at some time, spring up among us? And when such a one does, it will require the people to be united with each other, attached to the government and laws, and generally intelligent, to successfully frustrate his designs.[63]

There are those who think Lincoln was subconsciously talking about himself when he referenced the dangers of such burning ambition.[64] Perhaps. But whatever its source and whatever its dangers, Lincoln's ambition was defined and framed by race as well as other factors in his life and his culture. Certainly, issues of class played an important role too as he strove to make something of himself by rising up from his status as a "floating

CHAPTER TWO

piece of driftwood." His ambition was likewise framed by his manhood, eventually leading him by dint of his society's expectations in the direction of the professions and the law as the best means to satisfy his masculine desire for success.[65]

But race, in the form of that troubling stereotype white trash, and Lincoln's desire to shed its baleful effects subtly and powerfully molded Lincoln's ambition as well, determining its shape and its consequences. However messy his journey away from his poor rural roots might have been, it was not a race-neutral process, as has almost always been assumed by generations of biographers and writers for whom white was neutral and therefore invisible. Lincoln's rags-to-riches story is commonly seen as an embodiment of the American Dream. In reality, he was not trying to escape just poverty; he was trying to escape *white* poverty. And that escape was configured differently than if he had been an African American or a Native American or another nonwhite. Because of the cultural and social standards of his day, he was not compelled to break free from the presumptions associated with blackness. He did not, for instance, have to worry that people would automatically assume his sexual appetites were nearly out of control or that his skin color gave him some sort of inherent inability to comprehend complex ideas or concepts. Nor did he have to concern himself with shedding an image of savage barbarity, as he would have had he carried Indian blood in his veins. Instead, as he entered manhood, Lincoln felt compelled to push against a cultural image that was at once both racial and class driven. Throughout his life, he would approach the idea of equality as something primarily rooted in earning power, in one's economic opportunities; this approach had implicitly racial roots, in the white trash stereotyping he believed he had to battle. And there was that omnipresent racial foundation of fear as well. Not fear of the Other so much as the internal fear contained within the maddening contradictions of American whiteness.

THREE

■

The *Lebanon*

In 1841, on yet a third occasion, Lincoln encountered African Americans on a river, this time while traveling on a steamboat rather than a flatboat—and a well-appointed, modern steamboat at that.

The *Lebanon* was a "splendid" vessel, according to one passenger, and was used to perform all manner of tasks on the Mississippi and Ohio rivers as far north as St. Louis and as far east as Cincinnati. It was new (built in Pennsylvania less than two years previously) and substantial, displacing 141 tons and capable of carrying thousands of dollars' worth of cargo, along with many passengers.[1] It was a side-wheeler, and if its plans conformed to the standard construction of such vessels, it possessed two primary decks above the hold: the main deck, running the length of the vessel and carrying most of the ship's cargo, and the upper or "boiler deck," sporting the *Lebanon*'s saloon, washrooms, baggage compartments, and pantry. The poorer travelers, the "deck passengers," stayed on the main deck with the cargo, whereas the more well-heeled travelers could afford cabins on the boiler deck, which had a walkway ringing its length so that cabin passengers wishing a breath of fresh air did not need to mingle with the lower sorts on the main deck below.[2]

Lincoln was probably a cabin passenger, and it is likely that his friend and traveling companion, Joshua Speed, was as well. Speed was a young man on the make with Kentucky roots, like Lincoln, though his background was otherwise very different, hailing as he did from a family of wealthy slaveholders in Farmington, near Louisville. Hardworking, straightforward, and blunt almost to a fault, Speed moved to Illinois in 1834 and invested his time and money in a Springfield dry goods store, where he sold "groceries, hardware, books, medicines, bed-clothes, mattresses, in fact everything that the country needed."[3]

Speed was Lincoln's closest friend, and Lincoln was a man with very few close friends. The two shared their thoughts on deeply personal and intimate matters, such as Speed's courtship of his future wife, Fanny. "You well know that I do not feel my own sorrows much more keenly than I do yours," Lincoln wrote when Speed expressed misgivings about his match with Fanny. "You know my desire to befriend you is everlasting—that I will never cease, while I know how to do any thing."[4]

In the summer of 1841, Speed invited Lincoln to visit his family's home in Farmington. In a way, he was repaying the favor his friend had done for him in offering advice concerning Fanny, for Lincoln had experienced problems of his own with another young Kentuckian, named Mary Todd. They had broken off their affair earlier in the year under mysterious circumstances, leaving Mary angry and distraught, Lincoln deeply depressed, and tongues wagging. "Lincoln went crazy," Speed later claimed, adding that he "had to remove razors from his room, taking away all knives and other such dangerous things."[5]

Speed thought a change of scenery might do Lincoln good, and Lincoln enjoyed the respite at Farmington, a genteel place replete with Southern charm. He still suffered bouts of melancholy, however. When Speed's mother saw him in a down mood one morning, she felt moved to present him with an Oxford Bible, "advising him to read it, to adopt its precepts and pray for its promises." According to Speed, the episode "made a deep impression upon him."[6]

Now, Speed and Lincoln were returning to Springfield via the *Lebanon*. They boarded the vessel at the locks of the Louisville and Portland Canal (installed a few years before to bypass the falls of the Ohio River). Both men were somewhat the worse for wear, Lincoln from a sore tooth he tried and failed to have removed while staying in Kentucky and Speed from some undisclosed malady (Lincoln later opaquely referred to it as a "little indisposition"), which resolved itself as they traveled. The voyage aboard the *Lebanon* was circuitous, taking them home by way of St. Louis. According to Lincoln, nothing much happened on the voyage "except the vexatious delays occasioned by the sandbars."

But there was one matter of interest. At some point, Lincoln noted the presence of slaves aboard, a coffle of twelve black people. Unlike with the Offutt flatboat trip, we have direct, detailed evidence of Lincoln's reaction. "A gentleman had purchased twelve negroes in different parts of Kentucky and was taking them to a farm in the South," he later noted in describing the scene. "They were chained six and six together, a small iron clevis was around the left wrist of each, and this fastened to the main chain by a shorter one at a convenient distance from, the others; so that the negroes were strung together precisely like so many fish upon a trot-line."

An interesting little moment: Lincoln, the future author of the Emancipation Proclamation, staring intently at the sight of a dozen African Americans enslaved and chained together and on their way to some unidentified place and fate. It actually was more than a moment, lasting longer than that sudden, sharp encounter with the would-be thieves in 1828 or the hit-and-miss scenes of slave trades and auctions he might have witnessed on the streets of New Orleans. Aboard the *Lebanon,* Lincoln had more time to think about what he saw, perhaps standing at the rail of the boiler deck and looking down upon the slaves huddled together on the main deck below. He may well have encountered the slaves multiple times, whether he wished to or not. A few of the vessels that plied the Ohio River with slaves as cargo had specially built rooms for the purpose, but most did not. "The steamboats have no decks fitted specially for slaves," wrote one observer of riverboat slave traffic, "hence they are placed sometimes in one part of the boat, sometimes in another, and frequently are suffered to wander about the decks and guards at pleasure."[7]

What effect did this sight have on Lincoln? What was he thinking? What was he feeling? He did not record his impressions of the moment. He kept no diary or any other immediate record that has survived. But he did write one letter, after the voyage was concluded, that described the scene in detail. That letter is the earliest extended meditation by Abraham Lincoln on African Americans and their plight. As such, it is often utilized by historians to explore his early attitude toward slavery and African Americans, usually to Lincoln's credit, since elements of the letter can be read in a way that reveals him to have been a man of considerable compassion toward black people.[8]

CHAPTER THREE

It is entirely legitimate to use the letter in this way, but in doing so, we sometimes lose sight of the fact that this document was not just written about black people; it was also written about black people by a white person and to another white person. When we shift our focus slightly to take this into account, we find that Lincoln's point of view was more complex than traditional narratives allow.

In 1841, Lincoln was a relatively new member of the Illinois bar, having been licensed as an attorney five years previously. His entrance into the legal profession meant many things: money, a path to a political career, and a bit more stability for a man who had spent his entire adult life to that point eking out a living at various odd jobs. It also meant a degree of what might be termed respectability—meaning status and a certain amount of deference afforded him because of his professional standing. Underlying all of this was the understated fact that he had crossed a distinct, sharp racial barrier, one every bit as rigid—probably more so—as that of the flatboating culture of his youth. To be a lawyer in 1841 America was to be a white man, without exception. There were no nonwhite lawyers in the United States.[9]

As he was becoming a lawyer, Lincoln was also establishing himself in a second lily-white profession: politics. By 1841, he was serving his fourth term in the Illinois state legislature and eyeing a run at national office as a U.S. representative in Congress—a goal he would achieve in 1846. The law helped him earn a living, but politics fed his higher aspirations. "Lincoln's restless ambition found its gratification only in the field of politics," his law partner Billy Herndon observed. "He used the law merely as a stepping-stone to what he considered a more attractive condition in the political world." Not only did no nonwhites intrude upon that "attractive world" as fellow officeholders, but in most states in the North as well as the South, African Americans were not allowed to vote at all.[10]

A third facet of Lincoln's life in 1841, one closely related to his entry into the law and politics, was his relocation from New Salem—with its frontier rusticity and fringy white trash associations—to nearby Springfield and his eventual establishment of a comfortable, middle-class life in that town. Granted, Springfield was no prize, at least not to anyone from back East. Many of its buildings were ramshackle, its streets were often muddy quagmires, pigs and other animals wandered about at will, and the city's sewage system—such as it was—left much to be desired. But it was a town with at least pretensions of respectability.[11]

Lincoln moved to Springfield primarily to enhance his professional prospects, as he told Speed when he arrived in town in 1837. Referring to his recent entrance into the legal profession as an "experiment" whose prospects were uncertain, he said to Speed "in the saddest tone" (when Speed offered to loan him money to pay for a bed, mattress, and blankets), "'If I fail in this, I do not know when I can ever pay you.'" In the end, Speed offered to share his own meager accommodations, a room above the general store where he worked as a clerk. Lincoln eagerly accepted the offer, cementing their friendship.[12]

It was not an especially promising beginning, but Lincoln wanted much more than a shared room over a store. He wanted a wife, a home, a "settling down"—he wanted domesticity. And in his day, domesticity, like the law and politics, was culturally defined as white. In fact, hearth and home, along with an acceptably mannered and fashionable spouse, were rapidly becoming in the minds of middle- and upper-class Americans the heart and soul of respectable whiteness. Ambitious young men such as Lincoln were expected to make their mark in the world by engaging in proper manly pursuits outside the home, but they were at the same time expected to provide for and respect the establishment of a solid domestic realm for their wives and children—by all accounts, the very sort of place Abraham and Mary strove to create after they married. Much has been made of Lincoln's imperfect fit in this quintessential domestic environment, with various friends and later his wife struggling to teach him the manners, attire, and attitude befitting a respectable white gentleman presiding over a respectable household. But the fact remains that Lincoln wanted to be that gentleman. He wanted to fit into that domestic world as much as possible.[13]

The law, politics, and a solid domestic life: taken together, these three things dominated Lincoln's life choices in the 1830s and 1840s as he entered middle age—much as they would have for most similarly situated men of his era. They provided the filters through which Lincoln understood his daily life, and those filters were overwhelmingly associated with whiteness.

People who were not white did sometimes play small roles around the edges of his life—but only barely. Lincoln's law practice was overwhelmingly concerned with white people. Native Americans, to cite one example, were practically a nonfactor. In 1853, a woman named Mary Martin hired Lincoln and Herndon (it is not clear from the available records which partner represented her) to sue her husband, Samuel, for divorce, claiming that he was consorting with white women and "red women of the forest." By the time she filed the case, Samuel had left Illinois, and Mary eventually dropped the matter altogether. This was as close as Lincoln ever came to litigating a case involving an Indian.[14]

African Americans were also at best a drop in the bucket of his lawyer's life: only 24 out of over 3,800 cases involved black people.[15] In litigating these cases, he (or one of his law partners) directly represented only six black clients.[16] Such clients could sometimes be an indirect presence—part of an estate settlement, for instance, as in 1852 when Lincoln represented one of the plaintiffs, Leroy Hill, in a case involving the disposition of several slaves as part of a complex real estate and inheritance transaction. Similarly, in the 1841 case *Kane v. May and Eastham,* either Lincoln or John Todd Stuart (again, the court records do not clearly delineate which partner was involved in the case) helped negotiate an out-of-court settlement whereby their clients, William May and Marvelous Eastham, sold a slave girl to plaintiff Felicia Kane to satisfy an unpaid debt.[17]

But on this level, the human realities of slavery and the tactile, tangible realities of race were easily reducible to abstractions. Lincoln need not necessarily have contemplated the vagaries of race when he helped broker an agreement between his African American clients Mack and Frank Shelby and Abraham and Clarkson Freeman over the disposition of a town lot in Springfield. When he represented Mack's wife, Mary, in a divorce case stemming from Mack's drinking habits a few years earlier, he handled the case much as he would have had the Shelbys been white, at least on a strictly legal level; the paperwork was the same, and Lincoln's arguments would have been the same had the case reached fruition. And when Mary later changed her mind and dismissed the case, the dismissal would have been the same. It is unlikely Lincoln ever even saw the slaves in question in the 1845 case *Napier v. Woolridge,* when he and Stuart represented Clairborne Woolridge in his attempt to recover damages from Elias Napier because of Napier's failure to pay the balance on a $1,500 slave sale.[18]

The law, at least in these areas, was structured to present an ostensibly neutral mien. Legal treatises of the day did not usually differentiate between a black and a white set of rules governing debt collection, probate settlement, property negotiations, or the like. Thus, Sir William Blackstone's *Commentaries on the Laws of England*—the seminal text, first published in 1765, that Lincoln and nearly every other lawyer in America studied—rarely mentioned race. The word *Negro* appeared in the text only five times, in each instance referring to black slaves as examples of the old British principle that "when an innocent negro is seized and chained, or is driven to his daily toil by a merciless master, he still retains this species of liberty," namely, the liberty to "do whatever is not forbidden to do by *existing* law."[19]

Reading those lines may have reinforced Lincoln's general detestation of slavery as a system; so too may have Blackstone's emphasis on the supremacy of "natural law" over any man-made law such as that which created slavery. But otherwise, it would have done little to educate him in the vagaries of how race operated upon the realities of life in antebellum America, either in the courtrooms where he earned a living or elsewhere.[20] Legal thinkers such as Blackstone were not actually all that interested in the social impact of the law anyway. To them, the law functioned in the abstract realm of reasoned concepts—justice, fairness, equity, and the like—whose rightness or wrongness in a given case depended upon their intrinsic intellectual qualities, not their impact on the realities of everyday life and certainly not upon the messy and vexed relationships between black and white people in the streets of Springfield or elsewhere in America. Lincoln's legal education and his experiences in various American courtrooms told him that the law was in effect race-neutral. Its whiteness was invisible and undetectable because it was a universal given. This did not drain race from the actual proceedings in Lincoln's law office or in the courtrooms. Instead, it created a false appearance of color blindness.

Likewise, Lincoln's early political career had little to do with race, even less so than his law practice. The issues that dominated his tenure in the Illinois legislature were primarily economic and geared toward the concerns of entrepreneurs, farmers, and business developers—all of which were relevant to nonwhite people only on the outermost margins, if at all. Lincoln's general position on American economic development—a "commitment to the ideal that all men should receive a full, good, and ever increasing reward for their labors," as historian Gabor Boritt ably summarized it—was broad enough that it could well have included nonwhites. Later in the 1850s, he would articulate a reading of the Declaration of Independence allowing all Americans to prosper economically according to their situations and talents, blacks and whites alike. But on the whole, the economics-driven agenda that dominated his career in the Illinois legislature had little to say about racial issues.[21]

On those rare occasions when issues of race arose in the statehouse, Lincoln generally tried to steer clear of such things. He did nothing about Illinois' oppressive Black Laws (and in 1858, when African American abolitionist H. Ford Douglas asked Lincoln to join him in efforts to repeal those laws, he did not do so).[22] Lincoln did mount an occasional quiet assault on slavery—in 1837, he signed a petition in the Illinois legislature stating that slavery was founded "on both injustice and bad policy," and during his brief congressional term ten years later, he contributed to a vain attempt to outlaw slavery in the District of Columbia—but these actions had very little to do with race. Lincoln was a critic of slavery as an institution but not of the racial system that provided slavery's foundation. On both occasions, he skirted any such implications. In the 1837 petition, he distanced himself from the radical social notions of abolitionists by asserting that "the promulgation of abolitionist doctrines tends rather to increase than to abate [slavery's] evils." And Lincoln's preferred policy for abolishing slavery in Washington, D.C., involved a referendum on the matter by the city's "free white male citizen[s], above the age of twenty years." If slavery were to end in the nation's capital, it would require white permission, and whites would be in charge of when and how the end occurred.[23]

Nonwhite people had a more direct daily impact on Lincoln's home life, though again, this was limited. He and Mary employed servant girls from a wide variety of backgrounds, some white, others not. Mary hired several African American servants at various times, including Jane Jenkins, one of the Lincolns' few black neighbors; a woman named Mariah Vance;[24] and another, unidentified black woman whose cooking was so bad that Mary peremptorily (and rather loudly) dismissed her from service after only two weeks.[25]

Lincoln knew these black domestic servants and other African Americans too, among them his barber, William Florville. Sometime in 1860, he would make the acquaintance of an African American man named William Johnson, who later accompanied him to Washington, D.C., as his personal valet. Johnson may have worked at the Lincoln home in some similar capacity or as a gardener or handyman, and Lincoln held his work ethic and his general character in high regard, referring to him as "a worthy man."[26] Lincoln also sometimes interacted with Mariah Vance. (Mary ran off the black cook so quickly that he probably lacked the opportunity to do more than say hello.)

He had a more direct, business relationship with members of a group of Portuguese expatriates who lived in Springfield and nearby Jacksonville, having moved there from Madeira in stages during the early 1850s. Mary employed a Portuguese washerwoman (who later commented that Lincoln was "so kind . . . when he passa me, he patta my shoulder. I worka for him"), and she purchased produce from Portuguese farmers. Lincoln donated money to Springfield's Portuguese Presbyterian church, and in 1854, he lent money to Ritta Angelica da Silva, described in the Lincoln financial records simply as "a Portuguese woman."[27]

Lincoln's Springfield may have been more racially diverse than many people realized, but most of its white citizens would not have been too happy with that state of affairs. The *Sangamon Journal,* Lincoln's regular newspaper, focused overwhelmingly on white people and their concerns, with others of a different ethnic makeup either rarely making an appearance or doing so only in a dubious manner that played into prevailing stereotypes. One humorous tale printed by the *Journal* in January 1842, for example, told the story of a sharp horse trader "who had something of the appearance of the tribe of Abraham." Another noted Irish people's habit of being "deeply plunged into the sin of drunkenness." The *Journal* sometimes carried lurid tales of Native American misbehavior on the western frontier, and in 1844 under the headline THE GIPSIES — WHO ARE THEY? the paper speculated on European Gypsies' "swarthy hue," "dark piercing eyes," and the supposed fact that "they are without God in the world."[28]

African Americans likewise only appeared on the edges. A week before the *Journal* carried the full text of Lincoln's address to the Springfield Washington Temperance Society, it printed the speech delivered by Charles W. Campbell, "a colored man," before the "Washington Society of Colored People." On a less positive note, the paper published stories about drunkards who disgraced the neighborhood when in their cups by "preaching a negro sermon," as well as an account of the burning of a steam mill in a nearby county that was attributed to a gang of armed free blacks.[29]

The mores of Springfield and of Lincoln's professions were white at their core. In stepping firmly and with purpose into the three very white worlds of the law, politics, and domesticity, Lincoln was making a definite choice. It was a common choice, certainly, pursued by many thousands of young white men in similar circumstances. But it was still a choice—to stand firmly on ground that was associated with not just whiteness but respectable whiteness.

There were other options. Some people had begun to articulate a search-ing critique of white racial identity in America, advancing the then-radical notions that race was an artificial, social construct, not an immutable fact, and that white Americans needed to reexamine their own actions and be-liefs regarding race rather than continue to scapegoat and ostracize black people. Frederick Douglass, Gerrit Smith, William Lloyd Garrison, and many of their abolitionist allies argued that opposition to slavery as an in-stitution was not enough: racism had to be targeted as well. They wanted "to reintegrate cultural dichotomies that had long been present in Western culture," according to historian John Stauffer, "those of black and white, body and soul, sacred and profane, ideal and real, civilization and sav-agery, and masculine and feminine." The traditional idea of whiteness was predicated upon preserving those very dichotomies.[30]

But these people were generally considered to be fringe figures on the margins of polite white society. And Lincoln was never terribly interested in the fringes. He had made the deliberate choice to, in modern parlance, go mainstream. In doing so, he cared far more about polite white opinion than a Gerrit Smith or a Frederick Douglass ever would. It is within this context that we must understand his encounter with those African Ameri-cans aboard the *Lebanon*.

THE LETTER HE WROTE about the *Lebanon* slave coffle in September 1841 was to Joshua Speed's sister, Mary Speed. At that stage in his life, Lincoln had a complex, awkward perspective on women. Quite a few people who knew him believed that he didn't much like the company of ladies. "He didn't go to see the girls much," recalled neighbor N. W. Branson, adding that "he didn't appear bashful, but it seemed as if he cared but little for them." Dennis Hanks agreed, noting that Lincoln "didn't love the com-pany of girls." The exact reasons for this are unclear. Some felt he was overly self-conscious concerning his homely appearance and his lack of ed-ucation. Others believed that he found feminine company too "frivolous." And still others thought (contrary to Branson) that he was simply shy.[31]

Whatever the reason, Lincoln wasn't generally comfortable around members of the opposite sex. He didn't write many letters to women at all, composing a total of just four up to that point in his life—three to a New Salem woman named Mary Owens whom he once courted (she turned him down, noting that he was "deficient in those little links which make up the great chain of womans [sic] happiness") and one to the wife of Orville

The Lebanon   53

Browning, a friend and companion at the Illinois bar.[32] In addition, his tone in these letters was palpably different from that in his correspondence with men. Lincoln's letters to women tended toward stiffness, and he affected a self-deprecating tone that had an underlying feel of nervous humor. To Mary Owens, he complained that "this letter is so dry and [stupid] that I am ashamed to send it," and in another missive, he confessed, "I have commenced two letters to send you before this, both of which displeased me before I got half done, and so I tore them up."[33] With Mrs. Browning (to whom he felt compelled to explain the failure of his courtship of Miss Owens), Lincoln likewise displayed an unaccustomed awkwardness, beginning his correspondence by noting that "without appologising [sic] for being egotistical, I shall make the history of so much of my own life, as has elapsed since I saw you, the subject of this letter." He followed this with the observation that "in order to give a full and intelligible account of the things I have done and suffered *since* I saw you, I shall necessarily have to relate some that happened *before*."[34]

This same discomfited self-consciousness appeared in his letter to Mary Speed. "My friend," he began, "I have had some little difficulty in determining on which [member of the Speed family] to inflict the task of reading what I now feel must be a most dull and silly letter." But, he wrote, "when I remembered that you and I were something of cronies while I was at Farmington . . . I instantly decided that you should be the devoted one."[35]

"Something of cronies"—apparently, Lincoln and Mary Speed hit it off well during his Kentucky vacation. Mary was seven years older—thirty-nine at the time of Lincoln's letter—and unmarried. They seem to have engaged in a bit of playful flirtation, though it did not lead anywhere in serious romantic terms, perhaps because Lincoln was still more or less involved with that other Mary, Mary Todd. But Lincoln and Miss Speed had their moments. "While there [at Farmington], I once was under the necessity of shutting you up in a room to prevent your committing assault and battery upon me," he teased, referring to a who-knows-what bit of fun.

Lincoln informed her that the river journey had been one of almost unrelieved boredom. "By the way," he then wrote, "a fine example was presented on board the boat for contemplating the effect of *condition* upon human happiness," after which he launched into his extended description of the slave coffle.

The section on the coffle is abrupt, inserted right after Lincoln's assertion that the trip was mundane and entirely uneventful. He also underlined the word *condition*. Lincoln often underlined words to emphasize a point. But along with placing the sentence as an aside in his general narrative—something he rarely did when relating a story—the anecdote about the slave coffle has the feel of a continuation of an earlier conversation: perhaps a bit of philosophical musing between Lincoln and Mary during his stay at Farmington concerning the nature of happiness generally? Or maybe even a conversation about slavery itself. At Farmington, Lincoln was immersed in the peculiar institution. For one of a handful of times in his life, he was actually served by a slave, a valet who was assigned specifically to take care of him.[36]

The fact that he mentioned the slave coffle—and at such length and in such detail—is suggestive. Why bring it up at all? The overall point of the letter was to inform Mary of Joshua's good health and safe passage. The slaves were superfluous, having no direct bearing on the letter's purpose. Lincoln's description interrupted the letter's flow, as he himself acknowledged, writing "to return to the narrative" after he finished his account of the coffle.[37]

Nor was the mere presence of slaves on a steamboat so unusual as to merit special notice. They were in fact a common sight. "The number of slaves annually transported to the south-west by steamboats is very large," noted one observer. "There is scarcely a steamboat bound for New Orleans, which does not take down a cargo of slaves." Lincoln would have felt no particular urge to describe a sight that was common to river travelers in the South, merely by way of its uniqueness.[38]

He made a particular issue of the slaves, at length and for no reasons that are discernible within the framework of the letter itself. Speculation is all we have, but it does seem reasonable to surmise that his description of the slaves was the back end of a conversation begun at Farmington about a subject to which we are unfortunately not privy, given the lack of primary source documentation—a subject that concerned either human nature generally or the effect of slavery on its victims. Whatever the case may be, the passage suggests thoughtfulness; it was the first sign that Lincoln, at age thirty-two, was not heedlessly and hopelessly embedded in the accepted white racial mores of his day. Of course, he still wore the white skin he'd worn since birth. And he was still a decidedly white man firmly entrenched within the dominant white racial culture of his times. But he could, at least for a fleeting moment and in a small way, question those mores simply by noticing and then describing in considerable detail that which was not noteworthy to most other white Americans at the time—a collection of downtrodden slaves.

After describing the scene (where the slaves were "like so many fish on a trot-line"), Lincoln offered his assessment of their condition. "They were being separated forever from the scenes of their childhood, their friends, their fathers and mothers, and brothers and sisters, and many of them, from their wives and children," he wrote, "and going into perpetual slavery where the lash of the master is proverbially more ruthless and unrelenting than any other where." Lincoln thought he sensed a disconnect between their situation and their demeanor. "And yet amid all these distressing circumstances, as we would think them, they were the most cheerful and apparently happy creatures on board. One, whose offence [sic] for which he had been sold was an over-fondness for his wife, played the fiddle almost continually; and the others danced, sung [sic], cracked jokes, and played various games with cards from day to day." Lincoln referenced religion to prove his overall point about the effect of "condition" on happiness. "How true it is," he wrote, "that 'God tempers the wind to the shorn lamb,' or in other words, that He renders the worst of human conditions tolerable, while He permits the best, to be nothing better than tolerable."[39]

Lincoln's assessment here was complex, multilayered, and even a bit contradictory. On the one hand, it had a flavor of relativism about it, this idea of condition as the precursor for determining happiness. He seemed to be suggesting that a person's state of mind was dependent upon the circumstances of the moment, rather than an inner well-being that could resist the changing circumstances of one's time and place. Those circumstances, he implied, are everything. In this, Lincoln may have been following the writings on happiness as a philosophical construct by the seventeenth-century English philosopher William Paley (whose works he had read), emphasizing the relative aspects of happiness to a wide variety of changeable factors, rather than the innermost state of one's soul.[40]

On the other hand, there apparently was no doubt in Lincoln's mind concerning the objective reality of the slaves' condition: they were in fact bad off, regardless of their apparent demeanor. To him, they were, without a doubt, in "distressing circumstances." The slaves were held in bondage of course, but they were also being driven to some point farther into the Deep South, with its reputation for plantation brutality exceeding even that of the Upper South, and they were being separated from fathers, mothers, brothers, sisters, wives, children, and friends.

Lincoln used sarcasm in describing one slave as someone "whose of-fence for which he had been sold was an over-fondness for his wife." The tone was odd. His sense of humor normally did not run in such channels.[41] Somehow, he subtly reinforced the point that beyond the state of these par-ticular slaves' minds—their "happiness" or whatever—there was the objec-tive fact of injustice: that a man could be so punished for the quite human impulse of marital affection.

Lincoln here revealed a glimmer, tiny perhaps but real nevertheless, of recognition that no matter the outer appearances of contentment, no mat-ter the actual feelings of contentment evident in the slaves themselves, there was something fundamentally ugly and unjust at work. Right or wrong about the slaves' feelings and their demeanor, he by no means dismissed or belittled the moral import of what he witnessed. Those slaves and their sit-uation mattered.

They mattered enough, in fact, that he seems to have actively sought out information concerning their circumstances, which underscores one of the more striking elements in his letter to Mary Speed. How, after all, did he know that "the offence for which [one of the slaves] had been sold was an over-fondness for his wife"? Either he asked the owner or he asked the slave himself. The latter in particular would have entailed considerable ef-fort, depending upon the slaves' location aboard the *Lebanon*—possibly a trip from the boiler deck to the cargo deck. In any event, familiarizing him-self with the story of that one slave required more effort than the average white passenger would have undertaken.

Lest this seem to be almost too insignificant a matter to warrant attention, it is worth noting that often enough, other white people confronted with similar scenes gave no such indication at all. The "common sight" of slaves being transported to their fates aboard riverboats was rarely enough to spark outrage or even draw much of a passing glance from white passengers. Charles H. Titus, for example, was a New Englander who traveled aboard the same steamboat just four months prior to Lincoln and Speed's voyage. During a stopover in Louisville, Titus saw slaves everywhere around him, but he merely remarked that they "appeared to be cheerful and happy," adding that "an abolitionist is considered there [in Louisville] worse than a traitor." If Titus even tried to discern the reasons or exact circumstances of any of these slaves' predicaments, there is no record of the fact.[42]

Would Mary Speed—a wealthy white Southerner who was accustomed to such sights—have noticed? It is impossible to say. Underlying Lincoln's observations was the fact of his audience: this one particular white woman with whom he was on friendly terms and whose family had shown him hospitality and sympathy in a time of trouble. Lincoln would not have lightly risked offending the sensibilities of his best friend or his best friend's sister. Were his words therefore a genuine reflection of his reaction to the slaves he saw aboard the *Lebanon*? Or were they, rather, examples of Lincoln tailoring his response to his audience—maybe making a wealthy slaveholding woman feel a bit better about herself and her circumstances by suggesting that, however awful the condition of slavery might actually be, the slaves themselves were apparently happy and entirely unfazed by their lot?

The overall point of his anecdote, at bottom, was the slaves' contentment. They were victims of an unjust system, and yet, according to Lincoln's rendering, they seemed happy: they "danced, sung [sic], cracked jokes, and played various games." We know nothing of Mary Speed's particular personality or of her attitude toward slavery, but as a general rule, this was precisely what a slaveholding white Southerner wanted to hear. Slaveholders commonly told anyone who would listen that their human "property" was satisfied and had no need for freedom and its fruits. "Our slaves are happy and contented," declared Senator Jefferson Davis of Mississippi. "They bear the kindest relation that labor can sustain to capital." Many slaveholding Southerners agreed.[43]

The role of Mary Speed as his audience also helps to explain Lincoln's reference to God. It was highly unusual. The few religious references in his correspondence prior to 1841 were of the vaguest sort—as when he mentioned "the nineteenth century of the Christian era" in his address to Springfield's Young Men's Lyceum three years previously or when he used "The Saviour of the world" and his "twelve disciples" to illustrate a point in a legislative speech on economics. Even then, he tended to use religious images as handy ways to illustrate some broader points, rather than moral precepts. And even this he did infrequently; in most cases, Lincoln was much more likely to draw upon nonreligious examples or anecdotes.[44]

This is hardly surprising because, according to many people who knew him at the time, Lincoln was ambivalent about matters of faith. "When I first knew Mr. L[incoln] he was skeptical as to the great truths of the Christian religion," Joshua Speed later wrote. Lincoln was literate in the Bible of course; it was a book he knew from an early age. But by the time he reached youth and early manhood, his childhood faith was often at odds with his more rational, coldly intellectual side, to the point that he would sometimes question basic elements of Christian thought, such as Christ's virgin birth.[45] There were rumors that, as a young man, he had written "a pamphlet attacking the divinity of Christ," which friends persuaded him to burn because of the damage it might do to his political prospects.[46] To that end, he felt compelled to issue a public declaration in 1846 denying he was an "infidel." But in doing so, he chose his words so carefully that people reading them, then and since, have wondered about the true depth of his religious feelings.[47]

Even in his moments of deepest doubt, Lincoln retained a core belief in the existence of God, and he grew in his religious faith as he aged, particularly during his presidency. He may well have become more pious, especially during the Civil War when he increasingly turned to God in trying to explain the war's awful carnage.[48] But the available evidence leaves little doubt that the Lincoln of 1841 was a religious skeptic, a man who did not habitually cite the Bible or God in his letters or speeches and who rarely attended church at all. "I've never been to church yet [since arriving in Springfield]," he wrote to Mary Owens, "nor probably shall not be soon."[49]

In sum, referencing God was not normal behavior for Lincoln at that point in his life. Doing so with Mary Speed may have been playing to his audience—writing a letter to a woman whose mother he knew to be deeply religious and understanding, even at this early stage in his life, that he could make a larger moral point by couching it in biblical terms, given that he lived surrounded by devout Christians. The particular passage he employed, "God tempers the wind to the shorn lamb," is often attributed to the book of Proverbs, but it is not actually found there or anyplace else in the Bible. It originated in an eighteenth-century French saying ("*Dieu mesure le froid à la brebis tondue*," or "God measures the wind to the shorn lamb"), but Lincoln probably knew it simply as a common saying among the Christians around whom he had spent his life.[50]

Whatever the case may be, his precise meaning is open to several interpretations. Was he referring to a merciful God, saving African Americans from horrors they could not bear by giving them a false sense of contentment? Or could his letter be read as an implicit avowal of slavery's inevitability, like any other sin—lust, envy, anger, and so on? In this sense, God was apparently powerless to end the sin of slavery but could only ameliorate its worst effects—shades of Lincoln's second inaugural address twenty-four years later when he asked if "we shall suppose that American Slavery is one of those offences [*sic*] which, in the providence of God, must needs come."[51] There was also a hint of Lincoln's private battles with depression. "He renders the worst of human conditions tolerable, while He permits the best, to be nothing better than tolerable"—that last part had a rather dark tone, commensurate with a man whose mood was still often morose and worried.

Lincoln might therefore have been saying several things about slavery in this passage on God's mercy. But one point he did not make: he did not say that God hated slavery or slaveholders or their system. God was depicted with a very light touch in the letter to Mary Speed; there was no passionate declaration that human bondage was wicked and its defenders doomed to burn in hell, à la William Lloyd Garrison and his fellow abolitionists. Lincoln did not go in for such denunciations, and crusading invocations of God as an instrument to damn sinners and make them pay for their transgressions struck him as counterproductive. He made this point clear in a speech he gave in 1842 to Springfield's local chapter of the Washington Temperance Society:

> When the dram seller and drinker, were incessantly told . . . in the thundering tones of anathema and denunciation, with which the lordly Judge often groups together all the crimes of the felon's life . . . that they were the authors of all the vice and misery and crime in the land; that their houses were the workshops of the devil; and that their persons should be shunned by all the good and virtuous, as moral pestilences—I say, when they were told all this, and in this way, it is not wonderful that they were slow, very slow, to acknowledge the truth of such denunciations, and to join the ranks of their denouncers, in a hue and cry against themselves.[52]

Lincoln's particular understanding of human nature precluded such denunciations of drunkards or any other sinners—including slaveholders. But at the same time, Lincoln was not much given to empathy either, for drunks, slaveholders, or even their slaves. "I am not a very sentimental man," he once confessed. It was true. By the time he reached adulthood, he had learned to keep a certain distance from those around him, to eschew the overly sentimentalized and emotion-laden expressions common to his age, and to generally elevate reason above feeling as the best motivator for behavior and belief. Referring to the Founding Fathers in his address to Springfield's lyceum in 1838, he declared that "we, their descendants, [must] supply their places with other pillars, hewn from the solid quarry of sober reason. Passion has helped us; but can do so no more. It will in future be our enemy. Reason, cold, calculating, unimpassioned reason, must furnish all the materials for our future support and defence [sic]."[53]

His emphasis on "cold, calculating reason" manifested itself in relationships with other people as well as in politics. Few could honestly claim to know Lincoln intimately. He had "no strong emotional feelings for any person—mankind or thing," his friend and campaign manager David Davis believed. Elizabeth Edwards, Mary Todd's sister and the wife of one of Lincoln's political associates, agreed. "He was a cold man," she thought, and "had no affection." Many saw in him a manipulative, even somewhat aloof side. He "handled and moved man *remotely*," noted a fellow lawyer, "as we do pieces on a chessboard." Friends and associates found him distant and secretive. "Even those who were with him through long years of hard study and under constantly varying circumstances can hardly say they knew him through and through," his law partner Bill Herndon later wrote. "I always believed I could read him as thoroughly as any man, and yet he was so different in many respects from any other one I ever met before or since his time that I cannot say I comprehended him."[54]

If Lincoln openly avoided displaying his feelings, he was correspondingly reluctant to take an I-feel-your-pain approach toward other people. This reluctance is a striking facet of his letter to Mary Speed, as seen in his apparent lack of empathy for the enslaved black people aboard the *Lebanon*. He well understood the injustice and inherent unfairness of the slave *system*—the "condition" that would separate them "forever from the scenes of their childhood, their friends," and so on—but he did not express any particular empathy for the slaves as *people* in his letter. In fact, the entire thrust of his description of the slaves to Mary was an assertion that they were "the most cheerful and happy creatures on board" and, by implication, that they needed no sympathies. If we are to take Lincoln at his word, there was no pain for him to feel.

Nor was he, at least by that point, a terribly astute observer of the facts of slave life for its victims. It never seems to have occurred to him that the slaves on the *Lebanon*'s deck might be putting on a show for their white observers, knowing that it would be in their best interest to fake contentment or even joy, the better to escape the lash or lull their masters into a false sense of security. Modern scholars and psychologists call this masking, and by all accounts, slaves became quite good at it—showing the white men and women in power what they needed to see so that the slaves could survive in a white-dominated world.[55]

In that particular situation—surrounded by white people (many of whom might have felt nervous to be in such close proximity to slaves) and traveling aboard a steamboat that afforded opportunities for escape or mutiny—those slaves on the *Lebanon* may well have thought it expedient to feign a happy contentment with their lot. Others in a similar situation did so. A Northern traveler on a steamboat in Virginia, for example, remarked that a coffle of slaves on the ship "appear, in general, indifferent to their situation; whether they fully understand it I do not know."[56]

Like the vast majority of his white contemporaries, Lincoln was none the wiser. He had no special powers of discernment or insight on this matter, at least not in 1841. There is no indication in the letter to Mary Speed that he thought it possible the slaves might be putting the best and most politic face on a difficult situation, that they were not really happy or content. Then again, given Lincoln's limited exposure to African Americans or slavery thus far in his life, it may be asking too much to think that he understood the nuances of black slave life. Many a white Southern slaveholder who lived an entire lifetime among slaves and African Americans knew no better.

Even so, there is beneath Lincoln's narrative a quiet but steady throb of realization that slavery was, at its core, the "worst of situations," that there was a very human cost to the South's labor system. Lincoln did not need empathy or a keen reading of African Americans' lives and situations to understand that there was something fundamentally wrong in their enslavement. This letter illustrates a basic, contradictory feature of Lincoln's whiteness: Lincoln cared deeply about what other whites thought, and yet, at the same time, he was willing to point out something like the slave coffle even when there was no good reason for him to do so—indeed, when there might arguably have been good reasons for him to avoid the subject altogether. Even as Lincoln was deeply enmeshed in the web of whiteness that surrounded him, a web that he himself voluntarily and even enthusiastically entered, he could also, to at least some extent, stand outside that web and see, with a compassion lacking in so many other whites of his time, something as morally outrageous as that *Lebanon* slave coffle.

■

FOUR

The White A and the Black B

By the 1850s, Lincoln's whiteness had several components, accumulated over a lifetime of experiences living within what was a more or less typical white cultural and social environment. He possessed a benign but nevertheless distinct sense of whiteness defined by the savage and black Other, the sort that noted the difference between himself and nonwhites but assigned no particular malice to the fact. His sense of the nonwhite Other was not vicious or nasty, and he was capable of both noticing the plight of and feeling compassion toward Indians like the old man he encountered during the Black Hawk War or the slaves aboard the *Lebanon*.

There is some evidence that the pre-1850 Abraham Lincoln was able to connect his lifelong and consistent avowal of slavery's basic injustice to an appreciation of racism's basic injustice. He could see onboard the *Lebanon*, for instance, that slavery exacted a terrible human cost. This was no insignificant matter, not in an age when even slavery's most vociferous critics were often unable to mount any effective critique of the nation's pervasive racism, when some in fact rooted their antislavery ideals in their racism and their need to preserve white supremacy. This was not Lincoln.

But to whatever extent Lincoln appreciated racism's basic unfairness toward its nonwhite American victims—and it is impossible to truly gauge that extent—he did not openly challenge the presuppositions of white supremacy. He might mention that slave coffle to Mary Speed, might even deprecate its inhumanity. But he would not openly question Mary Speed's place in society as a white woman of privilege.

Nor did he use either of his chosen professions to critique American racism. As a lawyer, he showed no interest in using the law as a tool to challenge white supremacy, but then again, few lawyers in his day did so. Politics also was not for him a vehicle to critique white supremacy or the racial underpinnings of American society.[1]

All of this placed Lincoln somewhere in the middle of those whites who felt no empathy for nonwhite people and those on the more radical edge of white society who would have expressed to Mary Speed (and everyone else) their moral outrage—the William Lloyd Garrisons and Theodore Dwight Welds of the world, who understood both the racial oppression of black people and the structure of white supremacy sustaining that oppression.[2] There Lincoln's whiteness stood as he and the rest of the nation entered the tumultuous decade of the 1850s, a decade that would, in many sharp ways, lay bare not only the ugly undertow of slavery but also the toxic racial prejudice that coursed through all of American society, in the South as well as the North. Whether they wished it or not, all white Americans confronted—in numerous ways for the first time in the nation's brief history—the awful realities of caste and color. Some would try to challenge that reality; others would not. But race could no longer be ignored, not in the era of John Brown, Dred Scott, *Uncle Tom's Cabin,* the passion of Garrison and Weld, the countervailing passion of Hinton Rowan Helper and George Fitzhugh, and all the myriad other manifestations of the nation's ongoing sectional strife.

Lincoln knew where he stood. From an economic development–minded politician who rarely mentioned slavery in the 1830s and 1840s, he had become a single-minded, nearly obsessive opponent of slavery in the 1850s. No reasonable person could have misunderstood his point of view on this score: he hated slavery and said so, loud and often. He was not unsympathetic to white Southerners, he did not particularly like abolitionists, and he had no fixed ideas concerning exactly how slavery would end or when—but no one could doubt that he viewed slavery's eventual demise as an inevitable and desirable by-product of the American Dream. And the racial component, in particular the white component of his antebellum antislavery politics? That was more complicated.

ON THE SURFACE, white Americans of the antebellum era had ample cause to revel in their whiteness. After all, whites dominated American life at all levels, political, economic, social, and cultural. Still, even in this heyday of the white American, there was an undercurrent of fear and anxiety. White Southerners were the primary carriers of this anxiety, but white Northerners weren't far behind.

White Americans in the 1840s and 1850s did not possess a truly clear understanding of just what white was, but whatever it was, they often saw it as threatened and under attack. Much of this anxiety was due to slavery, as the South's slave system proved to be that rarity in human history—a slave population that actually grew by natural increase without constant replenishment from Africa. Some worried that this tendency for large plantations to increase the numbers of their black laborers posed a long-term threat to the stability and well-being of the surrounding whites. "Our wealthier planters, with greater means, and no more skill, are buying out their poorer neighbours, extending their plantations, and adding to their labour force," noted one Virginian, and "thus the white population has decreased, and the slave population increased. . . . One will discover numerous farmhouses, once the abode of industrious and intelligent freemen, now occupied by slaves."[3]

Race war was a constant, omnipresent fear among American whites. And it did not much matter whether one was proslavery or not. Slaveholding Americans of course had long-standing anxieties about possible slave uprisings inciting race-based violence with devastating results for whites. But many Northerners and even some of slavery's critics voiced similar concerns. "If the present state of things [in the slaveholding South] shall be continued for a century," warned one antislavery writer, "it is probable that it will end in a war of extermination between the black and the white population, or in an attempt by the blacks to conquer and exclusively possess one or more of the southern states of the Union as an independent kingdom for themselves." Others argued that the immediate emancipation schemes of radical abolitionists carried the real possibility of ruin if pursued too quickly or with too much vigor—or without a corresponding plan to get freed blacks out of the country as quickly as possible. "An immediate abolition of slavery . . . would be immediately followed by a desperate struggle for immediate ascendancy of the black race over the white race, or rather it would be followed by instantaneous collisions between the two races, which would break out into a civil war, which would end in the subjugation of the one race or the other," declared Henry Clay.[4]

Many whites cast a nervous eye toward the Caribbean, which made worldwide news for bloody slave uprisings that resulted in massacres of whites by rebellious and vengeful slaves. As early as the Saint Domingue rebellion of 1791, white Americans—especially Southerners—brooded about the possibility that blacks might see fit to emulate their Caribbean neighbors and start a bloodbath of their own in America. "The atrocities perpetrated were of a savage and relentless character," wrote one American journalist of the Saint Domingue revolt, and "in a short time no less than two thousand whites are supposed to have been massacred." Many white Americans could not help but wonder if they might be next, particularly in the wake of Nat Turner's spectacular (if short-lived) revolt in 1831. Actual armed violence by American black people against whites was rare, but this fact did not temper white America's paranoia.[5]

White racial anxiety was not just triggered by African Americans. Some saw the daily arrival of Irish and other supposedly nonwhite immigrants as a threat to the national character; indeed, such impulses gave rise to the burgeoning nativist movement of the 1840s and 1850s and culminated in the formation of the American, or Know-Nothing, Party. The nation's rapidly expanding western frontier also seemed to carry with it the threat of exposing white America to the dangers posed by intermingling with Indians and Mexicans. Although many welcomed the nation's growth, others worried about what might happen when whites collided with nonwhites on the frontier. "We have conquered many of the neighboring tribes of Indians, but we never thought . . . of incorporating them into our Union," argued John C. Calhoun. "We have never dreamt of incorporating into our Union any but the Caucasian race—the free white race. To incorporate Mexico, would be the very first instance of incorporating an Indian race, for more than half of the Mexicans are Indians. . . . I protest against such a union as that! Ours, sir, is the government of the white man."[6]

Whites reacted to these threats in different ways. At times, those underlying white anxieties led to sharp spasms of racial violence. In 1838, Lincoln himself noted a disturbing tendency among some whites to apply "lynch law" to African Americans who had in some fashion offended white sensibilities:

Negroes, suspected of conspiring to raise an insurrection, were caught up and hanged in all parts of the State [Mississippi]: then, white men, supposed to be leagued with the negroes; and finally, strangers, from neighboring States, going thither on business. . . . Thus went on this process of hanging, from gamblers to negroes, from negroes to white citizens, and from these to strangers; till, dead men were seen literally dangling from the boughs of trees upon every road side; and in numbers almost sufficient, to rival the native Spanish moss of the country, as a drapery of the forest.[7]

Some Northern whites erected legal barriers to the presence of any blacks in their midst, for fear that a horde of black emigrants could someday move in and drive whites entirely away. Lincoln's own state of Illinois created oppressive Black Laws in 1846 and 1853, which at first required every African American and mulatto to register a bond and certificate of freedom with the county court where he or she intended to reside; eventually, the laws banned free blacks from the state entirely.[8] Such was the temper of the times, as incredible as it may sound to modern ears. "Your State will be dotted all over with Negro cabins," warned an Indiana legislator, and "the white man will be driven out from the State, and his place be occupied by the African—for that will be the effect of permitting their immigration into the State. You will fill your land with Negroes, and the white man will either drive them out or leave the State himself, and seek another home."[9]

Some wanted the growing population of black people removed entirely from the United States. The 1840s and 1850s witnessed the flourishing of the American colonization movement, with a fair number of whites supporting removal of Africans from the United States not so much as a matter of justice to black people but rather as a way to preserve white racial purity. "Now that the days of [the black man's] majority have arrived, and as a young man who has come of age is provided with a home by his guardian, so the colored race, which now shows many signs of ability to take care of itself, should be provided with a suitable home by the older guardian race," argued a Northern legislator in 1852.[10]

If African Americans and other nonwhite people could not be removed physically, then they could at least be isolated and quarantined intellectually. Antebellum intellectuals tried to preserve whites' racial identities by throwing up scientific barricades to separate who was white and who was not, the better to maintain some degree of white racial purity. The rather vague sense that whites were superior to nonwhites, which had pervaded white thinking, was now being replaced by what was deemed incontrovertible, empirical evidence. During the 1840s and 1850s, for instance, scientists asserted that African Americans possessed smaller lungs and were thus consuming less oxygen, which contributed to the "habitually slower motions of the negro than the white man."[11] In 1839, University of Pennsylvania anthropologist and physician Samuel George Morton published *Crania Americana,* a statistical analysis of the differing sizes and characteristics of white and nonwhite skulls that supposedly proved with scientific rigor the innate superiority of the "modern white man." The American intellectual community seized upon Morton's findings as definitive proof of Caucasian superiority and implicitly a physiological guarantee of that superiority into the foreseeable future. At a minimum, Morton had explained just why things were as they were in America. Whites ran the country because science made it so, and this was a reassuring idea in an otherwise uncertain era. "One of the most singular features in the history of this continent is, that the aboriginal races, with few exceptions, have perished or constantly receded, before the Anglo-Saxon race," noted a review in the *American Journal of Science.* "These phenomena must have a cause; and can any inquiry be at once more interesting and philosophical than that which endeavors to ascertain whether that cause be connected with a difference in the brain between the native American race, and their conquering invaders?"[12]

Racial "amalgamation" was a persistent, nagging concern in the back of the minds of many antebellum white Americans, who worried about the possible consequences of sexual contact between whites and blacks. "Wherever in the history of the world the inferior races have conquered and mixed with the Caucasian, the latter have sunk into barbarism," argued Josiah Nott, a Philadelphia-trained surgeon living in Alabama who published and wrote about the scientific foundations of white racial identity. Nott agonized incessantly about the possible "adulteration of blood" that might result for whites from sexual contact with blacks, and he suggested that any interracial breeding could fatally harm the Caucasian future. "Every man conversant with the breeding of Horses, Cattle, Dogs and sheep, is aware of the effect of the slightest taint of impure blood," he warned.[13]

There were, then, a variety of nonwhite bogeymen inhabiting the minds of Lincoln's white neighbors during the 1850s: foreign slave uprisings, race wars caused by abolitionist zealots, so-called amalgamation and its attendant horrors. They had always been there of course, at least to a certain extent. But the many tumultuous sectional clashes between North and South that seemed to rise in drama and intensity after 1850 all had at their foundation some question related to black Americans and their relationship to whites. Scientific racial theories purporting to prove the vital importance of racial purity clashed with the agitation of a small but loud minority of abolitionists who appeared to want to erase racial boundaries entirely; though this was usually not the case, the mere suggestion that race relations should be altered in any way was greatly magnified as a controversy by the arguments of Nott and others. Add to this the growing numbers of immigrants from Europe and elsewhere who were not quite white—from the Irish Paddy to the Asian Celestial—as well as the many new Native American tribes suddenly living within America's borders following the war with Mexico, and antebellum America could seem a worrisome place, even to the white Americans who ran the country.

Shrewd politicians knew how to identify and exploit these fears, and in this respect, Illinois senator Stephen "Little Giant" Douglas was a master. His meteoric political career was built at least in part on his exploitation of all those white anxieties.

On one level, this was simply a matter of Douglas positioning himself as the nation's foremost champion of interests near and dear to ordinary whites' hearts. He was an ardent expansionist, which resonated with the many white yeoman farmers who wanted new farmlands carved out of the western territories. He was also a tireless champion of grassroots democracy and the inherent wisdom of the average, independent farmer who tilled the soil, cast his ballot as he saw fit, and with moxie and common sense steered the nation in the right direction.

When Douglas championed democracy, he by definition championed white interests. And one could charitably argue that he was (in this respect) an unwitting champion, without really understanding himself as such. Except that whiteness wasn't invisible to Stephen Douglas. He was an outspoken proponent of what he himself explicitly identified as white rights. "Our people are a white people," he told Congress when the issue of Illinois' racial exclusion laws was broached by his opponents. "Our State is a white State; and we mean to preserve the race pure, without any mixture with the negro. If you wish your blood and that of the African mixed in the same channel, we trust that you will keep at a respectful distance from us, and not try to force that on us as one of your domestic institutions." The audience in the gallery laughed.[14]

Douglas was quite willing to take advantage of white fears, to conjure up all those nonwhite bogeymen in whites' minds. One subtle but effective method was his consistent reference to the Republican Party as the "Black Republicans," the *Black* being a racially coded label with connotations clear to all his white listeners. Lincoln, for one, grew incensed at this. Douglas "called the new party *Black Republicans,*" Lincoln noted. "He might call names, and thereby pander to prejudice, as much as he chose: [but I] would not bandy such language with him."[15]

In response, Douglas made his purposes crystal clear. By using the term *Black Republicans,* he meant to tie the Republican Party inextricably to the dark, scary African American Others inhabiting white thoughts:

> This new republican party . . . abjures and ignores every question which has for its object the welfare and happiness of the white man— every question which does not propose to put the negro on an equality with the white man, politically and socially. . . . By this specious, but sophistical argument, they have succeeded in imposing on some weak- minded men, and some old women and children, until they have edu- cated a generation who really believe the negro is their brother.[16]

These references were repugnant, at least to some people, but they were effective, and they were part and parcel of the appeal exuded by the fore- most politician of his time. Although the value of Douglas's racial scare tactics are impossible to quantify—who can say which voters supported the Little Giant primarily out of racial fear and which supported him for some other reason?—he himself apparently believed they served him well, for he continued to reference the threats posed to the white race by African Americans, the abolitionists, and the Black Republicans throughout the 1850s.

For his part, Lincoln did not directly talk much about the white race at all. There is no evidence that he read *Crania Americana,* Josiah Nott's lec- tures, or any of the other pseudoscientific racism of his day. If anything, he was more exposed, on an intellectual level, to those few Americans who came at the issue of race from entirely the opposite perspective. His law partner William Herndon was a devotee of the transcendentalists, espe- cially Theodore Parker (with whom he briefly corresponded), and some of

CHAPTER FOUR

them were not only antislavery activists but also critics of the nation's racial caste system. Herndon once gave Lincoln a copy of Parker's "Effect of Slavery on the American People," which argued for "a solidarity in mankind" across racial boundaries and deprecated the dehumanizing effect of the institution on whites as well as blacks. Lincoln "read and returned it," Herndon wrote, and he was convinced that some passages in Parker's lecture directly influenced Lincoln when he later wrote the Gettysburg Address.[17]

On rare occasions, Lincoln did refer to black people as Others before white audiences and friends, but when he did so, he used the vehicle of humor. He had a real fondness for lowbrow "darky" jokes, of the sort found in the minstrel shows popular during his time. His friend Henry Whitney later wrote that "when he could select for himself [Lincoln] should prefer a 'nigger' show to an opera," and he sometimes attended the blackface shows available to him along with his wife, who also enjoyed such things.[18]

An acquaintance remembered that Lincoln once told a story about a balloonist who descended into a cotton field near New Orleans, the sight of which frightened the slaves in the field so badly that they all fled to the nearby woods—except for one black man. The listener recalled Lincoln describing this man as a "venerable darkey, who was rheumatic and could not run and who, as the resplendent aeronaut approached, having apparently just dropped from heaven, said: 'Good mawning, Massa Jesus; how's your Pa?'"[19]

The African Americans who inhabited Lincoln's humor were of this sort: thickheaded, stubborn, and just not terribly bright—a popular idea among whites. Another friend recalled a Lincoln story concerning "an ancient colored lady" who sold "game pies"—that is, meat pies—to eager customers along a Missouri highway. Her husband had grown too old and feeble to keep supplying the meat, but the old woman advertised the pies as game pies all the same. When her irate customers asked why she continued to call her meatless pies by that name, she replied, "I call 'em game pies 'cause that's their name. Game pies always was the name, and game pies is always a-going to be the name. That's all they is about it."[20] On another occasion, a friend recalled Lincoln speaking of "nigger mathematics" and describing a "darkey Preacher" named Pompey who had a reputation as a good mathematician. A local white man put that assertion to the test, asking Pompey the following question: if there were three pigeons sitting on a rail fence and one was shot, how many would remain? As Lincoln told the story, Pompey, "after a little wool-scratching," replied that two birds would remain. His questioner responded, "I knowed you was a fool, Pompey; der's none left; one's dead, and d-udder two's flown away."[21]

Lincoln's racial humor was handy in political settings—invariably white settings during which he regaled other whites. He once said of Democrats that their behavior recalled that of a "darky who, when a bear had put its head into the hole and shut out the daylight, cried out, 'What was darkening de hole?' 'Ah,' cried the other darky, who was on the tail of the animal, 'if de tail breaks you'll find out.'"[22] In March 1849, he received a letter from a Pennsylvania congressman named Moses Hampton, whom he had met while they both served in Congress and who, like Lincoln, had a reputation for wit and entertaining repartee.[23] "Do you remember the story of the old Virginian stropping his razor on a certain member of a young negro's body?" Hampton asked with a sniggering air, "which you told and connected it with my mission to Brazil—Now my good fellow, I am 'arter' that same mission, and my object in writing to you just now is to ask the favor that you will address a letter to [President] Taylor or Mr. Clayton [Secretary of State John M. Clayton] on that subject. . . . I want that appointment and *must have it.*"[24]

The point here is not the mere fact that Abraham Lincoln told such jokes, still less the seemingly endless (and fruitless) debate concerning whether such humor proves he was a bigot. Rather, the point is that these were jokes told by Lincoln the white man to other white men and presumably designed by Lincoln to have a positive effect on those men that would redound to his benefit. He told a joke about a "darky" and a bear to an audience of fellow Republicans not just as a form of entertainment but as a way to further reinforce his standing among them as a clever man and politician. It is a well-established fact, commented upon numerous times by Lincoln's friends, that he told his funny stories and jokes for good political effect. That political effect had a racial dimension, as well.

In this regard, Lincoln indulged in a significantly less vicious but comparable version of Douglas's tactics. Lincoln's jokes also made of the black an Other, and they did so as a political tactic that advanced his political interests among fellow whites. The difference between Lincoln and Douglas is vast and should not be understated: where Douglas made black people monsters to be feared, Lincoln made them buffoons. But even as buffoons, they were useful to and therefore used by Lincoln. This similarity to Douglas should not be overlooked either.

Privately, Lincoln apparently thought, at least in his more reflective moments, that race and color were poor means by which to define superior and inferior and to divvy up resources. This is clear from an interesting little fragment, written sometime in the 1850s, in which Lincoln deconstructed with lawyerly logic the fundamental absurdity of both slavery and its racial foundation.

He structured his thoughts as if he were interrogating an imaginary proslavery white person on the witness stand. "If A. can prove, however conclusively, that he may, of right, enslave B.—why may not B. snatch the same argument, and prove equally, that he may enslave A?" Lincoln continued, "You say A. is white, and B. is black. It is *color*, then, the lighter, having the right to enslave the darker? Take care. By this rule, you are to be slave to the first man you meet, with a fairer skin than your own." But Lincoln did not stop with this questioning of the facile concept of skin pigmentation as the deciding factor. He went after the even deeper substratum underpinning white supremacist arguments. "You do not mean *color* exactly?" he continued. "You mean the whites are *intellectually* the superiors of the blacks, and, therefore have the right to enslave them? Take care again. By this rule, you are to be slave to the first man you meet, with an intellect superior to your own." And still further: "But, say you, it is a question of *interest*; and, if you can make it your *interest*, you have the right to enslave another. Very well. And if he can make it his interest, he has the right to enslave you."[25]

It is to Lincoln's considerable credit that in an age such as his own, he could for a moment step back and clearly perceive the absurdity and injustice not only of slavery or even of racism as slavery's foundation but also of the very idea of white supremacy. Color, intellect, and interest were the foundation of antebellum whiteness, and Lincoln here called all three into question.

Few of his white neighbors did as much, not even those among his Whig and later Republican political allies who were adamantly opposed to slavery as an institution. Most antislavery Republicans refused to question white superiority at all and went out of their way in fact to emphasize that their desire to bring about the destruction of human bondage should in no way be read as a desire to deconstruct white privilege.[26]

However, this particular document from the 1850s was written by Lincoln in private, for his eyes only. Nothing like it appeared in any speech he delivered, nor does he seem to have voiced such sentiments to his colleagues and friends.

A cynic might point out that Lincoln deliberately hid his thoughts because he feared the backlash from white voters, most of whom would not be kindly disposed toward such musings—and there was probably truth in this. We have no idea and will never really know his purposes in writing this fragment or why he did not make his thinking public. What we do know is that the Abraham Lincoln of the 1850s was reluctant to antagonize white people for their racial views, even if privately he believed race was a poor way to order society.

There were many reasons for this. Lincoln was psychologically averse to open confrontation of any sort, much preferring solutions that worked around a given problem, rather than striking it head on. His profession also taught him the benefits of avoiding confrontation. As a lawyer, he saw himself as a negotiator who tried to settle disputes out of court whenever possible. "Discourage litigation," he advised fellow lawyers. "Persuade your neighbors to compromise whenever you can. Point out to them how the nominal winner is often a real loser—in fees, expenses, and waste of time. As a peacemaker the lawyer has a superior opportunity of being a good man." An acquaintance recalled overhearing a conversation between Lincoln and a prospective client in Lincoln's law office, during which Lincoln informed the client,

> Yes, we can doubtless gain your case for you; we can set a whole neighborhood at loggerheads . . . [but] you must remember that some things legally right are not morally right. We shall not take your case. But will give you a little advice for which we will charge you nothing. You seem to be a sprightly, energetic man; we would advise you to try your hand at making six hundred dollars in some other way.

Lincoln simply did not possess the temperament of a radical such as William Lloyd Garrison, who was entirely willing to set a neighborhood at loggerheads if it suited his purposes.[27]

And there was also Lincoln's ambition, which was no small matter. As mentioned earlier, Herndon observed that it was "a little engine that knew no rest," adding that Lincoln's "restless ambition found its gratification only in the field of politics."[28] It is entirely plausible that Lincoln chose not to make public his private questioning of race as a matter of political expediency—a calculation on his part that he could not hope to win elections if he openly challenged the principles of white superiority that animated nearly every voter in the lily-white audiences who listened to his speeches and voted accordingly. He had seen fit, long before 1850, to feed his ambitions by first escaping the white trash roots of his family background and then entering both the law and politics, two of the most rigidly and effectively segregated white pursuits in American life.

In his unwillingness to publicly vent his private musings concerning just why the white "A." might try to enslave the black "B.," he was echoing the same sensibilities that had animated the letter he wrote to Mary Speed years before, a letter that had no political context. In that letter, he might have, had he so chosen, given full voice to his sense of white supremacy's injustice without doing much more damage to his prospects than perhaps alienating the sister of his best friend. They were on much the same continuum, that letter and the fragment he wrote on slavery and white racism, expressing a rare sense of compassion toward blacks and an even rarer recognition of white supremacy's injustice, suppressed and qualified by a desire to avoid openly antagonizing his fellow whites. This last feature of his racial thought was thrown into sharp relief during his famous showdown with Stephen Douglas in 1858 for Illinois' U.S. Senate seat.

DOUGLAS WAS MANY THINGS to Lincoln: a high-profile political rival, the chief spokesman for a policy—popular sovereignty—that Lincoln equated with appeasement to proslavery elements, perhaps even at one time a competitor for Mary Todd's hand. On a private level, Lincoln simply did not like Douglas, an antagonism that was unusual in a man who by the 1850s had learned, sometimes the hard way, not to make politics too personal.

Douglas's perspective on slavery was more complex than either Lincoln himself or the subsequent judgment of history allowed. He was not truly proslavery, seeing in human bondage a backward institution that threatened the democratic foundations he so admired. But he did believe that slavery was appropriate, if only in the short term, for white Southerners, who needed slave labor for their particular economy and condition. For Douglas, this was entirely a matter of local autonomy. "There is a line, or belt of country, meandering through the valleys and over the mountain tops, which is a natural barrier between free territory and slave territory," he told a New Orleans audience, "on the south of which are to be found productions suitable to slave labor, while on the north exists a country adapted to free labor alone."[29] This had been the natural order in Douglas's America throughout his lifetime and before, and he was not much disposed to meddle with it or with slavery.

Douglas could afford to be so nonchalant about slavery's existence in the South because he simply did not like or care all that much about black people, whom he saw as a permanently inferior, degraded race that would (and should) remain under the domination of whites. "I have said over and over again," he declared in a Senate speech, "that, in my opinion, this government was made by white men for the benefit of white men and their posterity forever, and should be administered by white men, and by none other whatsoever." When challenged about the question of slavery in the West, he averred, "I am in favor of throwing the territories open to all the white men, and all the negroes too, that chose to go, and then allow the white men to govern the territory. I would not let one of the negroes, free or slave, either vote or hold office anywhere."[30]

When he geared up to challenge Douglas for the Little Giant's Senate seat in 1858, Lincoln might have chosen to ignore entirely his opponent's statements about African Americans. Certainly, this would have been the politically expedient approach. He well knew that Douglas's strategy was to tether Lincoln as tightly as possible to abolitionism, the better to portray him as a dangerous radical who, along with all the other Black Republicans, wanted to upend the nation's racial caste system and dispossess whites of their privileged place in society.

But Lincoln instead chose to make an issue of Douglas's race-baiting tactics and his bigotry generally, even though in doing so he played right into his opponent's hands. His reasons? That same impulse that led him to broach the subject of the *Lebanon*'s slave coffle to Mary Speed when there was no reason to do so.

He took direct aim at a habit of Douglas's that was as old as white supremacy itself: bestializing African Americans. He told a Lewistown audience, "[Douglas's] speech at Bloomington would leave us to infer that he was opposed to the introduction of slavery into Illinois; but his effort in Lewistown, I am told, favors the idea, that if you can make more money by flogging niggers than by flogging oxen, there is no moral consideration which should interfere to prevent your doing so." Elsewhere, he took issue with Douglas's—and what Lincoln saw as Douglas's Southern allies'—

comparisons of black people to hogs or horses. "It is said that the slave-holder has the same [political] right to take his negroes to Kansas that a freeman has to take his hogs or his horses," Lincoln said to his audience in Springfield, but "Southern men do not treat their negroes as they do their horses. There are 400,000 free negroes in the United States. . . . These negroes are free, because their owners, in some way and at some time, felt satisfied that the creatures had mind, feeling, souls, family affections, hopes, joys, sorrows—something that made them more than *hogs or horses*." Addressing the arguments made by Douglas and his Southern supporters in favor of the Kansas-Nebraska Act, Lincoln pointed out:

> Equal justice to the south, it is said, requires us to consent to the extending of slavery to new countries. That is to say, inasmuch as you do not object to my taking my hog to Nebraska, therefore I must not object to you taking your slave. Now, I admit this is perfectly logical, if there is no difference between hogs and negroes. But while you thus require me to deny the humanity of the negro, I wish to ask whether you of the south yourselves, have ever been willing to do as much?[31]

Addressing the various controversies surrounding Douglas's Kansas-Nebraska Act of 1854, which allowed white settlers in a given territory to vote on whether they would have slavery, Lincoln likewise attacked Douglas on a moral as well as political level. Douglas's approach made sense, Lincoln argued, only if there was no essential moral difference between a settler bringing into a territory a hog or a wagon, on the one hand, and bringing a black slave, on the other. But there was a difference, he pointed out. That slave was a person. "The Judge has no very vivid impression that the negro is a human," Lincoln argued, "and consequently has no idea that there can be any moral question in legislating about him. In his view, the question of whether a new country shall be slave or free, is a matter of utter indifference, as it is whether his neighbor shall plant his farm with tobacco, or stock it with horned cattle." Lincoln deserves credit for raising this issue at all in front of white voters, many of whom also did not possess a "very vivid impression" of black humanity. He could have brought a multitude of weapons to bear on Douglas and the Kansas-Nebraska Act without ever really tackling the moral issues of African Americans' status and treatment.[32]

When the debates began on August 21, 1858, Douglas was true to form. Delivering the first speech in Ottawa, Illinois, the Little Giant wasted no time in pushing the requisite racial buttons. He hardly used the term *Re-publican* without attaching it to *Black,* and he accused Lincoln and his al-lies of trying to "abolitionize" first the Whigs and then the Republican Party. He associated Lincoln with the nation's most prominent—and for many whites, its most scary—black man, "Fred Douglass," and other "lit-tle Abolition orators." "Are you in favor of conferring upon the negro the rights and privileges of citizenship?" Douglas thundered to the crowd (who responded with cries of "No! No!"). "Do you desire to strike out of our State Constitution that clause which keeps slaves and free negroes out of the State, and allow the free negroes to flow in, and cover your prairies with black settlements? Do you desire to turn this beautiful State into a free negro colony?" He then asserted, "If you desire negro citizenship, if you desire to allow them to come into the State and settle with the white man, if you desire them to vote on an equality with yourselves, and to make them eligible to office, to serve on juries, and to adjudge your rights, then support Mr. Lincoln and the Black Republican party, who are in favor of the citizenship of the negro."[33]

In case the audience missed his point, Douglas made his self-appointed championship of white America crystal clear. For him, this was not just about scapegoating African Americans; the Little Giant was unabashedly the Little White Giant, going to battle for white interests. "I believe this government was made on the white basis," he declared. "I believe it was made by white men, for the benefit of white men and their posterity for ever." Just for good measure, Douglas took a gratuitous swipe at those nonwhite Others who lurked in the back of white Americans' minds: "I am in favour of confining citizenship to white men, men of European birth and descent, instead of conferring it upon negroes, Indians and other inferior races."[34]

In Freeport six days later, he referenced an apocryphal image of Freder-ick Douglass riding about town while seated next to a white woman and driven by a white coachman. "All I have to say of it is this, that if you, Black Republicans, think that the negro ought to be on a social equality with your wives and daughters, and ride in a carriage with your wife, whilst you drive the team, you have a perfect right to do so," he jeered, adding a bit further along that Lincoln believed "the white man had no right to pass laws for the government of the black man without the nigger's consent."[35]

And so it went. In Jonesboro on September 15, he declared:

This government was made on the white basis, by white men, for the benefit of white men and their posterity forever, and should be administered by white men and none others. . . . [The Founders] desired to express by that phrase ["all men are created equal"], white men, men of European birth and European descent, and had no reference either to the negro, the savage Indians, the Fejee, the Malay, or any other inferior and degraded race, when they spoke of the equality of men.

In Charleston on September 18, he accused Lincoln of holding different principles in different sections of the state by telling the audience that Republican "principles in the North are jet black, in the centre they are in color a decent mulatto, and in lower Egypt [a nickname for southern Illinois] they are almost white." In Galesburg on October 7 and in nearly identical language during their final debate at Alton on October 15, he pronounced: "This government was made by our fathers on the white basis . . . and was intended to be administered by white men in all time to come."[36]

Douglas was quite successful in speaking to the worst angels of his white audiences' natures. When he told his Ottawa listeners that the government was created for whites only, the crowd responded, "Good for you" and "Douglas forever." When he again referenced Frederick Douglass's alleged carriage ride with a white woman and driver in Jonesboro, the crowd hooted "Shame!" "White men, white men," chanted the crowd in Freeport as Douglas enumerated the various ways in which he would defend their interests.[37]

Lincoln's response? He famously beat a retreat in the face of Douglas's implacable race-baiting. "Anything that argues me into his idea of perfect social and political equality with the negro, is but a specious and fantastic arrangement of words, by which a man can prove a horse chestnut to be a chestnut horse," he told their first audience.

I have no purpose to introduce political and social equality between the white and the black races. There is a physical difference between the two, which in my judgment will probably forever forbid their living together upon the footing of perfect equality, and inasmuch as it becomes a necessity that there must be a difference, I, as well as Judge Douglas, am in favor of the race to which I belong, having the superior position. I have never said anything to the contrary.[38]

His use of the phrase "inasmuch as it becomes a necessity" implied a lawyerly qualification regarding the need for racial distinction, and the insertion of "probably" somewhat ameliorated what was otherwise a dismal vision of America's racial future. But by the time the two men arrived in Charleston for their fourth debate, even those mild qualifications had largely disappeared—perhaps Lincoln sensed that the Little Giant was scoring points with his race-baiting and that he himself needed to sound more forceful in his refutations. "I am not nor ever have been in favor of making voters or jurors of negroes, nor of qualifying them to hold office, nor to intermarry with white people," he firmly declared. In language echoing his earlier pronouncement, he stated:

> And I will say in addition to this that there is a physical difference between the white and black races which I believe will for ever forbid the two races living together on terms of social and political equality. And inasmuch as they cannot so live, while they do remain together there must be the position of superior and inferior, and I as much as any other man am in favor of having the superior position assigned to the white race.[39]

Still, there were lines that Lincoln would not cross. He did not demonize black people. He shared in the general revulsion felt by whites concerning interracial sexuality, declaring in an earlier speech that "there is a natural disgust in the minds of nearly all white people, to the idea of an indiscriminate amalgamation of the white and black races."[40] But even if Lincoln may have been revolted by the idea, he did not seem to have been frightened by it, nor would he exploit those fears in others. During the 1858 debates, he actually poked a bit of fun at the whole subject. "I do not understand that because I do not want a negro woman for a slave I must necessarily want her for a wife," he said. "My understanding is that I can just let her alone. I am now in my fiftieth year, and I certainly never have had a black woman for either a slave or a wife. So it seems to me quite possible for us to get along without making either slaves or wives of negroes."[41]

Lincoln did not pose as an explicitly white champion of white interests, although in earlier speeches he had tried to speak to his white audiences' sense of self-interest in advancing arguments to keep slavery out of the western territories. "Whether slavery shall go into Nebraska, or other new territories, is not a matter of exclusive concern to the people who may go there," he suggested. Rather,

> the whole nation is interested that the best use shall be made of these territories. We want them for the homes of free white people. This they cannot be, to any considerable extent, if slavery shall be planted within them. Slave States are places for poor white people to remove FROM; not to remove TO. New free States are the places for poor people to go to and better their condition. For this use, the nation needs these territories.[42]

At times, Lincoln sounded as if he advocated a benign species of racial segregation. Knowing that a considerable number of whites in his audiences were in fact deeply worried about preserving white racial purity, he took a classic debater's approach by turning Douglas's arguments inside out, suggesting that opening up the West to at least the possibility of slavery was the best way to ensure racial amalgamation. By contrast, Lincoln argued, his and the Republican Party's platform of excluding slavery from the West entirely was a de facto method of racial separation. And though Lincoln would not go so far as to play directly on white sexual fears about lustful African Americans and others, he did state his belief that racial separation benefited whites and blacks alike. "From copious statistics he showed that where slavery existed, the *white* race was mixed with the *black* to an alarming degree, and thus proved that his policy of keeping them separate was decidedly more to be approved than that of Judge Douglas' who would bring them in contact," noted a newspaperman who recorded one of Lincoln's speeches.[43]

But if Lincoln seemed to want racial separation on the western frontier, he found in his reading of the Declaration of Independence a degree of political unity between whites and blacks—that document, he told white audiences, applied to both races equally. "There is no reason in the world why the negro is not entitled to all the natural rights enumerated in the Declaration of Independence, the right to life, liberty and the pursuit of happiness," he said. "I hold that he is as much entitled to these as the white man. I agree with Judge Douglas he is not my equal in many respects—certainly not in color, perhaps not in moral or intellectual endowment. But in the right to eat the bread, without leave of anybody else, which his own hand earns, *he is my equal and the equal of Judge Douglas, and the equal of every living man.*"[44]

Lincoln has been credited—appropriately—with affirming the basic rights of African Americans here, in the face of Stephen Douglas's ugly race-baiting tactics and perhaps even to the detriment of his own political prospects, given that so many white voters of his day were all too willing to deny African Americans even these minimal rights (as was the U.S. Supreme Court, which had done that very thing in the *Dred Scott* case). Lincoln has been praised by his many admirers for his willingness to speak out in this regard; conversely, critics of Lincoln have highlighted his famous and repeated assertions that he would not pursue racial equality.

Whether we focus in a positive way upon Lincoln's assertions of African American humanity or we focus negatively upon his unwillingness to espouse racial equality, our attention has always been directed to the black part of the racial equation, forgetting in the process that there was a white racial dimension to these issues. On the one hand, Lincoln's critique of Stephen Douglas was by proxy a biting indictment of the worst aspects of white racism that Douglas represented. But on the other hand, Lincoln was unwilling to expand this critique of Douglas into a broader and more far-reaching criticism of the white supremacy plaguing America as a whole.

His Declaration of Independence argument asserted that black people possessed rights already guaranteed them by the Revolutionary generation in 1787. This was a powerful and morally admirable stance, but it carried no corresponding implication that Lincoln's fellow whites needed to change their way of thinking, beyond a rather belated recognition that people of color possessed rights already guaranteed to them in 1787.[45] Moreover, those rights were, at bottom, economic: the right for African Americans to earn a basic living and compete in the American free enterprise game of life, no more and no less. This argument carried no overt criticism of white supremacy in general, nor did it require whites to alter much in their ways of thinking or living.

Rather than tell white people that they needed to take a hard look at themselves and how they had ordered the universe, Lincoln insisted that race was not a zero-sum game. White Americans were not required to give up anything or change anything substantial in order to honor his reading of the Declaration of Independence. "I do not perceive that because the white man is to have the superior position the negro should be denied everything," he said. There was room in American life, as matters stood in 1858, for black people to be given at least a reasonable shot at the American Dream.[46]

There were times when Lincoln regretted his white neighbors' bigotry. In a speech he delivered four years earlier in Peoria, Illinois, he mused at some length about just what might be possible if the slaves were suddenly freed. "What next? Free them, and make them politically and socially, our equals?" he asked. "My own feelings will not admit of this; and if mine would, we well know that those of the great mass of white people will not. Whether this feeling accords with justice and sound judgment, is not the sole question, if indeed, it is any part of it. A universal feeling, whether well or ill-founded, can not be safely disregarded."[47]

Coy as he was about his own private feelings concerning racial equality, Lincoln was not coy at all about his fellow whites. In his opinion, white America simply would not tolerate a mixed-race environment, and he had no inclination to have a tilt against the giant, unyielding windmill of white supremacy. His use of the word *safely* is revealing, suggesting that he saw white bigotry as something dangerous. It implies that Lincoln's unwillingness to openly confront white supremacy may have been about more than just preserving his own political prospects. It may also have been about avoiding measures that could unleash that torrid undertow of white racial fears that he understood was coursing just beneath the surface of antebellum American life.

Still, Lincoln saw potential or at least the possibility that his fellow whites could, if given the chance, rise above the muck and mayhem of their own dark fears and nightmares and recognize the basic humanity of black people. Speaking of the increasing numbers of free blacks in the slave South, he asked:

How comes this vast amount of property to be running about without owners? We do not see free horses or free cattle running at large. How is this? All these free blacks are the descendants of slaves, or have been slaves themselves, and they would be slaves now, but for SOMETHING which has operated on their white owners, inducing them, at vast pecuniary sacrifices, to liberate them. What is that SOMETHING? Is there any mistaking it? In all these cases it is your sense of justice, and human sympathy, continually telling you, that the poor negro has some natural right to himself.[48]

That was the problem with white race-baiters such as Stephen Douglas. They spoke to the worst features of whiteness, used those features to advance their own narrow political interests, and in so doing debased American public sentiment. "Public sentiment is every thing," Lincoln once observed. "*With* it, nothing can fail; *against* it, nothing can succeed. Whoever moulds public sentiment, goes deeper than he who enacts statutes, or pronounces judicial decisions."[49]

"Public sentiment" was by definition white sentiment: they were one and the same in an age when African Americans were not thought to have any real presence in the American polis. Douglas's insinuations, his dehumanization of blacks, and his amoral approach to their plight did more than just affect government policymaking. They also blunted the moral sensibilities and sound judgment of the entire white American community. Lincoln's feelings on this score were clear in the words scribbled on another of those private scraps of paper, written by him just prior to his first debate with Douglas. "Judge Douglas is a man of large influence. His bare opinion goes far to fix the opinion of others. . . . The susceptible young hear lessons from him, such as their fathers never heared [*sic*] when they were young," Lincoln wrote.

> If, by all these means, he shall succeed in moulding public sentiment to a perfect accordance with his own . . . in bringing all tongues to as perfect a silence as his own, as to there being any wrong in slavery—in bringing all to declare, with him, that they care not whether slavery be voted down or voted up—that if any people want slaves they have a right to have them—that negroes are not men—have no part in the declaration of Independence—that there is no moral question about slavery. . . . When, I say, public sentiment shall be brought to all this, in the name of heaven, what barrier will be left against slavery being made lawful every where?

At that point, Lincoln believed, white America was in every bit as much danger as black America, which reflected a species of racial unity in and of itself. "And then, the negro being doomed," he wrote, "and damned, and forgotten, to everlasting bondage, is the white man quite certain that the tyrant demon will not turn upon him too?"[50]

■

FIVE

The Broader Difference

Despite the dire warnings of alarmists such as Stephen Douglas, any significant change in the relationship between black and white Americans (and by extension the predicament faced by other ethnic minorities in America) before 1860 was highly unlikely. Discussions about the possibility were academic because in no significant sense did any American state—still less the national government—move toward either emancipation or easing the many galling restrictions imposed upon free black Americans, in the North and the South.

Lincoln summarized the situation well in another one of his searing moments of clarity and sympathy toward black people and their situation. During a speech in Springfield in June 1857, he observed of the African American that "all the powers of earth seem rapidly combining against him. Mammon is after him; ambition follows, and philosophy follows, and the Theology of the day is fast joining the cry." Warming to the subject, Lincoln offered an apt metaphor for both black suffering and white paranoia, declaring:

They have him in his prison house; they have searched his person, and left no prying instrument with him. One after another they have closed the heavy iron doors upon him, and now they have him, as it were, bolted in with a lock of a hundred keys, which can never be un-locked without the concurrence of every key; the keys in the hands of a hundred different men, and they scattered to a hundred different and distant places; and they stand musing as to what invention, in all the dominions of mind and matter, can be produced to make the impossi-bility of his escape more complete than it is.[1]

Lincoln's "they" in this passage was indeterminate: it may have indi-cated only proslavery extremists (his remarks were made while critiquing the *Dred Scott* decision), but he was not specific on this point. He made no explicit distinction between Northern and Southern treatment of African Americans. This was not just an antislavery statement; it was a description of American race relations in general. And there is a strong underlying sense here that Lincoln thought this ongoing white hand-wringing about African Americans was excessive and unjust.

But it was an isolated moment, this brief and oblique chiding of white America for its racial excesses. Lincoln was a passionate and consistent an-tislavery man. His criticism of slavery and its apologists was genuine, and it grew in intensity throughout the late 1850s as Lincoln increasingly came to believe that a conspiracy was afoot to enshrine in the pantheon of Amer-ican values the principle, as he put it, that "if one man chooses to make a slave of another man, neither that other man nor anybody else has a right to object." However, he was not the sort to dwell for long on the failings of his white neighbors, still less demand that they be corrected. His passionate hatred of human bondage was not matched by a passionate hatred of white supremacy.[2]

Rather than ask fellow whites to temper their unreasoning paranoia to-ward blacks, he devoted more time during the late 1850s to reassuring Americans that neither he nor his party posed any direct threat either to slavery where it existed in the South or to the nation's racial order as it ex-isted everywhere. His repeated and explicit assertions that he did not sup-port racial equality were designed to reassure nervous whites of this, and he made it a point to tell white Southerners that he bore them no enmity or really much in the way of criticism. "I think I have no prejudice against the Southern people. They are just what we would be in their situation," he pointed out. "When southern people tell us they are no more responsible for the origin of slavery, than we; I acknowledge the fact. When it is said that the institution exists; and that it is very difficult to get rid of it, in any satisfactory way, I can understand and appreciate the saying. I surely will not blame them for not doing what I should not know how to do myself."[3]

To some degree, this wariness of insulting white Southern sensibilities likewise fueled his actions or lack thereof during the 1860 presidential campaign. Contrary to myth, Lincoln was not the darkest of dark horses as the Republican presidential candidate. Though not on a par with more widely known antislavery men such as William Seward and Salmon Chase, he had achieved a national reputation as a firm antislavery man with his "house divided" speech in 1858 and his address at New York's Cooper's Union a year later, which had electrified Republican Party circles. By 1860, Lincoln had left a long paper trail of consistently antislavery speeches and writings, and insofar as he was known nationally, his name was firmly associated with the fight to end human bondage.

He knew it, too. He also knew that his record could be construed by nervous whites, especially in the South, as something more than it was: a moderate approach to slavery's long-term demise and an even more moderate, low-key approach to the attendant upheaval in America's race relations. He accordingly followed the custom of the day for presidential candidates and said nothing during the campaign, out of a concern that anything he did add to his already extensive public record on slavery would only serve to further inflame white public opinion in the South. "By the lessons of the past, and the united voice of all discreet friends, I am neither [to] write or speak a word for the public," he stated.[4]

For all his intelligence, his political savvy, and the fact that he was born a Southerner, Abraham Lincoln had a difficult time grasping the dark depths of white Southerners' fear and loathing of African Americans or their nearly uncontrollable dread at the thought of black people living among them without slavery's chains. A rational, reasonable man himself, Lincoln instinctively expected rational behavior in others, and so he could not quite understand the push toward proslavery extremism and secession in the South, which he believed were contrary to white Southerners' own interests. "In plain words, there is really no crisis except an *artificial one!*" he exclaimed in a speech in Pennsylvania during the secession crisis.

What is there now to warrant the condition of affairs presented by our friends "over the river [meaning the slaveholding South]"? . . . My advice, then, under such circumstances, is to keep cool. If the great American people will only keep their temper, on both sides of the line, the troubles will come to an end, and the question which now distracts the country will be settled just as surely as all other difficulties of like character which have originated in this government have been adjusted.[5]

The true "question which now distracts the country" was slavery and its disposition, but it was also the preservation of white supremacy that slavery institutionalized and nourished and that white Southerners saw as under assault by the North. In those overwrought, emotionally charged days following Lincoln's election, secessionists were blunt about the racial underpinnings of their revolution. Lincoln's Republicans "have demanded, and now demand, equality between the white and negro races, under our Constitution," complained one secession supporter in early 1861. "Our fathers made this a government for the white man, rejecting the negro as an ignorant, inferior, barbarian race, incapable of self-government, and not, therefore, entitled to be associated with the white man upon terms of civil, political, or social equality. This new administration comes into power, under the solemn pledge to overturn and strike down this great feature of our Union." Others evoked those age-old horrors of race war and amalgamation. Republicans would initiate "all the horrors of a San Domingo servile insurrection," according to one breathless critic, "consigning [the South's] citizens to assassinations and her wives and daughters to pollution and violation to gratify the lust of half-civilized Africans."[6]

White Southerners knew little at all about Lincoln, but they nevertheless peppered him with racially charged language and insults. He was frequently labeled with Stephen Douglas's favorite expression, *Black Republican,* and there were even those who speculated he might have mixed-race ancestry. The *Charleston Mercury* described him as "sooty and scoundrelly in aspect" and wondered, "After him what decent white man would be President?"[7] Some of Lincoln's Northern detractors harbored similar opinions. A British visitor to New York during the election related seeing a cartoon of Lincoln pasted to a store window, depicting him "spouting from a platform of rails, under which grins a half-concealed nigger."[8] And some of the many death threats he began to receive were racially charged. "If you don't resign we are going to put a spider in your dumpling and play Devil with you," growled a man named A. G. Frick in February 1861. After a profanity-laced, semiliterate harangue, he finished by saying, "Excuse me for using such hard words with you but you need it you are nothing but a goddam [*sic*] Black nigger."[9]

Despite such vitriol, Lincoln continued to believe that white Southerners would take stock of their situation rationally and remain in the Union. But the war came, and it would become a great grinding engine of racial fear, rumbling across the American landscape.

Some abolitionists actually welcomed that engine, seeing an opportunity to hitch a ride on its power and effect real, serious change in America. "For the statesman of the hour to permit any settlement of the present war between slavery and freedom, which will leave untouched and undestroyed the relation of master and slave, would not only be a great crime, but a great mistake, the bitter fruit of which would poison the lifeblood of unborn generation[s]," Frederick Douglass declared in a speech he titled "The American Apocalypse." William Lloyd Garrison struck a more somber tone, for the war was causing a painful conflict between his abolitionist principles and his pacifism, but he also expected the conflict to inevitably deliver the results he wanted. "There will be desolation and death on a frightful scale," he presciently predicted, "but if it shall end in the speedy and total abolition of slavery, the fountain-source of all our national difficulties, it will bring with it inconceivable blessings."[10]

But theirs was a minority opinion. Most Americans cringed at the thought of what the American apocalypse might entail. Fear management quickly became an integral part of Lincoln's job description when he assumed the presidency. And when the war inevitably churned up the nation's deep deposits of racial strife by making slavery and emancipation dominant issues, Lincoln became deeply engaged in white racial fear management. This was a subtle, overlooked dimension of the oft-told tale of his journey toward emancipation. As he slowly but steadily embraced freedom for blacks, he was simultaneously compelled to undergo another transformative journey involving whites, a journey that was, if anything, even more complicated and difficult than that which he undertook to achieve black freedom.

ALMOST FROM the moment he was elected, Lincoln was made aware of the fact that many white Northerners wanted nothing whatever to do with either emancipation or African Americans, no matter what the secession crisis brought. "The Party in Pennsylvania are thoroughly *Anti* Abolitionist and it is with difficulty we can keep them solid with the *Republican Party*," went a typical letter he received from a Philadelphian claiming to represent the "People's Party" in the state. "I respectfully ask that you will carefully weigh the appointments from this State and not give the *Negro* question to [*sic*] much prominence." Others were even more direct and even somewhat bizarre in the connections they made among Lincoln, the sectional crisis, and race. A Kentucky woman observed, in the middle of a rambling and nearly incoherent discourse on the war and its causes, that President-elect Lincoln should see to it that it "should be a Penetencherry offence [*sic*]" for any African American to help with the "amalgamation of the white race." "You damned old negro thief," snarled a man named J. B. Long, who enclosed with his letter an advertisement for a runaway slave and who had somehow convinced himself that Lincoln's mere election was enough to incite African Americans to mayhem. "If you dont find the above described slave, you shall never be inaugurated president of the United States—You old cuss."[11]

Racial amalgamation persistently haunted the imaginations of white Americans, many of whom connected Lincoln, the Republican Party, and the end of slavery with the dilution of white racial purity. "It must be your party's intention to exterminate the present race by force and establish a government of white, Black, yellow, red and every other color and mongrel order of People," asserted one Arkansas man. The racial overtones even reached members of Lincoln's administration. "We understand you have a very likely and intelligent mulatto boy you would dispose of on reasonable terms," read a sarcastic note from three men in South Carolina. "If you will let us know what you will take for the boy Hanibal [*sic*] known as Hanibal Hamlin [Lincoln's vice president] and your price is reasonable we will purchase him and are prepared to meet you with the cash at Richmond."[12]

Lincoln responded much as he had done throughout the years leading up to the war—by reassuring all who would listen that he wanted nothing to do with any scheme that might upset the order of things as they stood in 1860 with regard to either race or slavery. Briefly addressing a delegation of leaders from Washington, D.C., including the city's mayor, who had called upon him at Willard's Hotel when he first arrived in the capital on February 27, Lincoln pointed out that this was the first chance he had been given since the election to address the subject of slavery in a place where the institution existed. "I will take this occasion to say, that I think very much of the ill feeling that has existed and still exists between the people of the section from whence I came and the people here, is owing to a misunderstanding between each other which unhappily prevails," he said. "I therefore avail myself of this opportunity to assure you, Mr. Mayor, and all the gentlemen present, that I have not now, and never have had, any other than as kindly feelings towards you as to the people of my own section."[13]

In his inaugural address, he quoted extensively from his earlier speeches to this effect. He focused on the institution of slavery and its various legal and political dimensions, saying almost nothing about race beyond a rather quiet observation that African Americans threatened with removal to the South under the Fugitive Slave Act "deserved all the safeguards of liberty known in civilized and humane jurisprudence . . . so that a free man be not, in any case, surrendered as a slave." He also stated his belief that the Constitution's provision that "the citizens of each State shall be entitled to all previlages [sic] and immunities of citizens in the several States" applied to black as well as white Americans. This was a remarkable enough assertion, running entirely contrary to the arguments by many white Americans that African Americans possessed no citizenship rights or constitutional protections whatsoever.[14]

But beyond this Lincoln did not go, saying nothing else in his inaugural address about race and again devoting much of his time and attention to assuaging the anxieties of secession-minded white Southerners. "Will you hazard so desperate a step, while there is any possibility that any portion of the ills you fly from, have no real existence?" he asked. "Will you, while the certain ills you fly to, are greater than all the real ones you fly from? Will you risk the commission of so fearful a mistake?" And then came his famous closing paragraph, appealing to Americans' mystical sense of unity: "We are not enemies, but friends. We must not be enemies. Though passion may have strained, it must not break our bonds of affection. The mystic chords of memory, stretching from every battle-field, and patriot grave, to every living heart and hearthstone, all over this broad land, will yet swell the chorus of the Union, when again touched, as surely they will be, by the better angels of our nature."[15]

But of course, the white South ignored these overtures. As the war grew in scope and ferocity, Lincoln came under enormous pressure to do something about slavery, which many Northerners (whatever their racial views) understood was a vital cog in the Confederate war effort. Those pressures have been well and exhaustively documented: the Union army's manpower shortages, which caused Lincoln and his military commanders to increasingly consider using African American soldiers to fill the ranks; the ever-swelling numbers of runaway slaves, "contrabands" who crowded behind

Union army lines and whose exact legal status was unclear; the diplomatic advantages that might accrue among antislavery Europeans for Lincoln's administration if he redefined the war as a crusade against slavery; and (no minor consideration) the president's own moral conviction that finally ridding the nation of human bondage was the right thing to do.[16]

Among the throngs of visitors who arrived at the White House were antislavery-minded Americans who, for a variety of reasons and from a variety of perspectives, had concluded that slavery needed to go and that the president had to act. An endless stream of letters poured in, and for every letter he received warning him not to interfere with slavery, Lincoln now seemed to receive a matching letter insisting that he must do so—indicative perhaps of an American populace that was deeply divided and confused on the subject. Some individuals, such as an anonymous person styled "Omega," urged Lincoln to free the slaves in the name of the "Angel of Liberty." Others were more overtly religious. Thus, on June 20, he was visited by a delegation from the "Progressive Friends" who gave the president a memorial passed by a meeting of their organization asking for an emancipation decree, and on September 13—just nine days before Lincoln did in fact issue his preliminary emancipation decree—he received an antislavery memorial written by a multidenominational group of Christians from Chicago. Others were more secular and political in nature—such as a petition from twelve citizens of Portage County, Ohio, who called upon Lincoln to free the slaves and in so doing spread "liberty throughout the land."[17]

Lincoln approached these entreaties and the issue of emancipation on three different levels. The first was that of the president, and in this context, he was sensitive—with good reason—to the constitutional and political limitations under which he operated. "As commander-in-chief of the army and navy, in time of war, I suppose I have a right to take any measure which may best subdue the enemy," Lincoln observed. The qualifier *suppose* hinted that even in this area, he was not absolutely certain his authority would go unchallenged, especially given the hostility displayed by Supreme Court Justice Roger B. Taney. In an early war ruling—*Ex parte Merryman*—Taney had tried to severely limit Lincoln's constitutional prerogatives as commander-in-chief, and he could reasonably be expected to strike down an emancipation order should the opportunity arise. But even if Lincoln's power as commander-in-chief was constitutionally sound, it was bracketed by the war. Any emancipation order he issued as a war measure would have much more limited political and perhaps legal force once the war ended. And as an executive order, it could be rescinded at any time by a future president.[18]

The second level was that of a committed antislavery man. Lincoln's lifelong loathing of slavery certainly had not diminished when he became president. He stated on several occasions that, in his judgment, disagreement over slavery's fundamental immorality was the root cause of all the difficulties dividing the North from the South. "You think slavery is *right* and ought to be extended," he bluntly wrote to Alexander Stephens, a Georgian whom he had befriended from his days in Congress (and who would shortly become the Confederacy's vice president), "while we think it is *wrong* and ought to be restricted. That I suppose is the rub. It certainly is the only substantial difference between us." As Lincoln hated the war, so too did he hate slavery: the latter had begotten the former, and despite his early efforts while president to separate the two things, they constantly collided as phenomena that fed upon each other and that both were best eradicated.[19]

But Lincoln drew a sharp distinction between those first and second levels, between what he could actually accomplish as president and what he would like to do as an antislavery man. "He agreed with the memorialists [the delegation of Progressive Friends] that Slavery was wrong," noted an observer of the meeting, "but in regard to the ways and means of its removal, his views probably differed from theirs." "Ways and means" meant for Lincoln the Constitution and the restrictions it imposed upon his office. "I am naturally anti-slavery. If slavery is not wrong, nothing is wrong," he declared.

> And yet I have never understood that the Presidency conferred upon me an unrestricted right to act officially upon this judgment and feeling. . . . I understood, too, that in ordinary civil administration this oath even forbade me to practically indulge my primary abstract judgment on the moral question of slavery. I had publicly declared this many times, and in many ways. And I aver that, to this day, I have done no official act in mere deference to my abstract judgment and feeling on slavery.[20]

The scholarship on the emancipation issue confronting Lincoln has dwelled upon the interplay between Lincoln the president and Lincoln the antislavery man. But there was a third level, related to but distinct from the others: Lincoln the white man. On this level, Lincoln confronted the deep, abiding racial uncertainties beneath his pursuit of any emancipation policy. We can never know for certain, but perhaps he confronted a divided mind within himself. His mind may not have been divided over what he could do as president or over what should be done concerning slavery—for as the spring melted into the summer of 1862, he seems to have grown ever firmer in his resolve to find a way to end slavery and in his conviction that he possessed the power to do so. Yet it may have been divided over whether in ending slavery, he could expect some degree of accommodation for a multiracial society in postwar America, both within himself and from his white neighbors.

This was an exceedingly troubling issue—again, that matter of fear management. Lincoln had come to appreciate just how sensitive a racial nerve he was touching among whites whenever he in any way approached the issue of emancipation. There was terror there, unreasonable and unfounded terror—and he knew it.

Lincoln's thinking concerning the place and effect of emancipation on white America was succinctly expressed in a letter he wrote to Horace Greeley in March 1862, several months before he took his first serious steps toward making black freedom official Union war policy. Responding to a letter from Greeley urging the federal government to take action abolishing slavery in the nation's capital, Lincoln wrote, "I am a little uneasy about the abolishment of slavery in this District, not but I would be glad to see it abolished, but as to the time and manner of doing it." He then informed Greeley that should Congress see fit to pass a bill abolishing slavery, "I would like the bill to have the three main features—gradual—compensation—and vote of the people."[21]

All those features, in one respect or another, indicated Lincoln's healthy regard for the power (one might even say the menace) of the white dimensions of emancipation. Ease emancipation into the nation's fabric gradually, repay slaveholders for their lost "property," and remove as many African Americans as possible from the nation's shores—this was emancipation done up for white consumption, taking into account white interests and white anxieties. As Lincoln moved toward black freedom, he looked over his shoulder constantly, trying to gauge just how far he could push the white majority nation he led.

It appears that black people themselves hardly entered into the equation. Throughout those long, agonizing months during the spring, summer, and fall of 1862—as Lincoln wrestled interminably with the political, constitutional, and social implications of emancipation, groping his way toward the most momentous act of his presidency and arguably the most important single action ever taken by an American president regarding American race relations—he said next to nothing about or to African Americans. His mind was instead focused on white Americans: how they would react, what they might say or do, and what sort of consequences he could expect from white society should he finally take the nation in the direction of black freedom.

Until the late summer of 1862, he met with no black people. He publicly mentioned blacks infrequently and only in an incidental fashion or as an addendum to points he wished to make concerning white Americans—as in his December 1862 annual address to Congress, in which the subject of African Americans arose only in relation to his urgent requests that Congress adopt his colonization plan as the best policy for white America.[22]

Did this indicate a lack of concern or compassion for African Americans? No. Lincoln was still the same man in this regard that he had been in 1841, when he saw that slave coffle on the *Lebanon*. He still saw African Americans as human beings, and he had an innate sympathy for their plight, especially as the tumult of war made their situations in some cases worse. He seems to have taken a close interest in reports stating that Union military authorities had interfered with the opening of schools for African American children in occupied North Carolina. He worried about the fate of fugitive slaves, ordering the U.S. marshal for Washington, D.C., in February 1862 to stop arresting anyone suspected of being a runaway and instructing Secretary of War Edwin Stanton "that in common humanity [the fugitives] must not be permitted to suffer for want of food, shelter, or other necessities of life." In March when he was presented with a ceremonial bullwhip by a Massachusetts delegation—symbolic, they said, of the need to whip the rebels—Lincoln replied, "Let us not think only of whipping rebels, or of those who seem to think only of whipping negroes."[23]

His unwillingness to discuss at any length what emancipation might mean for African Americans indicated not a lack of concern for black people but rather the fact that, in the very early stages of his role as the Great Emancipator, his chief worry was emancipation's effect on white, rather than black, America. For President Lincoln, emancipation was, despite logic and surface appearances to the contrary, a predominantly white, not black, measure—at least in 1862.

This at least partially explains (even if it does not excuse) the words Lincoln spoke to the first African Americans who visited his White House in an official capacity in August 1862, in an extended dialogue concerning blacks, whites, and colonization. It was not—to put it mildly—Lincoln's finest hour.

The deputation consisted of five African American men, led by Edward M. Thomas, president of the Anglo-African Institute for the Encouragement of Industry and Art in Washington, D.C. They came at Lincoln's request; a few days previously, he had contacted members of the city's black community and asked them to appoint a delegation for a meeting at the White House, where "he [would have] something to say to them of interest to themselves and to the country."[24]

"And to the country" . . . those were revealing words. Lincoln was aiming for a much larger audience than the five black men in his office. In an age before formal news conferences and before presidents habitually delivered many speeches, Lincoln possessed few vehicles for shaping public opinion. When he wanted to communicate his views to the country, he typically used indirect, discreet methods: well-placed letters to the editors of prominent national newspapers, such as Horace Greeley, or private correspondence to political allies (and opponents) that he was certain would be leaked to the press. Or—as was the case in August 1862—arranging a meeting in the White House with prominent individuals, while seeing to it that his words were carefully recorded and made public "to the country."

The impetus for this particular occasion was a recent congressional act to support freeing the slaves in the District of Columbia—the only area in which Congress's emancipation powers could withstand constitutional scrutiny—and appropriating money for their relocation out of the United States. These actions enjoyed presidential support, especially the colonization efforts. From the outset of the war, Lincoln had been actively involved in various proposals to gradually emancipate and then colonize African Americans, sometimes in Africa, sometimes elsewhere. Only a month before, he had urged a group of Border State politicians to adopt their own plans for gradual emancipation, accompanied by some sort of scheme to get their newly freed slaves out of the country. "Room in South America for colonization, can be obtained cheaply, and in abundance," the president urged, "and when numbers shall be large enough to be company and encouragement for one another, the freed people will not be so reluctant to go."[25]

As the five African American men filed into his office, Lincoln greeted them warmly and then got right down to business. Colonization, he told them, was in their own best interest and the interest of African Americans as a whole. Understanding these men to be leaders in their community, he urged them to take a position at the forefront of the colonization movement. "It is better for us both, therefore, to be separated," he told them bluntly.

The president bolstered this observation with an extended monologue on just how race functioned between black and white people in America. "You and we are different races. We have between us a broader difference than exists between almost any other two races," he observed. "Whether it is right or wrong I need not discuss, but this physical difference is a great disadvantage to us both, as I think your race suffer very greatly, many of them by living among us, while ours suffer from your presence. In a word we suffer on each side."[26]

The suggestion that there was a "broader difference" between whites and blacks underscores the central role that African Americans played in Lincoln's thinking and in the minds of most other white Americans. Black and white was the most dominant and immediate racial problem of the age. Lincoln also seems to have felt that this profound difference between blacks and whites was intractable and insoluble, rooted in a "physical difference" that could not be surmounted. His dismissal of the moral dimension of race—"whether it is right or wrong I need not discuss"—underscores a certain fatalism in his thinking. He saw racial difference as a profound chasm, and it was here to stay, whether they (or he) liked it or not. "I do not propose to discuss this, but to present it as a fact with which we have to deal. I cannot alter it if I would. It is a fact, about which we all think and feel alike, I and you."[27]

But perhaps the most revealing part of Lincoln's speech was that ostensibly odd observation that whites "suffer from your presence"—odd because, as Lincoln himself well knew, black pain far outweighed anything inflicted on white America. "Your race are suffering, in my judgment, the greatest wrong inflicted on any people." Nor was this only about slavery. "Even when you cease to be slaves, you are yet far removed from being placed on an equality with the white race," Lincoln noted. "You are cut off from many of the advantages which the other race enjoy. . . . Not a single man of your race is made the equal of a single man of ours. Go where you are treated the best, and the ban is still upon you." Where, then, did white "suffering" come to bear on the matter? White suffering came partly from the war; partly from the fact that slavery was the war's root cause; and partly from the fact that, as Lincoln put it, slavery had "our white men cutting one another's throats, none knowing how far it will extend." But he also may have been talking about that unreasoning, irrational white fear that had gripped the white South and was the driving force behind the war and all its attendant evils. Maybe this was what he meant by whites' "suffering" from the presence of blacks, and it was the impetus behind his relatively rare use of such terrifying and violent imagery ("white men cutting one another's throats").[28]

Lincoln had always felt secession was an act of madness and the war still more so—a paroxysm of unreasonable, unfounded white Southern terror. But this sounded rather a lot like he was blaming black people for instigating that terror: not just for the war but at least indirectly also for white racism. Certainly, this was how Frederick Douglass took the president's meaning, and he did not like that at all. "Even Mr. Lincoln himself, must know quite well that the mere presence of the colored race never could have provoked this horrid and desolating rebellion," Douglass wrote.

> A horse thief pleading that the existence of the horse is the apology for his theft or a highway man contending that the money in the traveler's pocket is the sole first cause of his robbery are about as much entitled to respect as is the President's reasoning at this point. No, Mr. President, it is not the innocent horse that makes the horse thief, not the traveler's purse that makes the highway robber, and it is not the presence of the Negro that causes this foul and unnatural war, but the cruel and brutal cupidity of those who wish to possess horses, money and Negroes by means of theft, robbery, and rebellion.[29]

Douglass was not alone in his harsh reaction to Lincoln's meeting with the deputation of black leaders. The president's own secretary of the Treasury, Salmon Chase, thought that Lincoln would have been better served by offering a "manly protest against prejudice against color—and a wise effort to give freemen homes in America!" Most African Americans and abolitionists thought Lincoln's speech was at best misguided and at worst an onerous species of bigotry. Recalling Lincoln's words two years later, a black Philadelphian angrily paraphrased him as stating, "'You had better leave the country—the races cannot exist together.' 'If there had been no colored people, there would have been no war.'" The man predicted that "there will never be any reconstruction under President Lincoln, and his satellites mean another lease to slavery."[30]

Lincoln probably winced if he read these words. But the truth is that his audience was only partially those five African American men or black people as a whole. He was speaking to the rest of the country, and that country was overwhelmingly white. The best way to understand Lincoln's comments is to recognize that, on that particular day and in front of that particular audience, he had on his mind the third level—race, especially the white race. What he said was all about white fear: fear of a multiracial America and what that might mean for white insecurities about the supposed dangers of mixing with the black Other. It was a fear Lincoln knew to be palpable and powerful among his white neighbors. And though he had often in the past been dismissive of whites' anxieties about black sexuality, racial amalgamation, and the like, now that matters had come to a head—now that emancipation was indeed on the cusp of reality—it seemed to have been a fear at least partly shared by Lincoln himself. His secretary of the navy, Gideon Welles, recalled in an article written after the war that during this time, the president was convinced "it was necessary to rid the country of the African race." Why? Because, according to Welles, Lincoln believed "that the white and black races could not abide together on terms of social and political equality, [and] he thought they could not peaceably occupy the same territory—that one must dominate the other." Lincoln knew how that would turn out. "Africans were mentally an inferior race," Welles described Lincoln's thinking, and "any attempt to make them and the whites one people would tend to the degradation of the whites without materially elevating the blacks."[31]

Given that Welles wrote this over a decade after Lincoln's death, it is entirely possible that he exaggerated or perhaps even partially fabricated the president's thoughts. We cannot tell which of these words belonged to Lincoln and which to Welles or whether there was some mixture of the two here, fogged by the passage of time (Welles was seventy-five when he wrote this article). This is one of a handful of extant accounts suggesting that Lincoln worried about polluting the white race; amalgamation, that omnipresent white bogeyman, normally did not impinge much on his thinking.

There are reasons, then, to treat Welles's account with caution. But when coupled with Lincoln's remarks to that deputation of black leaders and set within the context of that difficult, anxious time, the account has at least a ring of truth. Perhaps this lies not so much in the specifics of what Lincoln actually thought and said but in the broad observation that, for all his admirable appreciation of African Americans' basic humanity and his courageous, unflinching recognition of slavery's evils, Lincoln not only understood his fellow whites' racial fears but likely also shared them to some extent and felt the need to mollify those anxieties rather than confront them directly. His tenacious advocacy of colonization was an expression of these sentiments.

Colonization was not a new idea for Lincoln in August 1862. He had long been an advocate of moving any freed slaves to some place outside the United States—usually Africa, though colonization's advocates had at times argued for a variety of other potential locations. As early as 1852 in a eulogy he wrote for his political hero Henry Clay, Lincoln praised Clay as the nation's leading voice of colonization. He pointed out that

> it was one of the most cherished objects of his direct care and consideration, and the association of his name with it has probably been its very greatest collateral support. . . . Every succeeding year has added strength to the hope of [colonization's] realization. May it indeed be realized! . . . If as the friends of colonization hope, the present and coming generations of our countrymen shall by any means, succeed in freeing our land from the dangerous presence of slavery; and, at the same time, in restoring a captive people to their long-lost father-land, with bright prospects for the future; and this too, so gradually, that neither races nor individuals shall have suffered by the change, it will indeed be a glorious consummation.[32]

Lincoln addressed a meeting of the American Colonization Society sometime in the mid-1850s, and he occasionally mentioned colonization when the subject of slavery's future demise arose. "The enterprise [colonization] is a difficult one," he admitted, "but 'when there is a will there is a way'; and what colonization needs most is a hearty will."[33] He sometimes presented colonization as a matter of justice for African Americans, an "ultimate redemption of the African race and African continent." But he also saw colonization in terms of what it might do to benefit white

Americans; in fact, when he spoke of colonization, Lincoln would occasionally lapse into openly speaking of American whites as a distinct racial category, something he rarely did. Colonization was a matter of two impulses, he said—"moral sense and self-interest"—and by "self," he meant white selves, telling a Springfield audience in 1857, "Let *us* be brought to believe it is morally right, and, at the same time, favorable to, or, at least, not against, *our* interest, to transfer the African to his native clime, and we shall find a way to do it." Alluding to the biblical tale of Moses and the Exodus, Lincoln argued that returning African Americans to Africa was a way for whites to avoid some sort of future calamity between the races when slavery's chickens finally came home to roost. "Pharaoh's country was cursed with plagues, and his hosts were drowned in the Red Sea for striving to retain a captive people who had already served them more than four hundred years," he observed. "May like disasters never befall us!" It was as close as Lincoln ever came to invoking the specter of a race war.[34]

Many of colonization's advocates viewed black removal as a means of preserving and purifying the white race—a position Lincoln himself voiced, telling the 1857 Springfield audience that "the separation of the races is the only perfect preventive of amalgamation" and that "such separation, if ever effected at all, must be effected by colonization." But in doing so, he did not indulge the more alarmist rhetoric of those white colonizers who saw removal as a way of saving white America from assault by bestial African American monsters. Quite the opposite: Lincoln saw colonization's supporters as affirming "that the negro is a man; that his bondage is cruelly wrong, and that the field of his oppression ought not to be enlarged."[35]

When the war began, Lincoln steadily and persistently clung to colonization as a necessary corollary for any emancipation scheme. His speech to the deputation of African Americans was only the most public manifestation of his ongoing commitment to relocating black people out of the United States. He worked with allies in Congress to advance congressional action on that front, and he told various Border State leaders that he would only consider emancipation if it was coupled with some sort of colonization plan. He pressed for approval of a plan to resettle African Americans in the Chiriquí Province of Central America and possibly Haiti.[36]

Colonization had lots of supporters among more conservative Republicans and Democrats, many of whom saw relocation as a means to rid the United States of African Americans' unwanted presence and to preserve the purity of the white race. But Lincoln did not indulge such vitriol. Whenever the subject arose in the first year of the war, he couched his support in much the same terms he employed in the 1850s, remarking that colonization was better for whites and blacks alike. In his first annual message to Congress, in December 1861, he pitched colonization as a matter of white self-interest. With African Americans on their way back to Africa (or some other location outside the United States), there would be more room for white immigration and expansion. "If it be said that the only legitimate object of acquiring territory is to furnish homes for white men, [colonization] effects that object; for the emigration of colored men leaves additional room for white men remaining or coming here."[37]

He sometimes sounded as if he were pleading with whites to see the wisdom of colonization, and where African Americans were concerned, he likewise seems to have believed they could be coaxed into supporting the project. Coaxing was crucial because Lincoln did not advocate forced removal. In his December message, he said he wanted colonization applied to "the free colored people already in the United States . . . so far as individuals may desire." When he issued his preliminary emancipation proclamation on September 22, he referenced his continued preference for colonization of "persons of African descent, with their consent." (The phrase *with their consent* had actually been supplied by Secretary of State William Seward, with Lincoln's apparent approval.)[38]

His tone whenever he mentioned colonization was persuasive, an appeal to his fellow Americans to act in their own self-interest and prevent the war from devolving into what he termed a "remorseless revolutionary struggle." He struck a similar tone when he recommended that both colonization and emancipation be done gradually and with monetary compensation for slaveholders. Lincoln saw such measures as cushioning the blow of emancipation for whites. Appealing to Border State leaders to adopt their own plans of gradual, compensated emancipation in May 1862, he declared that such an approach "makes common cause for a common object, casting no reproaches upon any. It acts not the pharisee. The change it contemplates would come gently as the dews of heaven, not rending or wrecking anything. Will you not embrace it?"[39]

"Gently as the dews of heaven" . . . this was how Lincoln wanted emancipation to occur. No doubt, he wanted the requisite changes in race relations to be gentle for African Americans, but his primary concern here was whites and how they felt about the jarring changes to come should slavery be placed on the road to extinction. Colonization got blacks out of the way of whites' wrath, and it removed them from competition with whites for the nation's resources. Gradualism eased primarily white sensibilities vis-à-vis the new order of things. Compensation put money in white pockets.

By December 1862, emancipation was official Lincoln administration policy. Within days of the Union army's September victory (of a sort) at Antietam, Lincoln issued his preliminary Emancipation Proclamation, giving Confederates ninety days to return to the Union or else face losing their slaves when Lincoln signed the final proclamation on January 1, 1863. The delay was further indication of his desire to ease Americans into the post-slavery era; no one seriously expected the Confederates to lay down their guns, but the delay gave Northerners—primarily white Northerners—time to adjust to the idea.

Between September and December, Lincoln received the usual mixed signals from his white constituents. "The People are jubilant over your emancipation message as a measure alike Military and Philanthropic," a Boston abolitionist assured him. Fifty-six citizens signed a petition that reached Lincoln in September, assuring him that they supported emancipation as "a measure intrinsically right, and necessary to secure for the country a righteous and secure peace." By contrast, some of Lincoln's Republican allies complained that his emancipation policies cost the party votes, and there were rumors that some Union soldiers might refuse to fight if the war became one to end slavery. Lincoln's own commanding general, George B. McClellan, had hinted as much in a letter he gave to the commander-in-chief in July, in which he cautioned that "military power should not be allowed to interfere with the relations of servitude" and that "a declaration of radical views, especially upon slavery, will rapidly disintegrate our present armies."[40]

Lincoln was concerned enough about white backlash against his upcoming January proclamation that he used the December message to push for a gentle-as-the-dews-of-heaven approach to emancipation. His plan was detailed and elaborate, proposing constitutional amendments that financially compensated any state that voluntarily abolished slavery, as well as the loyal slaveholders who resided within its borders. Lincoln would also have amended the Constitution to allow congressional appropriation of money and other necessary resources "for colonizing free colored persons, with their own consent, at any place or places without the United States."[41]

Lincoln devoted a considerable portion of his message to defending these propositions. And in doing so, his underlying message was consistently clear: a gradual, compensated approach to emancipation, followed by a fully funded colonization plan, was in the best interest of white America. In making this argument, he again assured white Americans that emancipation was not by necessity a zero-sum game, stressing that he could free African Americans without harming white interests. "It is insisted that [free blacks'] presence would injure, and displace white labor and white laborers," Lincoln observed (without being entirely clear about just who had made such arguments). "Is it true, then, that colored people can displace any more white labor, by being free, than by remaining slaves? If they stay in their old places, they jostle no white laborers; if they leave their old places, they leave them open to white laborers. Logically, there is neither more nor less of it."[42]

Not only would emancipation do white laborers no harm, but, Lincoln argued, the presence of free blacks, whether colonized or not, could also actually enhance white laborers' prospects. "Emancipation, even without deportation, would probably enhance the wages of white labor, and, very surely, would not reduce them. Thus, the customary amount of labor would still have to be performed; the freed people would surely not do more than their old proportion of it, and very probably, for a time, would do less, leaving an increased part to white laborers, bringing their labor into greater demand, and, consequently, enhancing the wages of it." Colonization might even increase white earning power. "With deportation, even to a limited extent, enhanced wages to white labor is mathematically certain," Lincoln asserted. "Labor is like any other commodity in the market—increase the demand for it, and you increase the price of it. Reduce the supply of black labor, by colonizing the black laborer out of the country, and, by precisely so much, you increase the demand for, and wages of, white labor."[43]

The structure of Lincoln's labor theory aside, he introduced—for the first and only time—the term *deportation* into the debates. It is not entirely clear if in using this word he actually meant the forceful removal of African Americans, whether they willed it or not. He had always been careful to delineate his colonization efforts as entirely voluntary, including in his proposed constitutional amendment. Still, Lincoln was a deliberate wordsmith; it may be that he was at this point introducing his willingness to acquiesce in some sort of colonization scheme that might not involve black consent—and in the name of mollifying white racial fear.

This had relatively little to do with the end of slavery. At the conclusion of his message, Lincoln asked his fellow Americans to embrace emancipation with typically Lincolnian eloquence. "The dogmas of the quiet past, are inadequate to the stormy present," he informed Congress. "The occasion is piled high with difficulty, and we must rise with the occasion. As our case is new, so we must think anew, and act anew. We must disenthrall our selves, and then we shall save our country." He also issued a ringing call for Congress and the nation to rally behind the rapidly approaching Rubicon he would cross by ending slavery. "The fiery trial through which we pass, will light us down, in honor or dishonor, to the latest generation. . . . In *giving* freedom to the *slave,* we *assure* freedom to the *free*—honorable alike in what we give, and what we preserve. We shall nobly save, or meanly lose, the last best, hope of earth."[44]

Those words are quoted often as examples of Lincoln's patriotism, his belief in American exceptionalism, and perhaps most of all his unswerving commitment to emancipation. They are a clarion call for Americans to embrace—to use another high Lincolnian phrase—the better angels of their natures, to push that god-awful war to a higher and finer calling, to make it count for something more than a mere bloodletting on a massive scale. Those words are Lincoln at his best.

But we are inordinately mesmerized if we believe that the words in that December message to Congress, coming as they did on the eve of his triumph as the Great Emancipator, are the only relevant passages in that message or, more generally, that Lincoln's nobler instincts—to give freedom to the free, come what may—are all that matter as we survey his actions in those dark and confusing times. He did end slavery, and in the process, he added an almost immeasurably valuable and positive dimension to the troubled legacy of American race relations by helping to lift African Americans from the terrible place in which slavery had placed them.

But there were other, less noble aspects of Lincoln's demeanor as he stood on the cusp of emancipation. As he gave freedom to black Americans, he worried incessantly about the concomitant reaction freed blacks would evoke among whites, as well as the deep, ugly reservoir of white racial fear that emancipation would expose and probably exacerbate. At times, Lincoln gave too much counsel to white fears; he sometimes sought too hard and too intensely for ways to circumnavigate white angst through dubious schemes such as colonization, when perhaps both he and the nation would have been better served by a direct and frank confrontation with the evils of white supremacy.

Abraham Lincoln's journey in 1861 and 1862, from a president who would do nothing about slavery where it already existed to a president who was willing to sign an executive order ending the legal protection of the slave system and thereby conferring liberty on 4 million African Americans, was remarkable. But the journey was not without difficulties, setbacks, and contradictions. Many of the problems were caused by the fears he encountered—and only imperfectly addressed—among whites, both within his society and perhaps within himself as well.

CHAPTER FIVE

Abraham Lincoln in 1848. This early photograph shows a young, upwardly mobile professional lawyer and politician—two of the most lily-white professions of Lincoln's age. (*Courtesy of the Library of Congress*)

"Mike Fink," by William Gropper, no date. The legendary flatboatman of the Mississippi River was famous for his feats of daring, strength, and marksmanship, including a racist tale of his having shot off an African American's protruding heel. Fink was a cultural icon of the predominantly white flatboating culture during Lincoln's boyhood trips down the Ohio and Mississippi rivers. (*Courtesy of the Library of Congress*)

"Practical Amalgamation," by Edward Williams Clay, 1839. As this illustration suggests, white Americans in Lincoln's day deeply feared and loathed any suggestion of social, sexual, or cultural "amalgamation" between blacks and whites. (*Courtesy Harry T. Peters Collections, The Smithsonian Institute*)

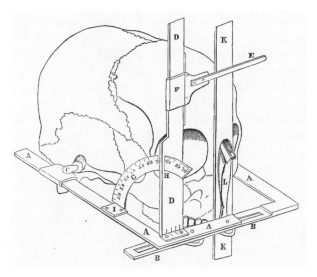

"Facial Goniometer." This illustration is from Samuel
George Morton's 1839 *Crania Americana*, which purport-
edly proved the superiority of the white race by
comparing skull size and characteristics with those of
nonwhites.

Josiah Nott, circa 1860. Nott was a South
Carolina–born physician and anthropologist whose theories concerning the innate
superiority of the white race were popular
among intellectuals in Lincoln's time.
(*Courtesy of the Library of Congress*)

"The Coming Man's Presidential Career," Jacob Dallas, *Harper's Weekly*, August 25, 1860. This cartoon from the election of 1860 illustrates the widespread belief among many Americans that race and the fate of African Americans would prove crucial during Lincoln's presidential tenure—perhaps to the detriment of a constitution that most whites believed was designed to protect white supremacy.

Theodore Parker, circa 1855. Parker was an abolitionist and radical thinker who believed that Americans had to effect fundamental changes to the structure of white supremacy, a belief shared by very few white Americans. (*Courtesy of the Library of Congress*)

"The Miscegenation Ball," by Kimmel and Forster, 1864. This viciously racist anti-Lincoln cartoon from the 1864 election depicts Lincoln's blessing being conferred upon blacks and whites interacting in ways most white Americans found unacceptable and revolting. (*Courtesy of the Library of Congress*)

ABRAHAM
AFRICANUS I.

His Secret Life,

AS REVEALED UNDER THE

MESMERIC INFLUENCE.

Mysteries of the White House.

J. F. FEEKS, PUBLISHER,

No. 26 ANN STREET, N. Y.

Abraham Africanus I, 1864. This front cover of a Democratic Party pamphlet was designed to play upon white voters' fears of a postemancipation America ruled by freed African Americans, with Lincoln's blessing. (*Courtesy of the Friends of the Lincoln Financial Collection in Indiana*)

■

Some Compunctions

And yet he acted. When the moment of truth came on January 1, 1863, Lincoln signed the Emancipation Proclamation into law. Some people wanted him to reconsider. "We think that the withdrawal of the Presidents [*sic*] proclamation from this State would harm the effect to quit our people and make them return to their allegiance to the United States Government, and would be most pleasing to the Union men," read a convoluted and syntax-challenged note from several Tennesseans to Lincoln in December. Others wanted the proclamation modified in some way that might avoid inflaming resentment among those slaveholders who had remained loyal to the Union. Emancipation for these people was not so much a conferring of freedom upon blacks as it was a punishment inflicted on whites, and they believed it should subsequently be applied with a light touch. "It is doubless [*sic*] known to you, that the Fed[eral] Army now holds entire military occupation of the northern potion [*sic*] of this State [Missouri] and of course extends over it the laws and authority of the U[nited] State's [*sic*] government and here of course the rebellion has ceased," wrote a Missourian to Lincoln. "As a consequence, emancipation is unnecessary as a military measure to quell the rebellion. And furthermore to execute on the people of this County [Country?] the penality [*sic*] of emancipation and that too after the object sought to be attained by it, has been already effected by other means, would involve in indiscriminate ruin, those who have rebelled and those who have opposed and deprecated the revolution in the Southern States."[1]

Others cited emancipation's possible political costs to the president and his party, especially (as always) in the Border States, such as Kentucky. "We were utterly astonished and *alarmed* at the feeling exhibited in this state regarding your late proclamation," wrote a Louisville man, adding that "citizens and soldiers, alike are condemning your course." They had a point: the Republicans suffered a shellacking in the November elections, losing key governorships in New York and New Jersey and control of several state assemblies, including in the president's home state of Illinois. There were many reasons—battlefield defeats, discontent concerning the Lincoln administration's internal security policies, and just a general war-weariness—but emancipation certainly had a major role. Democrats played a nasty game of racial politics that appealed to the white electorate's worst fears by charging that Lincoln now wanted to introduce full racial equality in America, in the North and the South. Those charges often found a receptive audience. "It is an abolition war," wrote a disgusted Indiana man in late November to a soldier in the field. "The elections in the different States will show how the majority of the people look on this war. . . . Those Eastern abolitionists are too tyrannical for white men to live with; and if they can succeed in getting the nigger freed they will put him into their manufactories at low wages or none. . . . We shall be a ruined people, and the Lord only knows where it will end."[2]

Others, however, urged Lincoln just as strongly to hold fast. "Emancipation is *the weapon* which, efficiently used can not only strike at the heart of the Rebellion but lay the foundation for a true and permanent republic," wrote two Republican supporters to Lincoln on Christmas Eve. "For God's sake, stand by the Proclamation," implored another man, named Green Adams. "No taking back, show the people you intend to stand firm by any policy you may adopt and the people will stand by you." Rumors that Lincoln might harbor contrary ideas bothered some. "We have heard that the President will recoil from his Emancipation proclomation [sic]," two men from New Orleans wrote to Secretary of the Treasury Salmon P. Chase. "We beg to express the opinion founded upon events transpiring here, that such a retrograde movement will be a great mistake."[3]

By the end of 1862, Lincoln found himself situated somewhere between a loud and insistent number of antislavery Americans and a more amorphous but powerful mass of whites who wanted nothing to do with "getting the nigger freed." Even within the loose collection of antislavery, pro-emancipation individuals, there were any number of fissures and disagreements—some wanted emancipation only, others wanted emancipation coupled with a degree of racial equality, and still others wanted blacks freed and then deported.

Whites who were opposed to emancipation tended to be a bit more straightforward. Most simply did not like black people and did not want to risk having freed African Americans move into their neighborhoods, competing with them for resources such as jobs and posing the threats that the ever-present black bogeymen always seemed to represent in most white Americans' minds. But even within the ranks of antiemancipation whites, there were disagreements, different levels of bigotry and racist assumptions, and—here was the important part, at least for Lincoln—different levels of potential for change, depending upon where one lived and how much importance one attached to slavery as a vital resource that should be denied to the Confederacy. Some whites, it seemed, would tolerate freeing blacks if in so doing they advanced the prospects of a Northern victory and damaged the Confederate war effort. "It is admitted upon all sides that the transfer of three millions of Slaves, from the productive force of the Rebels to that of the loyal States would *instantly* end the Rebellion; it follows that each Slave so transferred will proportionately contribute to that end," argued two fellow Republicans in a Christmas Eve communication to the president. "I should like to see every white man in the army returned to his family and his home, and his place filled by a negro," declared a more blunt commentator. "I should be glad to vote for a proposition that would call out a million of negro troops, that the whole white troops may be relieved from the dangers and fatigues of the army."[4]

Lincoln was laying a hefty political bet on this very assumption. He knew he could count upon the support of antislavery activists for his new emancipationist direction, but it was hard to say how many antislavery whites there actually were in the North or whether they were powerful or numerous enough to muster the political support he needed to prosecute the war. In all likelihood, he would need the hardened core of racial bigotry prevalent in other quarters of the white population to soften enough so that, at a minimum, emancipation and its attendant changes could be tolerated.

The best way to do this, Lincoln knew, was to appeal directly to whites' self-interest by pitching emancipation almost exclusively in military terms, as a necessity forced upon him by the need for black manpower in the armed forces, and the concomitant need to deny the Confederate South the slave labor that was vital to their survival. "Thousands upon thousands felt convinced that Slavery was not only the cause of the war, but was its strength and support," wrote an emancipation supporter to Lincoln. "These men have been and will continue to be, the main stays of your Administration, and they will rejoice at this new manifestation of the determination upon your part to save to the People, a Government which has vouchsafed to them such unparalelled [*sic*] prosperity and happiness." Lincoln could only hope such predictions would prove true.[5]

He of course knew white America well—he was embedded deep within its history, culture, and worldview. But in January 1863, he could not have known, at bottom, just where white America's basic sympathies lay. He could perhaps make an educated guess concerning what white Americans might tolerate in terms of ending slavery or (an even more difficult proposition) about changes in the nation's manifestly unequal caste system. But it would only be a guess, albeit a most important one. Frederick Douglass would later observe that "the sentiment of his country" (meaning, by and large, the white majority) was "a sentiment [Lincoln] was bound as a statesman to consult" when he contemplated emancipation. This was easier said than done.[6]

How could the president, after all, consult white sentiment? White America was not a measurable, definable entity. No one took its pulse with statistics, scientific opinion polls, or any kind of reliable indicator Lincoln could lean upon to estimate the impact of his actions. Hardly anyone in his time, himself included, thought much at all in terms of there even being a white America in any readily definable way—the ever-present quality of whiteness that was both everywhere and nowhere. A chief contributing factor to the almost insuperable complexity and mystery of America's race problem was the fact that the racial group that made the rules, set the boundaries, and created the nation's caste system rarely defined itself in any systematic way as a race or a caste. White America was largely an unknown quantity, as was its potential reaction to the Emancipation Proclamation.

But however much white America was a shifting, shadowy quagmire beneath Lincoln's feet, it was a key component of his proclamation. That was an underlying truth about the document and its circumstances: though it of course vitally concerned black Americans and their interests, a considerable number of whites saw it as important to them as well. And unlike African Americans, these individuals could vote and hold political office, and (at least until black soldiers were recruited in significant numbers) they were the foundation of the armed forces.

Many white Americans worried that emancipation might represent a potentially seismic shift in whiteness as well as blackness. Some saw this as a matter of economics and the labor force. "The only conflict is between white and black and not between free and slave labor, nothing is done by emancipation towards mitigating, much less toward eradicating the conflict and its cause," claimed one essayist. "On the contrary, emancipation at the South will only serve to open a new and more extended area for the conflict. . . . Black labor will stand forth as an obvious competitor with white labor for inadequate employment."[7]

Others argued that emancipation's creation of black soldiers would debase the valor and manhood of the Union's white troops. "This country cannot conquer and suppress this rebellion, unless [we] can employ the negro slave, and put Sambo, or some man meaner than Sambo, in command. Great God! Is that so?" wondered Congressman Charles Wickliffe of Kentucky. He continued:

> [We] still find it necessary at this time to blacken our record for the first time, by adopting into the army of the United States the African slave, and making him the equal and associate, by legislation, of the gallant soldier who may have distinguished himself in many a hard-fought battle; and that a captain Sambo and captain white somebody, and a colonel Sambo and colonel white somebody must stand side by side, day after day, on terms of perfect equality.[8]

Even when they tried to strike an enlightened note, many of Lincoln's fellow white Americans betrayed a nearly insurmountable preoccupation with racial difference and African Americans' inferior position in the order of things. "When we talk of emancipating the slaves of the rebels we know what we are saying, and are not indulging any rose-colored visions of African perfection," wrote the editor of *Harper's Magazine,* who actually supported the proclamation; he added that the African American

> [is] as compared with the historical white race, a backward and humble member of the human family. . . . We believe that, especially in the

passive virtues of mildness, docility [and] reverence, the negro is more than a match for the white man, and therefore his race is more likely to take emancipation safely than any similar number of white men with the same average culture or no-culture. He is willing to be taught, and glad to look up to a superior."[9]

A sense of white racial solidarity, though rarely articulated as such, could sometimes bind white Northerners to rebellious white Southerners. Democratic congressman James Brooks asserted, "For one, I am ready to say, that if the time ever arises when Georgia or Alabama, or Virginia or Louisiana is governed by negroes, with a negro judiciary, negro senators in Congress, and negro representatives, it is quite time for white people of the North to dissolve partnership with any such concerns." Even though the weariness and ugliness of the war had hardened a great many white Northerners into supporters of emancipation as an effective military weapon, others hesitated to embrace it because it seemed a bit too nasty, a bit too extreme a measure to inflict upon fellow white people—even rebels. "It would have afforded us pleasure at any time to see the negroes free," wrote one observer, "provided they got their freedom without injustice to the white race. As to wishing that the negroes should be emancipated though it should cause ruin to their white masters, we have never entertained any such feeling."[10]

However many telegrams of congratulations he received from abolitionists and however many people urged him to hold firm on his commitment to black freedom, Lincoln had to know that there were at least equal and probably larger numbers of white Americans who were hostile to the entire enterprise or who were extremely uneasy about what might come afterward. There were moments during that ninety-day interlude between the preliminary and final proclamations when the president sounded as if he might be wavering. Two religious leaders visited the White House in late December, and one of them (perhaps reacting to the widespread rumors that Lincoln was rethinking his emancipation policy) ventured to say, "We are confident you will come up to the mark, Mr. President." Perhaps with a humorous twinkle in his eye, Lincoln responded, "Oh, I don't know about that. You know Peter denied his Master." One man expressed doubt that this would be the case with Lincoln, whereupon, with a "half shrewd, half sad expression," Lincoln sank into a nearby chair and replied that "it is very hard sometimes to know what is right."[11]

But when New Year's Day dawned, his purpose was clear and his mind apparently set (though it was said that he stayed awake the entire night, brooding over what to do). When the sun rose, he might have quickly ventured outdoors to acquire a morning newspaper—something he often did—before he ate his usual spartan breakfast, then wrote out in longhand the final version of the proclamation. He sent it to the State Department to be printed and engrossed and settled in for the main task at hand: the traditional New Year's Day White House reception, with diplomats, cabinet members, and other high-ranking officials lining up to shake his hand and wish him (and Mary) their best for 1863.[12]

Secretary of State William Seward carried the official copy of the Emancipation Proclamation to the White House late in the morning. But Lincoln noticed a technical flaw in the language; it indicated, in the dense legal prose of the day, that the president had affixed his "name" to the proclamation, where it should have instead indicated that he had set it in his "hand," the more common legal form for an executive order. He ordered the document returned to the State Department for correction.[13]

Not until 2:00 P.M. did Seward return to the White House with the corrected copy. During the signing, Lincoln paused to be certain that his hand was as steady as possible. By that point, he had spent much of the day greeting dignitaries and well-wishers, and he worried that any sign of shakiness in his signature would communicate weakness and hesitation. "I never in my life felt more certain that I was doing the right thing," he declared. "But I have been receiving calls and shaking hands since nine o'clock this morning, till my hand is stiff and numb. Now this signature will be one that is closely examined, and if they find my hand trembled they will say 'he had some compunctions.'" Lincoln compensated by writing deliberately and firmly, and he signed his full name, rather than abbreviating "Abraham" as was his usual custom.[14]

Thereafter, he refused to back down. There is no credible evidence that he ever seriously considered reneging on the proclamation. He certainly could have done so. The proclamation was an executive order only, which he himself or any future president could rescind. Lincoln was also the sort of man who liked to leave his options open. Throughout his political career, he avoided burning bridges, narrowing alternatives, or taking irrevocable steps—residue perhaps of his long legal career, in which he learned that negotiation was preferable to confrontation. "Discourage litigation. Persuade your neighbors to compromise whenever you can," he advised fellow attorneys before the war; and compromise required keeping options open, in law and politics.[15]

But the Emancipation Proclamation was different. Along with reunification, it became one of the very few absolutes of his presidency, and it was not open to negotiation or compromise. Lincoln spoke of his commitment to emancipation in stark, absolute terms, which, again, was fairly unusual behavior. When he received a suggestion that he rescind the proclamation, he replied, "I should be damned in time and in eternity for so doing. The world shall know that I will keep my faith to friends and enemies, come what will." He told a delegation of Kentuckians that "he would rather die than take back a word of the Proclamation of Freedom." Once he had made the decision, a new air of self-assurance permeated his actions. When his private secretary, John Hay, briefed him on the reactions to emancipation in the leading newspapers, Lincoln was not much interested, replying that "he had studied the matter so long that he knew more about it than they did."[16]

Lincoln had concluded that both he and the Union could weather whatever storms were kicked up by emancipation among his white detractors. "The proclamation has been issued," he wrote to Gen. John Dix on January 14. "Now, that we have it, and bear all the disadvantage of it, (as we do bear some in certain quarters) we must also take some benefit from it, if practicable." The word from those "certain quarters" was that, despite some loud grumbling, white Northerners would acquiesce to emancipation and the enlistment of black soldiers, if for no nobler reason than their own self-interest. "Whilst much prejudice and feelings have manifest against negro enlistments at first it is daily giving away, and the thing will go quietly on I think," wrote one man to the president. "This is already apparent, as each negro will save a white man and reduces the chance of such being conscripted."[17]

"To use a coarse, but an expressive figure, broken eggs can not be mended," Lincoln wrote. "I can not retract it. . . . I made the peremptory proclamation on what appeared to me to be a military necessity. And being made, it must stand."[18] He was utterly dismissive of any suggestion that his administration consider abandoning emancipation. "I think I shall not retract or repudiate it," he wrote. "Those who shall have tasted actual freedom I believe can never be slaves, or quasi slaves again." A tone of incredulity entered his pronouncements on this score. "I am sure you will not, on due reflection, say that the promise being made, must be *broken* at the first opportunity," he wrote to one individual:

I am sure you would not desire me to say, or to leave an inference, that I am ready, whenever convenient, to join in re-enslaving those who shall have served us in consideration of our promise. . . . All recruiting of colored men would instantly cease, and all colored men now in our service, would instantly desert us. And rightfully too. Why should they give their lives for us, with full notice of our purpose to betray them?[19]

He saw the issuance of the proclamation as a watershed moment. "It is the central act of my administration," he told Francis Carpenter, an artist who visited the White House, and with a rare bit of hyperbole, Lincoln then added, "and the greatest act of the nineteenth century."[20] Whatever its practical applications (and there were many), it was also an eminently moral decree. In issuing the Emancipation Proclamation, Lincoln did the right thing. He knew it, too, and the moral dimension of emancipation only increased its profound nature. Thus, he did reference the Divine in his decision. "I can only trust in God I have made no mistake," he told serenaders in September, right after he announced his decision to free the slaves.[21]

It is such a tempting narrative device, alluring in its dramatic simplicity: the president who began the war with a personal desire to eradicate slavery but lacking the constitutional and political justification to do so finds both in the awful carnage of a bloody civil war. He then signs the Emancipation Proclamation as a necessary war measure and in the process finds the moral compass of his presidency and his nation. It is the story of a president's education, with Lincoln slowly but steadily growing in his maturity, political courage, and vision until he is ready on that New Year's Day in 1863 to make a final and firm commitment, on paper, not just to emancipation but also to the birth of a new, multiracial America. And once he did so, he never looked back.

There is much to be said for this version of Lincoln's emancipation story. It is both compelling and to a great extent accurate. But it also conveys a certain misleading simplicity, a linear story arc running along a relatively straightforward line.

It tends to work best when we conceptualize emancipation as an eminently black process, revolving around African Americans and Lincoln's attitude toward the black population, because the proclamation did lead him to rethink blackness in American life. Between 1863 and 1865, he would come to embrace ideas about African Americans that moved him steadily toward more radical antislavery positions, to the point that, just a few days prior to his assassination, he became the first president to endorse African American suffrage publicly.

Lincoln also showed signs of an increasing sense of empathy with African Americans. The potential was always there, dating from his days aboard the *Lebanon* and his appreciation for the plight of the slaves in that coffle. On an individual level, he was well disposed toward people who were not white, as indicated by his friendship with and support for his African American barber in Springfield, William Florville, and his compassion for the African American man named William Johnson who accompanied him from Springfield to Washington as the president's servant. Lincoln found Johnson a job in the Treasury Department following friction between the man and other White House employees, and when Johnson contracted smallpox and died in January 1864, Lincoln paid for his coffin, loaned money to his family, and repaid part of a loan Johnson had incurred at the First National Bank of Washington.[22]

As the war progressed and particularly after Lincoln had embraced emancipation, this private sympathy for individual African Americans seemed to gradually grow into a deeper appreciation for the problems of black people in general. He came to see himself as a caretaker of sorts. "How to better the condition of the colored race has long been a study which has attracted my serious and careful attention," he wrote in early 1864, "hence I think I am clear and decided as to what course I shall pursue in the premises, regarding it a religious duty, as the nation's guardian of these people."[23]

But did this same progression work on the other side of the equation? Did emancipation mark the beginning of changes in Lincoln's thinking concerning whiteness? In fact, it did—which was almost inevitable, blackness and whiteness being so tightly tethered together in American life. It is difficult to imagine how Lincoln could possibly rethink black without also changing the ways he thought about white. But the process was complicated, sometimes even contradictory, and it did not follow a simple, linear story line.

The Emancipation Proclamation did not erase Lincoln's worries and concerns about white racial attitudes overnight; the document itself suggested as much. It was excoriated in some quarters for its lack of passion, its utter absence of anything resembling the usual Lincolnian flair for dramatic and momentous language—possessing as it did "all the moral grandeur of a bill of lading," in historian Richard Hofstadter's dismissive phrase. Hofstadter saw this bland quality of the proclamation largely as a function of propaganda and politics, not race (though he did speculate that the president may have been so timid about emancipation because "there was in Lincoln something of the old Kentucky poor white").[24] But it would be a bit more accurate to suggest that the document's low-key tone reflected Lincoln's well-seated, well-considered, and practically lifelong respect for white racial opinion.

There was, first and foremost, Lincoln's ever-present Border State headache. The Border States were more than just the geographic boundary between North and South. In many ways, they also constituted the borders of white racial tolerance. This was a major reason why Lincoln wrote directly into the proclamation Border State exemptions from emancipation's operations. There were other reasons, to be sure: the continued strategic, military importance of the Border States; the political need to mollify the conservative and moderate elements that would be a factor in the upcoming 1864 presidential contest (and where Lincoln and the Republicans had made a poor showing in 1860); and Lincoln's worry that a Border State legal challenge to the proclamation might well end up in the Supreme Court, which was likely to strike down the measure as unconstitutional.[25]

But the foundation of all these other reasons was fundamentally racial. Lincoln had to worry about Border State political problems and legal challenges from disaffected whites because some of those whites were slaveholders themselves and also because they lived in the closest proximity to emancipated slaves. Whites would likely rub elbows with freed blacks in the border areas first and in greater numbers, and it was there that Lincoln probably thought he could expect the frictions created by black freedom to burst into flames soonest and hottest.

Better perhaps to ease whites into the whole emancipation project. Lincoln may have purposely struck a dry, legalistic "bill of lading" tone as a way of downplaying emancipation's momentous potential for change in white Americans' lives. He may also have chosen to sign the proclamation quietly and with so little public ceremony—only Seward and his son Frederick were present during the signing—because he wished to avoid unnecessarily antagonizing white sensibilities. We cannot know for certain, and Lincoln did not, as far as we know, reveal his inner thinking on these matters. But the quiet and understated tenor of the Emancipation Proclamation suggests that its author wanted to ease the nation's way into black freedom carefully and prudently. And prudence was most strongly advisable as an approach not toward black America or their white abolitionist allies but rather toward the mainstream of white society, wherein resided deep reservoirs of racial bigotry.

More generally, Lincoln still worried about the consequences of suddenly thrusting freed slaves into the midst of whites. Since the Emancipation Proclamation excluded the Border States, he was compelled to continue laboring for those states' leaders to see the light and pursue their own emancipation plans, and he wanted those plans to be both decisive in their eventual repudiation of slavery and gentle in their social impact. "Desirous as I am, that emancipation shall be adopted by Missouri, and believing as I do, that *gradual* can be made better than *immediate* for both black and white," he wrote to Gen. John Schofield, Union commander in Missouri, who had asked Lincoln whether the government might offer protection to slaveholders' property rights while the state transitioned to freedom, "my impulse is to say that such protection would be given." However, he hedged by pointing out that "I can not know exactly what shape an act of emancipation may take. If the period from the initiation to the final end, should be comparatively short, and the act should prevent persons being sold, during that period, into more lasting slavery, the whole would be easier. I do not wish to pledge the general government to the affirmative support of even temporary slavery, beyond what can be fairly claimed under the constitution."[26]

In various occupied areas of the South, Lincoln faced the question of how to redefine labor relations between the freedmen and white employers, and as with the Border States, he preferred a careful testing of the waters. He wanted black laborers to be fairly treated, but he was also sensitive to the concerns of their white employers. He signaled his support for "a system of apprenticeship," presumably as a kind of transitory mechanism for easing African Americans' presence among white laborers. Writing to Union general Nathaniel Banks concerning the course of reconstructing Louisiana, Lincoln gave his opinion that "it would not be objectionable for [Louisiana] to adopt some practical system by which the two races could gradually live themselves out of their old relation to each other, and both come out better prepared for the new."[27]

This was all policy and politics. On a personal level, Lincoln never did completely rid himself of some of the ingrained cultural habits resulting from a lifetime's immersion in a white supremacist culture. As had often been the case, those habits surfaced in his humor. He continued to attend blackface minstrel shows, and he would occasionally let fly jokes with distinct racial overtones. "Here comes forward a white man, and you ask him who will you vote for[?] I will vote for S[tephen] A. Douglass [*sic*]," Lincoln facetiously related during some reminiscences with visitors in August 1864. "Next comes up a sleek pampered negro. Well Sambo, who do you vote for[?] I vote for Massa Lincoln. Now asked the orator, what do you think of that[?] Some old farmer cried out, I think the darkey showd a damd sight of more sense than the white man."[28]

Reporter Henry Villard recalled a conversation Lincoln had with an unidentified acquaintance in the early days of his presidency. When this acquaintance expressed dismay that the president would probably be forced from the beginning of his White House tenure to address the ever-present slavery problem, Lincoln "told the story of the Kentucky Justice of the Peace whose first case was a criminal prosecution for the abuse of slaves," Villard recounted. "Unable to find any precedents he exclaimed at last angrily: 'I will be damned if I don't feel almost sorry for being elected when the niggers is the first thing I have to attend to.'" Three years later, while meeting with a delegation of representatives from the Committee for Recruiting Colored Troops who were seeking to equalize the pay of black and white laborers, Lincoln replied with a smile, "Well, gentlemen, you wish the pay of 'Cuffie' raised." When one of the delegates objected to Lincoln's use of *Cuffie*, the president was embarrassed and backpedaled, citing his Southern birth and his belief that in the South, "that term is applied without any idea of an offensive nature."[29]

Another reporter from California remembered relating to Lincoln a story about a politician from his state who had been compelled to tell the truth about a matter without actually knowing he had done so. Lincoln replied that this "reminded him of a black barber in Illinois, notorious for lying, who once heard some of his customers admiring the planet Jupiter rising in the evening sky." He described the barber exclaiming, "Sho! I've seen dat star afore. I seen him way down in Georgy!" "Like your friend," Lincoln told the reporter, "he told the truth, but thought he was lying."[30]

Nor was Lincoln uniformly the genial, friendly man of myth toward all African Americans. When he met the famous African American abolitionist and political activist Sojourner Truth in October 1864, he patronizingly referred to her as "aunty" and seemed ill at ease in her presence. One of

Truth's companions found the president's attitude distressing and his use of the term *aunty* offensive, as if she were his "washerwoman." Truth later found it politically advantageous to smooth over the manifestly rough edges of her meeting with Lincoln, but in fact the president had been brusque and even rather rude.[31]

As Frederick Douglass so aptly put it, "In his interests, in his associations, in his habits of thought, and in his prejudices, [Lincoln] was a white man." He remained so after emancipation. Although the proclamation was a transformative moment for Lincoln, it did not automatically erase all the assumptions, perceptions, and experiences acquired from a lifetime in America's white culture.[32]

Nor does the proclamation seem to have entirely ended Lincoln's interest in colonization—arguably the most prominent policymaking expression available for the angst felt by many antislavery whites such as Lincoln regarding the impact black freedom might have on whites and their interests. His long-standing commitment to colonization as a sine qua non for emancipation surely stemmed from a variety of sources (though he never explained his reasons in a systematic fashion). Chief among these would have been colonization's usefulness as a palliative for white bigots who worried that black freedom would result in black neighbors and black competitors for jobs and other resources. Lincoln well understood this. "My first impulse would be to free all the slaves, and send them to Liberia," he said in 1854, followed by his admission that his "own feelings will not admit" allowing blacks to be freed and remain in America as equals. "And if mine would," he added, "we well know that those of the great mass of white people will not. Whether this feeling accords with justice and sound judgment, is not the sole question if indeed, it is any part of it."[33]

Lincoln pressed for colonization right up to the edge of emancipation, making it the centerpiece of his December address to Congress. After he signed the Emancipation Proclamation, however, his public support for colonization evaporated. He would never again couple emancipation with any colonization plan. In fact, he would never again publicly endorse colonization at all.

But in reality, Lincoln did not totally discard colonization after signing the proclamation. He still received pressure from some in the North to make good on the speech he delivered to the deputation of black leaders in August 1862. "The Country is distracted with the Negro question [and] dissatisfied with all other plans, save that which you projected in your Address to the Negro committee which waited on you at the Executive Mansion," wrote a colonization supporter to the president in March 1863. "Throughout the Union that plan gave pleasure. . . . It gave at least a safety valve to the high pressure under which free Negroes and 'contrabands' were being forced into the free loyal states. . . . [But] so soon as it was known that the plan was delayed—that efforts were to be made by extremists to place the negro on a par with the white man—again dissatisfaction became apparent." Lincoln was never entirely immune to such worries.[34]

He did continue to meet quietly with colonizationists of various stripes, and he offered surreptitious, low-key approval for several colonization projects.[35] At the very end of the war, Gen. Benjamin Butler claimed that Lincoln voiced his persistent fears of a "race war" and instructed Butler to investigate the possibility of shipping African American soldiers off to Panama or some other foreign destination so as not to unduly alarm whites by leaving armed blacks in their midst.[36] Historians have long debated the veracity of Butler's testimony, for many of its details are suspect—Lincoln rarely even mentioned the possibility of a race war, and as we will see, he considered black soldiers' service a ticket to inclusion in the American community, not a ticket out of the country—but other evidence suggests that colonization continued to inhabit at least some small corner of the president's thought until his death.[37] He told a Republican congressman that he still harbored deep worries concerning what should be done with "these people—Negroes—after peace came."[38]

If he did at some point abandon the idea of colonization—or at least diminish its importance—he seems to have done so for reasons other than colonization's efficacy as sound policy. "I am glad the President has sloughed off that idea of colonization," John Hay wrote in July 1864. "I have always thought it a hideous and barbarous humbug." To Hay, Lincoln's "sloughing off" appears to have been caused by his understanding of colonization's tendency to produce fraud and corruption among those officials charged with its administration. "The thievery of Pomeroy and Kock have about converted him," Hay believed, referring to charges that Republican senator Samuel C. Pomeroy and Bernard Kock (a British entrepreneur and ardent colonizationist) had either badly mismanaged or outright stolen money and resources intended for colonization efforts in Chiriquí and Haiti.[39]

If Lincoln did continue to quietly lend a hand to colonization after January 1863, as the available evidence suggests, why did he do so and why would he have kept such support out of the public eye? White racism had certainly not disappeared. Some whites accepted emancipation as a legitimate war measure, but others definitely did not, and African Americans found themselves targets of all manner of discrimination and abuse. In February 1863, Lincoln received disturbing reports that white soldiers recuperating at a hospital in Philadelphia had indiscriminately assaulted African Americans in their midst. That summer, ugly riots erupted in New York City, during which angry white mobs targeted African Americans as the cause for the war, the draft (the catalyst for the riots), and all the woes suffered by white New Yorkers.[40]

The Confederates did their part to feed the flames of racial strife. Their outrage concerning the North's decision to embrace black freedom was predictable enough. The Confederate Congress labeled it a "gross violation of the usages of civilized warfare, an outrage on the rights of private property, and an invitation to an atrocious servile war." One Confederate congressman wanted to go still further and use the proclamation as an excuse to fly the "black flag" (that is, take no prisoners) and "proclaim a war of extermination against all invaders of our soil." Whatever the politicians thought, Confederate soldiers acted on their convictions, and word reached Lincoln of atrocities committed against African American soldiers by their Confederate enemies. In one particularly gruesome and highly publicized incident, Confederate soldiers commanded by Gen. Nathan Bedford Forrest massacred black soldiers who were trying to surrender, in what was manifestly a paroxysm of violent white rage.[41]

If Lincoln saw colonization merely as a political tool for easing whites into the new realities created by emancipation (what historians Phillip Magness and Sebastian Page aptly dub the "lullaby thesis"), then he had more reason, not less, to trumpet his support for colonization after 1863.[42] Yet he did not do so. His involvement in colonization, which was so public and open before January 1863, was so surreptitious afterward that a fair number of his contemporaries and subsequent historians assumed he had totally abandoned the idea.

Why? Speculation is all we have, but this colonization conundrum seems to illustrate a private matter, rather than a political or public one: Lincoln's split mind on emancipation even after he signed the proclamation, a split that had less to do with the politics of race (as the lullaby thesis would suggest) and more to do with his personal misgivings and an ambivalence that centered on whites. He was not split on the proclamation as either a necessary war measure or a moral commitment to African Americans. He was split on how emancipation would affect American white people, on what emancipation meant to whites, and on what moral commitment he might have (if any) to white people as such.

This split mind worked both ways. Lincoln worried about white prejudice and bigotry, but at the same time, his willingness to defy white prejudice grew steadily stronger. While part of him worried about the state of white opinion, another part felt that white public opinion had grown and progressed during the war. Speaking to British abolitionist George Thompson, Lincoln employed another of his apt metaphors, likening (white) American public opinion to a slowly ripening fruit tree. "A man watches his pear-tree day after day, impatient for the ripening of the fruit," he observed. "Let him attempt to *force* the process, and he may spoil both fruit and tree. But let him patiently wait, and the ripe pear at length falls into his lap!" As with the pear tree, so went Americans' attitudes toward slavery. "We have seen this great revolution in public sentiment slowly but *surely* progressing, so that, when the final action came, the opposition was not strong enough to defeat the purpose."[43]

Be that as it may, he knew that "the opposition"—that is, white antipathy toward both emancipation and African Americans in general—still had teeth. Democrats continued to mount furiously racist assaults on Lincoln as a way of garnering votes. And as the Union army advanced ever further into the crumbling Confederacy, sullen and angry white Southerners, facing the twin prospects of military defeat and slavery's demise, were a matter of concern.

But Lincoln was dencreasingly charitable in describing white slaveholders, those whom he had tried so hard to mollify before the war and whom he had described as people much like himself and other Northerners.[44] In a thoughtful speech he delivered at a Sanitation Commission fair in Baltimore in April 1864, he described slaveholders not as fellow whites deserving of sympathy but as predators. "The shepherd drives the wolf from the sheep's throat, for which the sheep thanks the shepherd as a *liberator,* while the wolf denounces him for the same act as the destroyer of liberty, especially as the sheep was a black one," Lincoln said in an extended soliloquy on the different meanings of the word *liberty* as applied by Northerners and Southerners. "Plainly the sheep and the wolf are not agreed upon a definition of the word liberty; and precisely the same difference prevails today among us human creatures. . . . Hence we behold the processes by which thousands are daily passing from under the yoke of bondage, hailed by some as the advance of liberty, and bewailed by others as the destruction of all liberty." His use of the wolf imagery left no doubt about where his sympathies lay. "Recently, as it seems, the people of Maryland have been doing something to define liberty; and thanks to them that, in what they have done, the wolf's dictionary, has been repudiated."[45]

He was also considerably less understanding toward Northerners who did not wish freed Southern blacks to relocate in their direction. When he received a letter from Massachusetts governor John Andrew in February 1864 complaining about interference from loyal Virginia authorities in Massachusetts' recruiting efforts for African American soldiers, Lincoln replied that

[if] it be really true that Massachusetts wishes to afford a permanent home within her borders, for all, or even a large number of colored persons who will come to her, I shall be only too glad to know it. It would give relief in a very difficult point; and I would not for a moment hinder from going, any person who is free by the terms of the proclamation or any of the acts of Congress.[46]

His tendency to see the war increasingly in terms of divine retribution or as a calamity visited by God on both sides for the sin of slavery meant that he was more and more unwilling to excuse the sins of either white Northerners or Southerners. Both were culpable for what had been wrought upon African Americans. "If God now wills the removal of a great wrong, and wills also that we of the North as well as you of the South, shall pay fairly for our complicity in that wrong," he wrote to Kentucky newspaperman Albert G. Hodges in April 1864, then "impartial history will find therein new cause to attest and revere the justice and goodness of God." This statement foreshadowed what would be his more famous formulation of much the same sentiment in his second inaugural address ten months later.[47]

Lincoln had concluded that he would risk white ire, come what may. His response to one Kentucky Unionist was indicative of this determination. The Unionist wrote the president in July 1864, saying that he would only speak out in favor of emancipation if the federal government escorted freed blacks out of his state. "[Kentucky] certainly will not be asking too much," the Unionist said, "to ask to have them colonized out of her border when emancipated. . . . The only drawback to successful emancipation, is a disinclination to have the negro population freed and kept among us." Lincoln—the native Kentuckian who once was so terribly worried about Kentucky's white Unionists—simply ignored the man and his missive.[48]

Heated complaints from whites who felt put upon by the mere presence of black soldiers in their midst likewise met with little in the way of presidential sympathy or action. An outraged Marylander groused to Lincoln, "For three months we remained under guard, night and day, of negro soldiers, compelled to endure every species of humiliation and insult from a class whom we had been educated to regard and treat as servants." The president did nothing. The more alarmist pronouncements by nervous whites invited his contempt. "As to any dread of my having a 'purpose to enslave, or exterminate, the whites of the South,' I can scarcely believe that such dread exists," he wrote to John McClernand, a Democratic politician and general. "It is too absurd."[49]

From fearing white racial paranoia, Lincoln had come around to the idea of using it as a weapon. At one point, he actually thought of playing upon white Southerners' worst nightmares about the dark African American Other as a way to persuade them to surrender. "The bare sight of fifty thousand armed, and drilled black soldiers on the banks of the Mississippi, would end the rebellion at once," he enthused to Andrew Johnson.[50]

He was also increasingly protective of the freedmen against the bigoted or predatory practices of whites. When Union troops occupied ever larger swaths of Southern land, bringing Arkansas, Louisiana, and significant portions of the coastal areas of the Carolinas directly under military supervision, a myriad of questions arose concerning the new relationships between whites and blacks in those areas. African Americans were no longer slaves—this much was clear. But beyond this simple fact lay a host of nettlesome questions about how the new racial order should proceed.

In January 1864, Lincoln received a letter from Alpheus Lewis, a cotton entrepreneur looking for opportunities to trade with planters in the occupied areas. Lewis wanted some presidential guidance on the manner in which the government would approach labor relations between blacks and whites. Lincoln's response to Lewis was telling. "You have enquired how the government would regard and treat cases wherein the owners of plantations, in Arkansas, for instance, might fully recognize the freedom of those formerly slaves, and by fair contracts of hire with them, re-commence the cultivation of their plantations," he wrote. "I answer I should regard such cases with great favor." The president then laid down a fairly clear set of guidelines. "As [to] the principle, [I would] treat them precisely as I would treat the same number of free white people in the same relation and condition. Whether white or black, reasonable effort should be made to give government protection."[51]

This was arguably the most color-blind statement made by an American president to that point in the nation's history. Historians examining Lincoln's approach to labor relations between blacks and whites have (understandably) focused their attention on what he said and thought about black laborers.[52] But it is worth noting that his words carried implications not just for the freedmen whom he sought to protect but also for their white laboring counterparts and employers.

In the summer of 1863, Lincoln was invited to address a meeting of "Unconditional Union men" in his home state of Illinois, led by James C. Conkling, a friend and fellow lawyer. The president chose to write a letter to Conkling instead, a letter that was widely reprinted in Northern newspapers. Lincoln used the opportunity to answer his critics on the impossibility of compromise with the Confederacy (as some war-weary Northerners continuously urged) and to offer a spirited defense of the Emancipation Proclamation's constitutionality and practical value to the Union war effort. On that last score, he sounded the familiar themes of military necessity that he had employed to ameliorate white angst. "I think the constitution invests its commander-in-chief, with the law of war, in time of war," he wrote. "The most that can be said, if so much, is, that slaves are property. Is there—has there ever been—any question that by the law of war, property, both of enemies and friends, may be taken when needed? And is it not needed whenever taking it, helps us, or hurts the enemy?" He also made the familiar appeal to white self-interest: "I thought that whatever negroes can be got to do as soldiers, leaves just so much less for white soldiers to do."[53]

Underneath this familiar rhetoric, however, was a new, subtle, and powerful subtext aimed at American whites regarding the existence of a moral responsibility to African Americans that they could not avoid or rationalize away. In making this case, Lincoln tried a new tack, by appealing to white Americans' sense of shame. As a longtime critic of slavery, he had usually avoided trying to pin a sense of guilt on Southern white slaveholders. ("They are just what we would be," he had said of them before the war.) Nor had he ever said much concerning white Americans' generally shoddy treatment of their African American brethren. But now—just two months after the black soldiers of the 54th Massachusetts had been slaughtered in an assault on Battery Wagner in South Carolina—Lincoln wrote that after the war, "there will be some black men who can remember that, with silent tongue, and clenched teeth, and steady eye, and well-poised bayonet, they have helped mankind on to this great consummation [of democracy]; while, I fear, there will be some white ones, unable to forget that, with malignant heart, and deceitful speech, they have strove to hinder it."[54]

"Malignant heart" and "deceitful speech"—this was unusually hard language for Lincoln to aim at his fellow whites. The words were not in this case aimed just at Confederate sympathizers in the North or at those Southerners who had tried to wreck the Union. The context of the letter suggests that Lincoln was also shaming those whites who would rescind emancipation's promise of freedom, particularly to the black men who had fought and died alongside whites.

His statements in the Conkling letter indicate that a primary source of this newfound toughness was the fact that when he saw African Americans, as often as not he saw them as soldiers—which placed them on a relatively even par with whites and also required a degree of respect from America's white majority. "Sambo" did not degrade white soldiers because in Lincoln's eyes, the black heroes of Battery Wagner and elsewhere were no longer Sambos—they were men.

He insisted that black soldiers be shielded from white Southerners' racist wrath. "Having determined to use the negro as a soldier, there is no way but to give him all the protection given to any other soldier," he declared in an April 1864 speech, referencing the slaughter of black soldiers at Fort Pillow and promising that the reports of atrocities committed by Confederate soldiers there (at the time only rumored) would be "thoroughly investigated." "If there has been the massacre of three hundred there, or even the tenth part of three hundred, it will be conclusively proved; and being so proved, the retribution shall as surely come." When the rumors proved to be true, Lincoln's reaction was swift and angry. In May, after noting that it was "quite certain a large number of our colored soldiers, with their white officers, were, by the rebel force, massacred," he requested from each cabinet member a written recommendation for government action. This in itself was an unusual step. Lincoln eventually decided not to seek an eye-for-an-eye solution by executing Confederate prisoners (as some urged him to do), observing that "blood cannot restore blood." But the attention he devoted to the entire affair was extraordinary.[55]

Whenever reports reached him of abuse directed at African Americans by whites, there was no suggestion of presidential tolerance of white excesses. "Complaint is made to me that . . . our military are seizing negroes and carrying them off without their own consent, and according to no rules whatever, except those of absolute violence," he wrote to Gen. George Thomas, who commanded Union soldiers in the area of Kentucky where these complaints originated. "See that the making soldiers of negroes is done according to the rules you are acting upon, so that unnecessary provocation and irratation [sic] be avoided." He sounded more angry and impatient in early 1865, writing to a white officer commanding an African American regiment that he had heard dismaying reports "that you are forcing negroes into the Military service, and even torturing them— riding them on rails and the like—to extort their consent." The president insisted that "the like must not be done by you, or any one under you. You must not force negroes any more than white men."[56]

In a conversation with two newspaper correspondents in the summer of 1864—when the bloodletting in the Wilderness campaign had caused tens of thousands of Union casualties—Lincoln set in sharp relief the black contribution to the war effort and the pragmatic political perspective he took concerning white objections to black soldiers. Pointing out that the preferred Democratic Party strategy was to fight the war with white soldiers only, he declared, "The slightest acquaintance with arithmetic will prove to any man that the rebel armies cannot be destroyed with democratic strategy. It would sacrifice all the white men of the north to do it. There are between one and two hundred thousand black men now in the service of the Union." Under the Democrats' approach, he said, "these men will be disbanded, returned to slavery and we will have to fight two nations instead of one. I have tried it. You cannot concilliate [sic] the South, when the mastery & control of millions of blacks makes them sure of ultimate success. You cannot concilliate the South, when you place yourself in such a position, that they see they can achieve their independence. The war democrat depends upon conciliation."[57]

Conciliation meant, at bottom, white Northerners making common cause with white Southerners. But this represented a strategy that Lincoln felt was no longer viable, that is, treating the war as an affair between and among white men only. He knew the war was no longer solely a white man's war. Nor was the Union army solely a white man's army. In his mind's eye, Lincoln had stopped seeing the army as an exclusively white instrument. He made it a point to identify and describe the army as a mixed-race entity, referencing in his 1864 annual address to Congress the "thousands, white and black, [who] join us as the national arms press back the insurgent lines."[58]

Before emancipation, he had shoved black people and their concerns as far into the background as possible, treating them either as dangerous distractions or even, in his least charitable moments, as a cause of the war that had white men "cutting each other's throats." But it had now become as much a black as a white war through the "manhood" and battlefield sacrifice of black soldiers. These individuals had elbowed their way into the front ranks of the war's conversation, and according to Lincoln, white America now had to make room for them.

As a good politician, Lincoln frequently pointed out that it was in whites' best interest to allow black participation in the war. But he was also increasingly given to dismissing the extremes of white racist paranoia. Further, he was more and more willing to buck white resistance to what he deemed were basic issues of fair treatment for African Americans.

Also—and this was no small matter—Lincoln had slowly come to the realization that "white" was a vested interest. Whites were not simply the invisible majority, everywhere and nowhere, ubiquitous and strong because of their very invisibility. When the war began, Lincoln, like nearly everyone else, had reflexively treated white interests as the nation's interests, considering them one and the same. But years of war, battles over emancipation and race, and his ongoing confrontations with the bumptious and painful conflicts between whites and blacks had finally opened his eyes to the fact that white racial identity was merely a faction (albeit a very powerful faction) in a multiracial America. It was not America itself.

This realization was apparent in a bit of correspondence in August 1864 that Lincoln dictated to his secretary, John Nicolay, in response to a racist screed he had received from a Washington, D.C., resident named John McMahon. McMahon fired off a brief little telegram to the president on August 5, writing that "the following lines will give you to understand what is justice and what is truth to all men." And those lines of "justice" and "truth"? "Equal Rights and Justice to all white men in the United States forever. White men is in class number one and black men is in class number two and must be governed by white men forever." Lincoln responded with a sparkling little gem of wisdom. "The President has received yours of yesterday, and is kindly paying attention to it," wrote Nicolay on Lincoln's behalf. "I will thank you to inform me, for his use, whether you are either a white man or black one, because in either case, you can not be regarded as an entirely impartial judge." Just for good measure, Lincoln added an extra little dig. "It may be that you belong to a third or fourth class of *yellow* or *red* men, in which case the impartiality of your judgment would be more apparent."[59]

As the end of the war drew closer, Lincoln had not shed all of his worries about the power and prejudice of white America. But he did come to understand that "white" was not "neutral" and that a white point of view was not de facto an objective or a just perspective. It was instead merely one interest in a bubbling, sometimes fractious multiracial nation. In that day, merely seeing America in this way was itself an accomplishment.

■

SEVEN

Abraham Africanus the First

Lincoln's last recorded encounter with an African American occurred on April 14, 1865, the day before he was assassinated. April 14 was an extraordinarily busy day for the president. Gen. Robert E. Lee had surrendered at Appomattox five days previously, and the capital was buzzing with excitement and activity, foretelling the end of the war. In the morning, Lincoln's eldest son, Robert, arrived and ate breakfast with his father. After breakfast, the president conferred with a succession of diplomats, congressmen, and other notables, followed by an 11:00 A.M. cabinet meeting during which Gen. Ulysses S. Grant presented a report on Confederate general Lee's recent surrender. The president also discussed with his officials various mopping-up details related to the Union victory.[1]

By the time Lincoln ushered Vice President Andrew Johnson into his office at 3:00 P.M. for a talk, he was probably exhausted. At some point, according to the story, an African American woman named Nancy Bushrod elbowed her way past the White House guards and interrupted Lincoln's conference with Johnson. She poured out her heart to the president: her husband, Tom, was a soldier in the Union army but had not yet been paid, she had tried vainly to find work in the capital city, and she and her children were nearly destitute. "You are entitled to your soldier-husband's pay," Lincoln said. "Come this time tomorrow and the papers will be signed and ready for you." She showered him with praise and thanks, after which he added some kindly paternal advice: "My good woman, perhaps you'll see many a day when all the food in the house is a single loaf of bread. Even so, give every child a slice and send your children off to school."[2]

This little bit of Lincoln lore must be taken with more than the usual grain of salt. It originated in a pamphlet called *She Knew Lincoln,* published in 1930 and written by a woman named Esther May Carter, who had met Bushrod and recorded her story. But this was many years after the fact, and Bushrod's version of events does not have independent corroboration. Her story also smacks somewhat of Lincolnian mythmaking, with the familiar themes of extraordinary presidential compassion—she had Lincoln telling the guards who tried to block her path, "There is time for all who need me. Let the good woman come in"—and Lincoln's supreme valuation of education, a long-standing staple of the Lincoln legend.

However much of the Bushrod tale may be fact or myth, it illustrates a more fundamental point: as president, Lincoln encountered more people with a skin color other than his own than at any other time in his life. Or, more to the point, the largely homogeneous whiteness that had characterized his surroundings since birth was at least somewhat diluted by the usually quiet, persistent presence of people who were not white.

Black servants had long been a mainstay in the Executive Mansion— appropriately enough, since the building was constructed largely using slave and free black labor. During the nation's early years, African Americans had served as White House cooks, laundresses, maids, butlers, coachmen, and gardeners.[3] In the late 1850s, however, the black servants were entirely expunged at the insistence of President James Buchanan, who installed an all-British staff, thinking they would be more discreet and protect his privacy.[4]

Lincoln's arrival signaled a return to a mixed-race staff.[5] His White House included a number of African American servants: his personal valet, the aforementioned William Johnson, whom Lincoln brought with him from Springfield; a Treasury Department employee named William Slade, who served as a presidential messenger; a cook named Cornelia Mitchell (she had previously worked for a well-to-do Southern family and knew how to prepare Southern cuisine); a waiter named Peter Brown; and Mary Lincoln's seamstress (and confidante), Elizabeth Keckly, whose memoirs would become a mainstay of Lincoln literature.[6]

When Lincoln ventured outside the White House, he found in Washington, D.C., the most racially cosmopolitan town in which he had ever lived. He had resided there briefly once before, from December 1847 until March

1849 during his brief stint in the U.S. House of Representatives, and he had encountered both free African Americans (working as servants in the boardinghouse where he stayed) and slaves being sold on the capital's streets. Returning as president fifteen years later, he would have found a city that hosted over 9,000 free blacks and around 1,800 slaves. That population grew as Washington became home to mounting numbers of runaway slaves before emancipation and freedmen refugees and African American soldiers and their families afterward.[7]

The available evidence suggests Lincoln enjoyed in Washington the same amiable relations with African Americans that characterized his interactions with his black barber, Billy Florville, and most of the other black people he had encountered throughout his life. As we have seen, he took good care of his African American valet, William Johnson, even after Johnson's death, and the other black servants in the White House claimed Lincoln likewise treated them with extraordinary compassion and kindness. Elizabeth Keckly saw in him a gently humorous, somewhat distant but amiable man who exhibited remarkable patience with his wife's erratic behavior and treated Keckly herself with courtesy, calling her "Madam Elizabeth."[8]

The First Lady was not exactly patient or forbearing, but toward Keckly and other African Americans, she was (like her husband) a tolerant sort. As a white woman from a wealthy slaveholding family, Mary was more familiar with the peculiar institution than her husband, though what she might have shared with him on the subject is anyone's guess.[9] One of her cousins remembered Mary was "horrified" when she read of stories about slavery's cruelty in a New Orleans newspaper, and she had never been enamored of slavery and its abuses, which she saw in abundance while growing up in Kentucky.[10]

But (as always) there was a distinction between what Mary thought about slavery and what she might have thought about race. She was comfortable around African Americans, and that comfort gave her if not color blindness at least a blurred perception of the color line. A poor relationship with her stepmother (her mother died when Mary was a child) caused her to turn with unusual fervor to an African American maid named Mammy Sally, who gave her crucial emotional support. Sally was, according to another member of the Todd family, "a jewel of a black mammy" whom Mary seems to have genuinely revered.[11]

However, Mary interacted with Sally—and most African Americans in her life—as a master or an employer. Her "model was the dynamic between mistress and family slave," historian Jennifer Fleischner has observed. Rarely did she encounter a black person on a basis of equal power.[12] She was also prone to the prejudices common among whites in her time. She sometimes described African Americans as "darkeys" (though she avoided using the term *nigger,* having been taught by her parents that the expression was too vulgar), and both she and Abraham liked to mimic black dialect. During his Senate race in 1858, she scoffed at the idea that her husband might ever "countenance social equality with a race so far inferior to [his] own."[13]

When she arrived at the White House in 1860, Mary brought with her an unusual combination of genteel white compassion, casual racial condescension, and startlingly liberal views concerning emancipation. An abolitionist named Jane Grey Swisshelm, who became acquainted with Mary during the war, felt that she was pressuring her husband to adopt some emancipation policy "as a matter of right," and Mary's close friendship with Republican antislavery senator Charles Sumner probably exerted a decisive influence on her thinking in this regard as well.[14]

Keckly's memoir gives the impression that she—along with other White House domestics—became adept at "handling" Mary, who could be moody and unpredictable. Still, Keckly came to know Mary well enough that she felt confident in approaching the First Lady for help concerning a project near and dear to Keckly's heart: relief for the thousands of destitute freedmen the war had created. Keckly became a leading figure in the Contraband Relief Association and began to solicit funds to distribute for the "benefit of the suffering blacks." "I told Mrs. Lincoln of my project," she recalled, "and she immediately headed my list with a subscription of two hundred dollars. . . . She made frequent contributions, as also did the President."[15]

In addition, Abraham and Mary found time to visit a contraband camp located near the cottage on the outskirts of the city known as the Soldier's Home, which the Lincolns employed as a summer residence. The president was a frequent visitor. He became acquainted with Mrs. Mary Dines, an African American nurse who lived in the camp (and was sometimes employed to look after the Lincoln children), and a black minister named Ben, who, according to Dines, occasionally sang favorite hymns at the request of the president. Dines herself sang spirituals for Lincoln and claimed that the songs sometimes brought tears to his eyes.[16]

Presidents generate circles around themselves that foster a particular atmosphere, and the Lincolns created in their White House a circle that was markedly open and compassionate for its time. Even allowing for the romanticization and sentimentality that characterized recollections of all things Lincoln (would the normally reticent Lincoln really have cried when he heard Mrs. Dines sing?), it is nevertheless notable that none of the African Americans who interacted with the president on a daily basis in his inner circle found evidence of the racial bigotry that infested so much of white America.[17]

But this was the private Lincoln, a matter of his personal traits as a compassionate white man—admirable enough but fairly limited in its importance. Plenty of white Americans in Lincoln's era were cordial in their everyday dealings with individual African Americans, while still harboring decidedly bigoted attitudes toward nonwhite people in general. It was entirely possible for a white American at that time to simultaneously treat black people as relative equals in private and yet think of and treat them as the alien Other in public.

During most of his career, Lincoln had said and done little to combat the scary black Other that haunted the white public mind. He was not himself especially prone to the dominating white fear and loathing of black people; he rarely invoked the race war specter or black men as a danger to public safety or anything of that sort. Before the war, he had avoided talking about such things at all if he could possibly help it, and when a political opponent such as Stephen Douglas did so, Lincoln's response was generally annoyance. "Let us discard all this quibbling about this man and the other man— this race and that race and the other race being inferior," he declared.[18]

But if he was not given to exploiting white fears of black people, he also was not often willing to openly confront or criticize those fears. However compassionate and understanding Lincoln may have been toward Keckly, Johnson, and the other African Americans within his White House circle, his kindnesses were extended behind the scenes, in private. This is not to say that Lincoln self-consciously hid such things from the (overwhelmingly white) public eye, but those actions did remain private, and in the process, they helped keep blacks firmly entrenched as a frightening nonwhite Other in the public realm.

Unfortunately, Lincoln did his part to encourage such thinking, at least during the early days of the war. In that August 1862 meeting with the deputation of African American leaders about colonization, he treated them as quite distinct Others, men of color who stood apart from the white mainstream. "You and we are different races," he told them at the outset.

"We have between us a broader difference than exists between almost any other two races." It is difficult to imagine words that could more pointedly shove black people outside the white mainstream—and these were public words too, which Lincoln no doubt knew would be widely disseminated, telling much of white America just who "we" and "they" were. In this instance, Lincoln did not demonize blacks, but he made it quite clear they were different, with an identity that stood apart from white America.[19]

That ill-considered meeting was a low point for Lincoln in many ways. For one of only a few times in his life, he pushed nonwhite people beyond the pale of an American public square dominated by whites. During the 1850s, he had won plaudits from antislavery activists—and a good deal of enmity from the more bigoted quarters of white society—for doing just the opposite, for trying to pry open the lily-white door to the American public square and allow nonwhite people inside via the inclusive language of the Declaration of Independence. On August 14, however, he took a step backward, bending to the predominant white norm by casting black America as an alien presence in the nation's polis.

But in this regard, January 1, 1863, once again seems to have been a watershed moment. After emancipation, Lincoln took steps that began to slowly erode that image of the black Other. Not only did he meet with more and more African Americans, but he did so in a public fashion that communicated to white America, in ways subtle and otherwise, that African Americans belonged in the public square.

Black Americans weren't the only Others, of course, though no other nonwhite people carried their resonance and impact on the white mind, especially during a war that seemed to so many Americans to be all about slavery and the black place in American life. Preoccupied as he naturally was with such matters, Lincoln rarely found other ethnic concerns intruding upon his daily affairs.

Native Americans, second only to African Americans in potency as a white racial foil, were for the most part background noise during the Lincoln administration. The president dutifully submitted treaties to Congress that were negotiated with various tribes, usually without comment. He did not interact much with either Caleb Smith or John Usher, the two men who served as his secretary of interior (and therefore head of the Office of Indian Affairs) during the war. Lincoln did see fit to appoint a fellow Illinoisan, William P. Dole, as commissioner of Indian affairs, but his dealings with Dole were minimal as well.[20]

Lincoln had never been given to hating Indians, any more than he demonized blacks, but as with black Americans, he had never done much to lessen the sting of the Native American "savage" image in the white mind either. When he actually met with tribal leaders during the war, he revealed himself as a rather run-of-the-mill white man. "Three Indians of the Pottowatomies [sic] called today upon their Great Father," John Hay noted in April 1861. "The President amused them greatly by airing the two or three Indian words he knew. I was amused by his awkward efforts to make himself understood by speaking bad English, e.g., Where live now? When go back Iowa?"[21]

On only one occasion did Lincoln take the opportunity to express in any detail his ideas concerning just where Native Americans might fit into the larger scheme of the nation's destiny. His opinion mirrored that of mainstream white America—Indians had to remake themselves in the image of white farmers. In March 1863, Lincoln met with Cheyenne, Kiowa, Arapaho, Comanche, Apache, and Caddo leaders in the White House's East Room. "[The] Indians are fine-looking men," remarked a reporter. "They have all the hard and cruel lines in their faces which we might expect in savages; but they are evidently men of intelligence and force of character."[22]

Following a lecture given by a university professor on the nature of the earth (he used a globe as a visual aid and explained to the tribal leaders how that "great ball" functioned), Lincoln took over. "There is a great difference between this palefaced people and their red brethren, both as to numbers and the way in which they live," he said.

> We know not whether your own situation is best for your race, but this is what has made the difference in our way of living. The palefaced people are numerous and prosperous because they cultivate the earth, produce bread, and depend upon the products of the earth rather than wild game for a subsistence. . . . I can only say that I can see no way in which your race is to become as numerous and prosperous as the white race except by living as they do, by the cultivation of the earth.[23]

That qualification—"we know not whether your own situation is best for your race"—was vintage Lincoln, typical for a man who was normally reluctant to make statements of absolute certainty. Otherwise, his lecture was a fairly common white take on Indians and their difficulties, even down to an assumption that Indians were by and large more bloodthirsty than whites. "Although we are now engaged in a great war between one another, we are not, as a race, so much disposed to fight and kill one another as our red brethren," Lincoln observed.[24]

According to the reporters who were present, the Indians received Lincoln's message with approval. But they could have been forgiven if they found it patronizing and rather shallow. Dominated as his presidency was with white and black America, the president (understandably enough) did not devote a great deal of scrutiny or intellectual depth to red America and its problems.

But in the late summer of 1862, there was a brief moment when Indian problems pushed through even the momentous events of the war and impending emancipation to occupy a good deal of Lincoln's attention. In August, the Sioux living in and around western Minnesota staged a bloody uprising, spurred by resentment over years of treaty violations, corruption among the government's Indian agents and officials, conflicts over annuity payments, and the resulting widespread hunger and poverty. Bands of Sioux warriors put to death at least 1,200 white settlers and laid siege to both the town of New Ulm and nearby Fort Ridgely. The army rushed soldiers to the area, who joined with local militia to eventually quell the uprising, killing and capturing over 1,000 Sioux.[25]

Military trials of the captured Indians quickly followed. Although the Indians had been promised status as bona fide prisoners of war, the markedly unsympathetic soldiers who conducted the trials treated the Sioux as common criminals, sentencing 303 of them to death. The trials were a mockery of justice by anyone's standards, with the defendants often convicted on flimsy or hearsay evidence or in some cases simply because they were Sioux.[26]

As commander-in-chief, Lincoln had to sign off on the handiwork of these military tribunals. When those 300-plus death sentences landed on his desk, the temptation must have been great to rubber-stamp the verdicts and get back to the business of running the war. A few people called on Lincoln to show leniency, but many others wanted vengeance and warned him of the consequences should he hinder the executions. "I apprehend serious trouble with the people of this state who are much exasperated against the criminal Indians," telegraphed Lincoln's military commander on the scene, Gen. John Pope. "I feel that a great necessity is upon us to execute the *great majority* of those who have been condemned by the Military Commission," urged a missionary who had witnessed the uprising and knew of the heated feelings of revenge it generated among Minnesota's whites. "This is required as a satisfaction to the demands of public justice." A private citizen who wrote Lincoln was more blunt and lurid. "Those who sit in opulent homes, with their wives and daughters around them, may be more disposed to pardon savage barbarity than those who have had a wife or a daughter ravished, a son slain, or a child dashed against a stone," wrote one Thaddeus Williams.

> Mr. President, if a being in the shape of a human, but with that shape horribly disfigured with paint and feathers to make its presence more terrible should enter your home in the dead hours of night, and approach your pillow with a glittering tomahawk in one hand, and a scalping knife in the other, his eyes gleaming with a thirst for blood . . . would not a curse of vengeance, eternal and deep, (if *not* loud,) escape your lips?[27]

Even those who sympathized with the Sioux were wont to view them through the lens of that long-familiar assumption about Indians as irredeemable and barbaric savages. Indian Commissioner Dole wrote to Secretary of the Interior Caleb Smith that the executions were "more of the character of revenge than the infliction of deserved punishment" and that they were "contrary to the spirit of the age, and our character as a great, magnanimous and christian people." That said, Dole argued that "these Indians perpetrated most horrible and atrocious crimes, and were guilty of barbarities which shock every feeling of humanity, and are only known in Indian warfare. . . . These people are a wild, barbarous, and benighted race."[28] This from a man who actually wanted to stay the hand of the executioner and who was the administration's primary Indian agent.

Lincoln's response to all of this was to apply the brakes to what seemed a runaway rush to judgment and execution by both the Minnesota white population and his own people on the scene. He telegraphed Pope to send him the names and trial records of the condemned men. "And if the record does not fully indicate the more guilty and influential, of the culprits, please have a careful statement made on these points and forwarded to me," he added. Lincoln then reviewed each case separately, using his trained lawyer's eye, and tossed out all but thirty-eight convictions.[29]

It is hard to characterize these actions as presidential compassion, since when all was said and done, Lincoln still authorized the largest mass execution in American history. He did nothing when Congress expelled the remaining Sioux from Minnesota in April 1863. Nor did he intervene when the remaining Sioux prisoners languished in disease-ridden internment camps (one of which was located in Lincoln's home state of Illinois).

It is, however, also fair to point out that in reviewing and then commuting so many sentences, Lincoln treated the Sioux not as aliens but as people who deserved the same consideration as that given to white Union soldiers whose court-martial sentences he also routinely reviewed (and just as often commuted). None of the communications regarding the Sioux suggest that Lincoln viewed them any differently than he would have viewed a similar number of similarly situated whites.

Nor did Lincoln perpetuate any of the common stereotypes and epithets routinely applied to the Sioux. When he mentioned the uprising in his 1862 annual address, his tone was comparatively restrained. He noted that "the Sioux Indians, in Minnesota, attacked the settlements in their vicinity with extreme ferocity, killing, indiscriminately, men, women, and children," but he offered no further condemnation. And he told Congress that perhaps the entire system of dealing with the Indians ought to be overhauled.[30]

Admittedly, none of this likely had much of an impact on the whites, many of whom (especially out West) approved of the treatment the rebellious Sioux received and probably wished Lincoln had not seen fit to commute all those death sentences. Savages they were, and they remained so in the white mind no matter what the president might do or say. However laudable Lincoln's intercession may have been in preventing executions of the Sioux on a far greater scale, the entire affair of the uprising and its aftermath was in the end no more than a relatively minor matter to a distracted country.

And African Americans? They *were* the distraction, all the more so after January 1863. There were those who saw in emancipation the future ruin of white America. A Missouri critic pointed to what he called the degraded state of affairs in the Caribbean islands where slaves had been emancipated, warning that "we find no evidence in these countries that either the white or black races have been benefited by the change emancipation has wrought; but we have evidence that it has produced the most deplorable results—physical, moral, and intellectual. . . . I fancy I see a mongrel population controlling [Missouri's] destiny."[31]

CHAPTER SEVEN

Mongrel population was yet another of the endless phrases invoking white fears concerning black sexuality, racial amalgamation (what would soon be called miscegenation), and the creation of a mixed-race America, with all the horrors this prospect sparked in white Americans' minds. "The general understanding among Abolitionists and Republicans is, that such of [emancipated slaves] as please to do so, might come North and mingle among the white race," declared an angry anti-Lincoln newspaper editor named Dennis Mahoney.

Are you in favor of this being done? I tell you candidly I am not . . . because the incorporation of persons of the negro race among the white race will be productive of evils for which not all the good that philanthropy can accomplish, will be able to compensate. . . . Imagine what a state of society you would have when crowds of debauched negroes gather in your towns and villages and hamlets.[32]

Other whites grumbled indelicately about the need for discussing black people or their problems at all—what had come to be called in common slang "the nigger question" that had dominated so much of American life. "We are tired, disgusted and sickened out with the 'nigger' question," complained a writer in the *Christian Banner*. "In every political speech, in every newspaper, at the corner of every street, in social circles, at churches, in prayer-meetings, in kitchens, in workshops, and barber-shops, and everywhere else where two or three people are met together, the 'nigger' topic is first, last, and forever."[33]

Antislavery activists and abolitionists of course held far different opinions, but even they tended to agree that the Emancipation Proclamation now meant the future of white America would be linked to black America, for better or worse. "If, then, emancipation be the price of national unity and of peace, and if a people, to be emancipated, must draw the sword in their own cause, then is the future welfare of the white race in our country indissolubly connected with an act of justice, on our part, towards people of another race; then is it the sole condition under which we may expect . . . domestic tranquility," argued antislavery and social activist Robert Dale Owen.[34]

Such were the burdens Lincoln now carried as the author of the Emancipation Proclamation: the whole panoply of white fear, paranoia, indifference, and even (in the case of abolitionists) expectations. His public actions, great or small, in relation to African Americans would be closely scrutinized by whites. Lincoln had hitched his political fortunes, as well as the future of his party and in many respects the Union, to emancipation, and emancipation, as much as the Union, would be his calling card for most American whites from January 1863 onward.

Lincoln had to know this, had to know that the eyes of white Americans—already fixed so steadily upon him as president and commander-in-chief—would stare that much more keenly at any of his public actions related to blacks. Not just his words but also any interaction with black people in the fishbowl that was the American presidency would communicate to white Americans just where Lincoln believed African Americans belonged in the nation's public square.

Lincoln could have emancipated the slaves and then ignored the various troubling issues concerning African Americans' postslavery future. He could have chosen to never again publicly meet with any black people in the White House. The message to white America would have been clear: black soldiers were good enough to stop Confederate bullets and black people in general did not deserve to be slaves, but they otherwise had no place in American public life. White Americans did not need to make room for them. Whites could continue to treat blacks as distinct, alien, and inferior (or terrifying) Others, useful only in a limited capacity to further the ends of a still predominantly white-owned and white-operated America.

A considerable segment of white America wanted to believe that very thing—that emancipation did not have to seriously disrupt the nation's race relations or disturb the structure of white supremacy, if only the president would either carefully quarantine the freedmen in the South or again take up the colonization project. "Let us get rid of it [the race problem between whites and blacks] by insisting that the negroes shall be left where they are till the South itself chooses to be rid of them and to find some other place for their future abode than the United States," argued Mahoney.[35]

There were sound political reasons for Lincoln to court the support (and votes) of these white Americans by keeping black Americans at arm's length. But he did not do this. After 1863, there would be no more meetings with black people on a par with that of the deputation—that is, a public separation of blacks as "them," distinct, different from, and by presumption inferior to the white "us." In fact, Lincoln's various public encounters with black Americans sent quite the opposite message.

At least two of those occasions had an overtly religious atmosphere. In August 1863, he met with Leonard A. Grimes, an African American Baptist minister, abolitionist, and conductor on the Underground Railroad. As pastor of the Twelfth Street Church in Boston, Grimes had agitated against the Fugitive Slave Act in the 1850s, and during the war, he recruited soldiers for the fabled 54th Massachusetts Volunteer Infantry. Grimes "is, emphatically, a practical man," read an 1863 sketch of his life, and "[takes] a suitable part in every thing that tends to the welfare of his race."[36]

On August 21, 1863, Grimes led a twelve-man committee from the American Baptist Missionary Convention to the White House for a meeting with the president. Their object was to secure presidential approval for their attempts to minister to the spiritual needs of African American soldiers serving on the front lines. (Grimes had in fact been offered the chaplaincy of the 54th Massachusetts, an offer he turned down, citing other duties.) The president was entirely amenable to the plan and wrote for Grimes a generic pass that he and his fellow ministers could present to Union army authorities as they approached military facilities. "The object is a worthy one," Lincoln wrote in the pass, "and I shall be glad for all facilities to be afforded them which may not be inconsistent with or a hindrance to our military operations."[37]

A year later, Lincoln met in his White House office with a delegation representing the "loyal colored people of Baltimore," led by three African American pastors. The occasion was more involved and formal than the meeting with Grimes, with the Reverend S. W. Chase reading from a prepared statement. "The loyal colored people of this country everywhere will remember you at the Throne of Divine Grace," Chase read. "May the King Eternal, an all-wise Providence protect and keep you, and when you pass from this world to that of eternity, may you be borne to the bosom of your Saviour and your God." The committee then presented Lincoln with an ornate Bible in a walnut case, inscribed as a "token of respect and Gratitude."[38]

Lincoln's reply was equally formal. "It has always been a sentiment with me that all mankind should be free," he said. "So far as able, within my sphere, I have always acted as I believed to be right and just; and I have done all I could for the good of mankind generally. . . . In regard to this Great Book, I have but to say, it is the best gift God has given to man." Reporters who were at the meeting noted that Lincoln "spent some time in examining the present, and expressed himself highly pleased; and after a pleasant conversation the party separated—the President taking each of them by the hand as they passed out."[39]

These presidential meetings were unremarkable, low-key affairs. Lincoln had held similar meetings with religious leaders throughout the war. Evangelical Lutherans, Reformed Presbyterians, Quakers, Jewish clergy from Philadelphia—all had filed in and out of the president's office at one time or another. Their behavior and Lincoln's reception were nearly indistinguishable from one another or from the delegations led by the Reverends Chase and Grimes.[40]

But then, that is really the point: the meetings with white clergy and black clergy were identical. Lincoln's treatment of black religious leaders was notable precisely because it was so typical, because those meetings did not stand out in any particular way. Black men walking into the White House and meeting with the president—they were normal.

This was partially a function of Lincoln's relative lack of racial prejudice and his cordial personal relations with African Americans, including Elizabeth Keckly, William Johnson, and other black people in his life. But these were public meetings, conducted in his office and reported in mainstream white newspapers that were read by white audiences. Lincoln made no apparent attempt to disguise or downplay the presence of blacks in the White House. He did not, say, make them wait an inordinate amount of time or use a servant's entrance, nor did he meet with them in some other, less prominent, less "white" place. He sent no signal that he thought of them as anything other than normal Americans engaging in a normal ritual of calling upon their president.

He had compelling political reasons to do otherwise. That meeting with the Baltimore delegation occurred less than two months before the presidential election of 1864, in the heat of a campaign in which Democrats tried their level best to portray the president as a rank abolitionist and betrayer of the white race. Race hatred was thick in the air. "Thou shalt swear that the negro shall be the equal of the white man," read a vicious anti-Lincoln screed called *The Lincoln Catechism*. "Give to a negro that asketh not, but from the poor white man turn thou away. . . . Is it disloyal to speak of white men as a superior race? It is, very," according to "Abraham Africanus the First." Antiadministration political cartoons depicted Lincoln with black features, and Democratic stump speakers everywhere assured their audiences that a vote for Abraham Lincoln was a vote to both dismantle white supremacy and dilute white racial purity by mixing it with black, "tainted" blood. "May the Blessings of Emancipation extend throughout our unhappy lands," read a sarcastic Democratic campaign pamphlet called the "Black Republican Prayer," "and the illustrious, sweet-scented Sambo nestle in the bosom of every Abolitionist woman, that she may be quickened by the pure blood of the majestic African . . . [and] that we may become a regenerate nation of half-breeds and mongrels."[41]

In such a superheated atmosphere of white racism, Lincoln might well have chosen to make the African American as much of an Other as possible, the better to assuage the sensitivities of those white voters who might be vulnerable to such appeals—moderate and conservative Democrats and Republicans, as well as constituents in the all-important Border States. He did not necessarily need to behave in an uncharacteristically nasty and crudely racist manner; he needed only to ignore black America as much as possible to avoid antagonizing conservative whites. The president and his party were very sensitive to that portion of the electorate, enough so that Lincoln replaced the vice president of his first term, antislavery New Englander Hannibal Hamlin, with Andrew Johnson from Tennessee as a way to court Border State and conservative votes.[42]

But Lincoln would not court white votes by shoving black people beyond the pale of polite American society. His meetings with those black ministers in 1863 and 1864 sent precisely the opposite message. Instead of pushing black people away, he folded them into the normal, everyday life of his presidency.

He did so again, in a different context, in June 1864 during a visit to Grant's headquarters at City Point, Virginia. By this time, Grant had locked Lee's army firmly into its trenches around Petersburg and was settling in for a lengthy siege. The president arrived on a steamer at City Point's wharf, a bit out of sorts and seasick from choppy seas. "I know it would be a great satisfaction for the troops to have an opportunity of seeing you, Mr. President," Grant told his commander-in-chief. "I am sure your presence among them would have a very gratifying effect. I can furnish you a good horse." Despite his illness, Lincoln readily assented.[43]

The troop review was a staple of Lincoln's presidency, a ritual he had repeated numerous times throughout the war. The review served an important military purpose of course, showing the men their commander-in-chief and providing the sort of morale boost Grant predicted. But by the summer of 1864, Lincoln's troop reviews had come to serve other purposes as well.

They had become public and even quasi-political ceremonies in which "Father Abraham" cemented his strong bond with thousands of ordinary young white men in blue uniforms, men who found his sometimes rustic appearance, decidedly unmilitary mannerisms, and folksy simplicity charming and democratic—and who voted accordingly. The soldier vote would be a key factor in returning Lincoln to the White House in 1864, five months after his review of the City Point army.[44]

Troop reviews were more than just military rituals. They were part of the wartime American polis, and at City Point that June, President Lincoln included black men in the ceremony. There were plenty available, for Grant's siege army around Petersburg included thousands of black soldiers. Their lot was not easy. They served in segregated regiments with white officers, were often assigned the most disagreeable tasks, and faced ongoing discrimination. They had until recently—the very month Lincoln steamed for City Point, in fact—been paid considerably less money than their white counterparts.[45]

African American soldiers had proven their value on the battlefield, despite all of these obstacles, and General Grant, among others, was convinced of their worth. "Mr. President, let us ride on and see the colored troops, who behaved so splendidly in Smith's attack on the works in front of Petersburg last week," Grant suggested as they rode down the line. "Oh yes, I want to take a look at those boys," the president replied. The retinue proceeded to the camp of the Eighteenth Corps, where, according to Union general Horace Porter, the soldiers' reaction was electric. "The enthusiasm of the blacks now knew no limits," he recalled; "they cheered, laughed, cried [and] sang hymns of praise." Lincoln removed his hat and offered some now-forgotten words of thanks and congratulations. "The scene was affecting in the extreme, and no one could have witnessed it unmoved."[46]

Again, it is tempting to see Lincoln's actions here solely in their private, personal context. But the larger—and white—public audience was no small consideration. White officers and enlisted men would have seen their president passing a unit of black men, and they would have seen him treat those black men in exactly the same fashion as they themselves were treated. Had he wanted to do so, Lincoln could probably have avoided reviewing those black men and potentially avoided wounding the racial sensibilities of some white soldiers—white soldiers who would vote in the all-important 1864 election or at least communicate in their letters with white family members who would vote. But there is no evidence that the president reviewed those black men in a manner that differed in any way from the troop reviews he had conducted with scores of white soldiers. He was saying something to white Americans. Black soldiers were not Others—they were, to at least some extent, "us."

The best example of Lincoln's efforts to defang the scary black Other, however, involved not black ministers or soldiers but rather an individual who was the most famous—and to considerable numbers of whites the most frightening—black person in America: Frederick Douglass.

Douglass's lionization as an American hero and the foremost African American leader of the nineteenth century can obscure how in his own time the more racist segments of the American white population reviled him as the epitome of the dangerous black man. Physically handsome and imposing, he was blessed with a superior intellect. He had extraordinary speaking and writing skills, and above all, he was uncompromising and outspoken in his principles. Consequently, Douglass was a nightmare for those whites who truly feared the consequences of allowing black men liberty of thought and action.

It seemed as if every white person who believed in white supremacy had an opinion about Frederick Douglass. Some tried to explain him away as a clever mimic. "He exhibited remarkable ease of delivery, which he has so readily acquired while mingling with distinguished speakers of the superior race," sniffed one critic who had attended one of Douglass's lectures. Others cast aspersions on his manhood. People "are wishing to know why Fred. Douglass does not go into army and fight for his race," wrote a white supremacist and anti-Lincoln editor named C. Chauncey Burr. "Several loyal league sisters in Rochester, New York [where Douglass lived] . . . gave him more peaceful inclinations, and persuaded him that it was far better to be a living black Adonis than to be a dead and charred lump of patriotism." Still others felt threatened. "We hate the present negro literature—especially that of Fred's," wrote journalist George Graham, "which by abusing the white, is intended to elevate the black man."[47]

Not for nothing did Stephen Douglas repeatedly use Frederick Douglass as a black specter to taunt Lincoln and frighten white voters during their 1858 debates. He claimed with sardonic glee that Douglass was one of Lincoln's chief advisers and repeatedly invoked an image of Frederick Douglass riding about the country in a carriage with a "beautiful young lady"—a white lady, of course—and her mother, while the white husband and father drove the carriage.[48] For his part, Lincoln studiously avoided mentioning Frederick Douglass at all. No reference to him appears in any of Lincoln's prewar speeches.

As a leader of the abolitionist movement and a prolific journalist, Douglass became one of the Lincoln administration's chief gadflies during the first two years of the war. Douglass naturally saw the conflict as a struggle to end slavery from the very beginning, and he waxed indignant at the president's foot-dragging on emancipation. "The present policy of our Government is evidently to put down the slave-holding rebellion, and at the same time protect and preserve slavery," he wrote in September 1861. "Can the friends of that policy tell us why this should not be an abolition war? Is not abolition plainly forced upon the nation as a necessity of national existence?"[49]

Lincoln did what he had always done with Douglass in the past: he ignored him. No references to Douglass appear in any of his pre–Emancipation Proclamation speeches and correspondence, and there is no indication in the relevant primary sources—John Hay's diary, for example—that Lincoln gave much thought to Douglass or his criticisms.

After January 1863, Douglass's opinion of the president softened considerably. "In the hurry and excitement of the moment, it is difficult to grasp the full significance of the change in the attitude of even the present administration," he noted a month after the Emancipation Proclamation became law.

> During this very administration slavery has been [an] all commanding and all controlling political power at Washington as well as at Richmond. The saying that cotton is king was never an empty boast. It was king and ruled us as with iron. But thank Heaven, this rule is now to a considerable extent broken. Notwithstanding the deficiency of the Emancipation Proclamation which exempts Tennessee from its operation, and leaves the slaves still in the hands of the rebel masters in so called loyal districts in Louisiana it is a tremendous change in the attitude of the Government and a heavy blow at the rebellion.[50]

Douglass had shifted from an administration critic to a cautious but committed ally. Still, the president might have continued to hold him at arm's length, for the reasons to do so were just as compelling after emancipation as before. Douglass was still a polarizing figure to many whites, and Lincoln faced enormous reservoirs of white anger and mistrust.

But when Douglass arrived at the White House in the company of Senator Samuel C. Pomeroy of Kansas on August 10, 1863, the president not only met with him, he also saw to it that Douglass and Pomeroy were ushered in immediately without having to wait with the long line of other people crowded around the president's door. Pomeroy's presence may have helped. He was a well-respected and powerful member of the Republican Party's radical wing, at times as much of a critic of Lincoln's supposedly slow emancipation policies as Douglass was. (Pomeroy would later try to engineer Lincoln's replacement as the 1864 Republican presidential nominee with the radicals' favorite, Secretary of the Treasury Salmon Chase.) He was the sort of man Lincoln would need to placate in his ongoing and sometimes delicate task of holding together the fragile coalition that was the Republican Party.

Nonetheless, it was Douglass's card delivered to the president, followed immediately by an interview in Lincoln's office, that did the trick. It was a bold thing, the president meeting with Frederick Douglass—his first public reception of an African American since the deputation a year previously. People noticed. "I knew they would let the nigger through," growled one of the white men in the crowd waiting to see the president as Douglass was escorted past.[51]

In his careful reconstruction of the meeting, historian James Oakes relates an amiable, pleasant conversation between Douglass and Lincoln. The chief topic was African American military service (at that point, recruitment of black soldiers had been official Union policy for about eight months), with Douglass both congratulating Lincoln for a recent retaliatory order aimed at punishing Confederates who harmed black prisoners of war and simultaneously quietly chiding the president for having waited so long to issue the order.[52]

Lincoln's reply indicated that the white population outside his office walls was as much a concern to him as the black man standing before him. "[The] country needed talking up to on that point," he told Douglass, and by "country," the president meant white America. If he had issued the retaliatory order immediately on the heels of emancipation, Lincoln argued, "it would be said—'Ah! We thought it would come to this. White men were to be killed for negroes.'" Instead, the president continued, he had waited until black soldiers proved their worth in white eyes at places such as Fort Wagner, the better to ease white public acceptance of measures designed to protect those brave men. Even so, "the wisdom of making col-

ored men soldiers was still doubted," he told Douglass, "[and] their enlistment was a serious offense to white prejudice."[53]

Oakes points out that this first meeting between Douglass and Lincoln
"confirms how sensitive Lincoln was to the prejudices of white Americans."[54] This was certainly true. Amiable as their conversation may have
been, hovering nearby was that unpredictable, snarling, irrational whiteness that both Lincoln and Douglass, each in his own and very distinct
way, had known their entire lives. "I knew they would let the nigger
through"—the president was familiar with the churning resentment behind
that voice.

That first brief encounter between Lincoln and Douglass apparently
elicited little public comment. Moreover, it was a meeting held at Douglass
and Pomeroy's request, not Lincoln's, and as always, the president might
easily have avoided a face-to-face encounter with such a controversial
black man. Douglass was keenly aware of this. "I could not know what
kind of reception would be accorded me," he recalled years later. "I might
be told to go home and mind my business . . . or I might be refused an interview altogether."[55]

Their second encounter occurred a little over a year later. This time, it
was the president who summoned Douglass. He did so not as an authority
figure being importuned by constituents but rather in the spirit of a president soliciting advice from a leading voice in a constituency he respected.

The context was quite different from their first interview, when emancipation and black military service were still relatively new. By the summer
of 1864, black soldiers were commonplace, and emancipation was an established staple of the Lincoln administration's war effort—and to a great
many Americans, victory seemed further away than ever. Lincoln was being assailed in all quarters, talk of a negotiated peace with the Confederacy
was in the air, and Lincoln had severe doubts about his prospects for reelection.

When he arrived at the White House, Douglass found the president in
an anxious state of mind. "The increasing opposition to the war, in the
North, and the mad cry against it, because it was being made an abolition
war, alarmed Mr. Lincoln," Douglass remembered. This time, however,
Lincoln spoke not so much about the latent power of white racism but
rather about securing emancipation and the freedmen's future as free men
if the war were to end before the Constitution could be amended to permanently abolish slavery. "He saw the danger of premature peace," Douglass

believed, "[and] he wished to provide means of rendering such consummation as harmless as possible."[56]

To that end, Lincoln wanted Douglass to help him find ways to get more African American men into the army, not just to win the war but also to reinforce emancipation. Even without a constitutional amendment, the president reasoned, white Americans would surely hesitate to reenslave black soldiers—so the more black soldiers, the better. Douglass agreed but pointed out that Southern slaveholders "knew how to keep such things from their slaves, and probably very few knew of his proclamation." Lincoln replied that he wanted Douglass to "set about devising some means of making them acquainted with it, and for bringing them into our lines."[57]

While they conferred, one of Lincoln's secretaries interrupted to say that the governor of Connecticut, William Buckingham, was waiting to see the president. "Tell Governor Buckingham to wait," Lincoln replied, "for I want to have a long talk with my friend Frederick Douglass." Douglass was shocked. "This was probably the first time in the history of this Republic when its chief magistrate found occasion or disposition to exercise such an act of impartiality between persons so widely different in their positions and supposed claims upon his attention." He might have added that this was the first time in American history that a president made a white man wait for a black man's business to be concluded in the White House.[58]

Their third and final encounter took place in a still more public, prominent place and before a much larger white audience, in March 1865—only a few weeks before Lincoln's death. By this point, with the collapse of the Confederacy imminent, with his own reelection for another four-year term secured, and with the Constitution amended to forever outlaw slavery, Lincoln could be reasonably sure that white public opinion had shifted enough to at least accept the peculiar institution's demise and without the concomitant attempts to compensate slaveholders or deport African Americans. White racism still remained intact of course, but one suspects Lincoln breathed a little easier.

So too did Frederick Douglass. The night before Lincoln's second inauguration, he had tea with Salmon Chase, former secretary of the Treasury and newly installed chief justice of the U.S. Supreme Court. Chase was an ardent antislavery radical who "had conquered his race-prejudice, if ever he had any," according to Douglass. So the notion of America's highest judge inviting a black man to both dine at his home and assist his daughter in "placing over her honored father's shoulders the new robe then being made, in which he was to administer the oath of office to the re-elected President," was not perhaps so strange. Nevertheless, the idea of a black man, any black man, moving so calmly and without adverse comment through the highest circles of the nation's capital was exceedingly new.[59]

So was Douglass's attendance at the inaugural ceremony the next day and—even more radical—his decision to attend the presidential reception and ball at the White House that evening. Too radical, perhaps, at least for some of the white men who stood guard at the White House entrance. When Douglass arrived, the guards refused him entrance. Nonplussed, Douglass shouted to a white friend and dignitary who was on his way inside. "Be so kind as to say to Mr. Lincoln that Frederick Douglass is detained by officers at the door." When the president was informed of the situation, he gave orders for Douglass to be admitted, the first time a black person was ever afforded such an opportunity.[60]

Lincoln went still further. He might have chosen to simply allow Douglass to stand in the back of the room unnoticed or afforded him a perfunctory handshake and a few words—the better perhaps not to offend the (white) cream of Washington high society. But when Douglass entered the room, "amid a scene of elegance such as in this country I had never witnessed before," the president spied him, moved to him in the crowd, and exclaimed ("loud enough for all to hear," according to Douglass), "Here comes my friend Douglass . . . I am glad to see you. I saw you in the crowd to-day, listening to my inaugural address; how did you like it?" When Douglass tried to beg off—embarrassed perhaps by the stares of the "thousands waiting to shake hands with you"—Lincoln insisted. "No, no, you must stop a little, Douglass; there is no man in the country whose opinion I value more than yours." Douglass replied, "Mr. Lincoln, that was a sacred effort."[61]

Unfortunately, we have no record in Lincoln's words concerning what he thought of this and his other two encounters with Douglass or exactly what his purposes might have been. Our accounts come directly from Douglass himself, most written quite some time after the fact, and we must allow that he—like any other person—might have permitted distortions of bias and fuzzy memory to cloud what actually occurred.

But such caveats aside, Douglass came away from all three meetings impressed with the president. "Douglass always felt extremely comfortable around Lincoln, more so than around most other white men," historian John Stauffer observes. "Indeed, Douglass sensed a kindred spirit in Lincoln."[62]

No doubt, Lincoln found a level of personal rapport with Douglass as well. Douglass's résumé as an American rags-to-riches story fit well with the dominant narrative of Lincoln's own life. Douglass was also a man—no small matter and one that may explain what was apparently Lincoln's far different treatment of Sojourner Truth. Lincoln was never too comfortable around women, and he often viewed female visitors to the White House as at best a nuisance. Douglass would have found a much readier rapport with Lincoln than had Truth or the other women who accompanied her to the White House during her October 1864 visit.

But in all three meetings, Lincoln brought into play not just his private regard for Douglass but also a public dimension, looking figuratively (or, in the third meeting, almost literally) over his shoulder at white reaction as he met with the most famous black man in America. There was an escalation of the stakes in the three meetings, as if Lincoln was growing steadily bolder in his willingness to defy white public opinion—from a quiet meeting initiated by Douglass to a meeting called by the president himself and finally to a very open and warm rapport with Douglass in front of a crowd of white onlookers.

By meeting with Douglass and by more generally making his White House a hospitable place for black people, Lincoln was—in his own way and on his own timetable—slowly but surely eroding the image of the black Other that so dominated white America. He had begun the process of normalizing black people in front of white America, something no American president had ever before attempted.

Conclusion

Frederick Douglass was not the only African American present at Lincoln's second inaugural ceremony. Prior to 1865, black people were theoretically not allowed to attend presidential inaugurals. I qualify this with *theoretically* because crowd control in a city with the size and sprawling layout of the nation's capital could not have been tight, and given Washington's substantial black population (free and slave), some African Americans were surely able to mingle on the crowd's edges at any given event.

But in 1865, the president's inaugural ceremony was officially opened to African Americans. By at least one account, they took full advantage. A French observer wrote to his wife that "thousands of negroes" milled about in the crowd during the ceremony, applauding frequently throughout the president's address. Several companies of black soldiers were present, as were African American chapters of the Odd Fellows and the Masons.[1]

A few grainy photographs exist of that crowd, but most of the faces are an indistinct blur, the product of an imperfect technology in its infancy. One focuses on the speaker's platform and the front portico of the Capitol. Lincoln is another blur—albeit a faintly recognizable, tall, and angular blur—seen holding his speech and speaking in front of a small table, a glass of water near at hand. Above and to Lincoln's left, squeezed among a host of other onlookers, is John Wilkes Booth.

If Booth wanted to get as far away as possible from those "thousands of negroes," he could not have done much better, perched as he was on one of the highest points above and behind the president, far removed from the masses of people below. All of the faces that are distinguishable around him are white. Whether he intentionally arranged his position in the crowd for that reason is of course unknown, but he certainly would have preferred it that way.

Booth was a true believer in white supremacist principles. "That means nigger citizenship. Now, by God! I'll put him through," he would exclaim to friend and fellow conspirator David Herrold a month after Lincoln's inaugural when he again stood listening to a presidential speech and heard Lincoln offer his support for African American suffrage. In his private correspondence, Booth clearly indicated that one reason he targeted Lincoln for assassination was his belief that the president was a betrayer of the white race. "This country was formed for the *white* and not for the black man," he seethed. "And looking upon *African slavery* from the same stand-point . . . I for one, have ever considered *it,* one of the greatest blessings (both for themselves and us) that God ever bestowed upon a favored nation." As the architect of emancipation, Booth reasoned, Lincoln was destroying not just the white race but also the blacks, who were immeasurably better off in bondage.[2]

Booth was an extreme example of the white presence that haunted Lincoln throughout the war: worried, resentful, above all terribly afraid to lend even a modicum of encouragement to the freedmen lest white racial privilege be somehow compromised. Not all of white America was as extreme or vengeful as Booth of course. But all knew that times were changing, that whatever came next for America's race relations after the war and emancipation would be unprecedented. White America would, as it turned out, maintain its privileged position in the nation's life. But it would never quite be the same.

What sort of white America did Lincoln represent, standing on the cusp of victory in 1865? Was he the man Booth thought he was? Was he a white man who, in the eyes of Booth and others of his ilk, was willing to "betray" the white race—or at least call upon his fellow white Americans to begin to change their ways?

His second inaugural address could be read that way. That storied speech was rich in layers of meaning about the nature of the American experiment, the need for magnanimity and healing, and even (a rare thing for Lincoln) thoughtful reflection on God's will. In addition to all these things, the address carried an implicit message: the war was punishment for the sins of white America. The relevant passage is now justly famous as a high-water mark in presidential rhetoric:

> If we shall suppose that American Slavery is one of those offences [*sic*] which, in the providence of God, must needs come, but which, having continued through His appointed time, He now wills to remove, and that He gives to both North and South, this terrible war, as the woe due to those by whom the offence came, shall we discern therein any departure from those divine attributes which the believers in a Living God always ascribe to Him?

"North and South" America was, in essence, white America. And Lincoln averred that the war was divine retribution for the pain and suffering inflicted by whips wielded by white hands on black backs: "If God wills that [the war] continue, until all the wealth piled by the bond-man's two hundred and fifty years of unrequited toil shall be sunk, and until every drop of blood drawn with the lash, shall be paid by another drawn with the sword, as was said three thousand years ago, so still it must be said 'the judgments of the Lord, are true and righteous altogether.'" Booth could not have liked such talk.[3]

Yet in many ways, Lincoln was still the white man he revealed himself to be in that 1841 letter to Mary Speed concerning the *Lebanon*'s slave coffle—a mixture of motives and impulses. He was capable of transcending the disdain, indifference, and casual cruelty that marked so many of his white neighbors' perceptions of African Americans. But he was also sensitive to the power of white prejudice, of that "universal feeling, whether well or ill-founded, [that] can not be safely disregarded." He thought twice before offending white sensibilities, even when he privately believed those sensibilities were wrongheaded.[4]

Having been born into a society that taught him, in ways great and small, the fundamental superiority of white people, he may never have entirely shed that belief. His particular brand of white supremacy, to be sure, was of a relatively benign nature. He exhibited little of the racial malice and paranoia that animated so many of his fellow white Americans, and (unlike Stephen Douglas), he would not exploit those fears for his own political gain. Lincoln was far more likely to crack an off-color joke at a black person's expense than he was to invoke the specter of a race war or runaway black sexuality or otherwise conjure up a frightening black or savage Other.

He knew white racial fears, what they were and how strong they could be. He likely shared at least some of those fears himself, dating back to his days as a boy traveling through the alien racial landscape of the Mississippi River and confronting those African American thieves one evening near New Orleans. And he knew the fears white Americans carried within themselves—fears of descent into the pit of white trash and all the ignominy that implied. Those fears helped propel his ambition and his drive. But he rarely spoke of his anxieties as a white man in nineteenth-century America, and his inner fears, whatever they were, did not master him.

These basic elements of his whiteness never really changed. They were present in Lincoln when he became president, and they were exacerbated by the various travails of the Civil War. As he was buffeted back and forth by crosscurrents of politics and opinions concerning whether his administration should pursue emancipation and some sort of racial equality, Lincoln's worries about the consequences of black freedom in terms of his support among white Americans increased, leading to some of his more unfortunate decisions. These included his ongoing pursuit of colonization, his poorly conceived meeting with the deputation of black leaders in August 1862, his early efforts to keep black people at arm's length, and his unwillingness to risk offending white public opinion.

But after he crossed the Rubicon of emancipation, there is evidence of growth, a maturing process that roughly paralleled his increasing embrace of a degree of African American equality.[5] Where his slowly developing appreciation of black Americans' problems involved a growing sense of sympathy, his changing point of view concerning whites involved rather the opposite: a certain hardness, a diminishing of the sensitivity he had always displayed in regard to the opinions and judgments of white America. By around mid-1864, he had steeled himself against whatever backlash he might incur from whites. He would risk their wrath, whatever the consequences.

Where did this hardness come from? The war itself likely played a key role. Having by 1864 witnessed so much carnage and destruction, Lincoln, like nearly every other American, had developed a tolerance for risk-taking and casualties—in this context, the political casualties he might suffer from his wholehearted embrace of emancipation, his public meetings with a prominent black man such as Frederick Douglass, and his endorsement of some measure of black suffrage. Lincoln had seen men fight and die by the hundreds of thousands—indeed, he had in many cases sent those men to their deaths himself—and he knew some at least were African American men. Their battlefield valor and courage played no small part in bolstering Lincoln's resolve when confronting white intransigence and hostility.

One wonders too if Lincoln was so willing to risk white ire because he had by the end of the war finally shed those white trash insecurities that had driven him since his early days. He had known from the time he was a boy that if he wanted to get ahead, if he wanted to avoid falling into the pit of failure and marginalization that was the white trash stereotype, he had to avoid wounding the sensibilities of more prominent and well-to-do whites. Those insecurities and concerns probably stayed with him throughout most of his adult life. But by war's end, he was a victorious commander-in-chief and a two-term president (the first president reelected to a second term since Andrew Jackson). He had arrived, so to speak, and perhaps a sense of inner self-satisfaction served as a bulwark against his worries about offending polite white society.

Still, we should not exaggerate the extent of Lincoln's newfound hardness. If we were to view his progression in racial matters as a kind of two-track approach—one track being his attitude toward African Americans, the other toward his fellow whites—then it would be fair to say he had progressed further down the former than down the latter. By 1865, he was on record as supporting some form of black suffrage, a position that would have been unthinkable by any president only a few years previously. He happily signed the Thirteenth Amendment ending slavery, calling it a "King's cure for all the evils" of the war. Though he differed with the more radical members of his own party concerning the nature and scope of Reconstruction, those differences were reconcilable, and there were signs that the president was moving quite steadily in the radicals' overall direction at the time of his assassination.

Booth knew what he was about when he snarled that Lincoln stood for "nigger equality." Maybe not quite yet, but the president was getting there.[6] Lincoln's position vis-à-vis white America was not nearly so clear-cut or so openly radical. There were signs by 1865 that he had the potential to reexamine and critically appraise what it meant to be white in America, but this remained potential only. The bullet of a lone and very angry white man saw to that.

■
Notes

Introduction

1. Text of speech available at http://teachingamericanhistory.org/library/index.asp
?documentprint=39.

2. On the various controversies surrounding the monument, see Kirk Savage, *Standing Soldiers, Kneeling Slaves: Race, War and Monument in Nineteenth-Century America* (Princeton, N.J.: Princeton University Press, 1997), 89–128.

3. Text of speech available at http://teachingamericanhistory.org/library/index.asp
?documentprint=39.

4. See, e.g., David B. Chesebrough, *Frederick Douglass: Oratory from Slavery* (Westport, Conn.: Greenwood Press, 1998), 71; John Stauffer, *Giants: The Parallel Lives of Frederick Douglass and Abraham Lincoln* (New York: Hachette, 2008), 187; David W. Blight, *Frederick Douglass and Abraham Lincoln: A Relationship in Language, Politics, and Memory* (Milwaukee, Wis.: Marquette University Press, 2001), 16–17; and James A. Colaiaco, *Frederick Douglass and the Fourth of July Oration* (New York: Palgrave Macmillan, 2006), 195–198. All these works suggest that Douglass's overarching purpose was not to demean Lincoln but to elevate the freedmen.

5. Lerone Bennett, *Forced into Glory: Abraham Lincoln's White Dream* (Chicago: Johnson, 2000).

6. See, e.g., David R. Roediger, *The Wages of Whiteness: Race and the Making of the American Working Class,* 2nd ed. (New York: Verso, 2007); Roediger, *Working towards Whiteness: How America's Immigrants Became White—The Strange Journey from Ellis Island to the Suburbs* (New York: Basic Books, 2006); Noel Ignatiev, *How the Irish Became White* (New York: Routledge, 2008); Matthew Frye Jacobson, *Whiteness of a Different Color: European Immigrants and the Alchemy of Race* (Cambridge, Mass.:

Harvard University Press, 1999); and Nell Irvin Painter, *The History of White People* (New York: W. W. Norton, 2010).

7. For a very useful overview of the literature and its premises, see Peter Kolchin, "Whiteness Studies: The New History of Race in America," *Journal of American History* 89 (June 2002): 154–173.

8. James Oakes, "Natural Rights, Citizenship Rights, States' Rights, and Black Rights: Another Look at Lincoln and Race," in *Our Lincoln: New Perspectives on Lincoln and His World,* ed. Eric Foner (New York: W. W. Norton, 2009), 299n.

Chapter 1: Seven Negroes

1. R. Gerald McMurtry, "The Lincoln Migration from Kentucky to Indiana," *Indiana Magazine of History* 33 (December 1937): 385–421, records an incident when the young Lincoln was said to have encountered a black servant named Minerva at the home of Col. David D. Murray, en route from Kentucky to Indiana, in December 1816. Benjamin Quarles, *Lincoln and the Negro* (New York: Oxford University Press, 1962), 17, thus describes this as Lincoln's "first recorded experience with a Negro." But McMurtry's source here strikes me as unreliable; I have therefore identified the 1818 flatboat encounter as the first recorded encounter with an African American.

2. Francis Fisher Browne, *The Everyday Life of Abraham Lincoln* (1887; repr., Lincoln: University of Nebraska Press, 1995), 89.

3. Dawn E. Bakken, "A Young Hoosier's Adventures on the Mississippi River," *Indiana Magazine of History* 102 (March 2006): 1; Nathanial Grigsby, Silas Richardson, Nancy Richardson, and John Romine, Interview with William H. Herndon, September 14, 1865, in *Herndon's Informants: Letters, Interviews and Statements about Abraham Lincoln,* ed. Douglas L. Wilson and Rodney O. Davis (Urbana: University of Illinois Press, 2007) (hereafter referred to as *HI*), 116. "*The* rich man" quote is in Lincoln to Andrew Johnston, September 6, 1846, in *The Collected Works of Abraham Lincoln,* 8 vols. and supp., ed. Roy P. Basler (New Brunswick, N.J.: Rutgers University Press, 1953) (hereafter referred to as *CW*), 1: 384 (emphasis in original). Also see Nathaniel Grigsby to William H. Herndon, September 4, 1865, *CW* 1: 94. The reference to Thomas Lincoln's flatboat trips is in A. H. Chapman, written statement, in *HI,* 100.

4. The 1820 census for Spencer County, Indiana, lists Allen Gentry in the 10–16 age range; census available at http://us-census.org/pub/usgenweb/census/in/spencer/1820.

5. See William G. Greene to William H. Herndon, June 7, 1865, *HI,* 26; Anna Gentry, Interview with William H. Herndon, September 17, 1865, *HI,* 131; and Lincoln to Jesse W. Fell, enclosing autobiography, December 20, 1859, *CW* 2: 511.

6. Nicknames are found in John Russell Bartlett, *Dictionary of Americanisms,* 3rd ed. (Boston: Little, Brown, 1860), 155. The "covered shed" quote is from (of all people) Edgar Allan Poe, writing a travelogue; see "Dots and Lines, No. 11; or, Sketches of Scenes and Incidents in the West," in *The Ladies' Companion,* vol. 11 (New York: William Snowden, 1839), 69. On general flatboat construction techniques at this time, see Henry Howe, *Historical Collections of Ohio,* 2 vols. (Norwalk, Ohio: Laning Printing, 1896), 2: 276; Michael Allen, *Western Rivermen, 1763–1861: Ohio and Mississippi Boatmen and the Myth of the Alligator Horse* (Baton Rouge: Louisiana State University

Press, 1994), 67–69; and Erik F. Haites, James Mak, and Gary M. Walton, *Western River Transportation: The Era of Early Internal Development, 1810–1860* (Baltimore, Md.: Johns Hopkins University Press, 1974), 13–15.

7. Logan Esarey, *History of Indiana from the Exploration to 1922*, 3 vols. (Dayton, Ohio: Dayton Historical, 1922), 1: 306; Emory R. Johnson, Thurman William Van Metre, Grover G. Huebner, and David S. Hanchett, *History of Foreign and Domestic Commerce in the United States*, 2nd ed. (Washington, D.C.: Carnegie, 1922), 242; Robert Baird, *View of the Valley of the Mississippi, or the Emigrant's and Traveler's Guide to the West*, 2nd ed. (Philadelphia: H. S. Tanner, 1834), 127; and Haites, *Western River Transportation*, 20–21.

8. Esarey, *History of Indiana*, 306–307; Bakken, "Young Hoosier's Adventures," 3.

9. James D. B. De Bow, *The Industrial Resources, etc., of the Southern and Western States*, 3 vols. (New York: John Street, 1852), 2: 137.

10. Emerson Bennett, *Mike Fink, Legend of the Ohio* (Cincinnati, Ohio: J. A. and U. P. James, 1853).

11. Quoted in Bakken, "Young Hoosier's Adventures," 1.

12. Examples of this explicit association of flatboats with white people can be found in Nelson W. Evans, "The First Steamboat on the Ohio," *Ohio History* 16 (1907): 310; Seymour Dunbar, *A History of Travel in America* (Indianapolis, Ind.: Bobbs-Merrill, 1915), 271; and John C. Leffel, *History of Posey County, Indiana* (Chicago: Standard, 1913), 50. Allen, *Western Rivermen*, 175–176, the best modern study of flatboats during this period, argues that on the whole, flatboating in the Ohio Valley region was a white pursuit.

13. Fink legend is in Emerson Gould, *Fifty Years on the Mississippi* (St. Louis, Mo.: Nixon-Jones Printing, 1889), 50.

14. Quarles, *Lincoln and the Negro*, 17; also Louis A. Warren, *Lincoln's Youth: Indiana Years, 1816–1830*, 2nd ed. (Indianapolis: Indiana Historical Society, 2002), 13–14.

15. Andrew R. L. Cayton, *Frontier Indiana* (Bloomington: Indiana University Press, 1996), 190–191.

16. Kentucky law is quoted in William Jay, *Inquiry into the Character and Tendency, of the American Colonization and Antislavery Societies*, 6th ed. (New York: R. G. Williams, 1833), 133.

17. Richard D. Sears, *The Kentucky Abolitionists in the Midst of Slavery, 1854–1864: Exiles for Freedom* (New York: Edwin Mellen Press, 1993), xviii–xix. On Kentucky's general black population numbers during this era, see Marion B. Lucas, *A History of Blacks in Kentucky: From Slavery to Segregation, 1760–1891* (Lexington: Kentucky Historical Society, 2003), xv–xvi.

18. Erastus R. Burba, Interview with William H. Herndon, May 25, 1866, *HI*, 257. David H. Donald, *Lincoln* (New York: Simon & Schuster, 1995), 165, makes a similar observation about Lincoln's overall lack of direct experience with slavery.

19. John L. Blake, *A Geographical, Chronological, and Historical Atlas, on a New and Improved Plan* (New York: Cook, 1826), 103; Nell Irvin Painter, *The History of White People* (New York: W. W. Norton, 2010), ix.

20. On associations of whiteness with beauty and aesthetic value, see Painter, *History of White People*, 71, 103.

21. On the relationship between whiteness and citizenship, see David R. Roediger, *The Wages of Whiteness: Race and the Making of the American Working Class,* 2nd ed. (New York: Verso, 2007), 21–23; Matthew Frye Jacobson, *Whiteness of a Different Color: European Immigrants and the Alchemy of Race* (Cambridge, Mass.: Harvard University Press, 1999), 17, 22–24, 29–31; and Painter, *History of White People,* 34, 107.

22. Noah Webster, *Webster's 1828 American Dictionary of the English Language,* available at http://www.1828-dictionary.com/. Lincoln was directly familiar with *Webster's;* see David Turnham, Interview with William H. Herndon, September 15, 1865, *HI,* 121.

23. James Barclay, *A Complete and Universal English Dictionary* (London: J. P. and C. Rivington, 1774); Thomas Dilworth, *A New Guide to the English Tongue* (London: Richard and Henry Causton, 1798), 134; John Bunyan, *The Pilgrim's Progress* (New York: P. P. Collier, 1909), 163; and Daniel Defoe, *The Life and Adventures of Robinson Crusoe* (London: A. J. Valpy, 1831), 72. On Lincoln's familiarity with these books, see Turnham, Interview with Herndon; Dennis E. Hanks, Interview with William H. Herndon, June 13, 1865, *HI,* 41–42; and Robert Bray, *Reading with Lincoln* (Carbondale: Southern Illinois University Press, 2010), 1–2, 34–36, 44.

24. This observation was made as long ago as 1954, in Gordon W. Allport's seminal *The Nature of Prejudice,* 25th ed. (New York: Basic Books, 1979), chap. 2. More recent research suggests that this preference of white over black and other ethnic groups acts very powerfully upon white children, even when social and environmental stimuli are minimal; see Nilanjana Dasgupta, "Automatic Preference for White Americans: Eliminating the Familiarity Explanation," *Journal of Experimental Social Psychology* 36 (2000): 316–328.

25. See, e.g., Meagan M. Patterson and Rebecca S. Bigler, "Preschool Children's Attention to Environmental Messages about Groups: Social Categorization and the Origins of Intergroup Bias," *Child Development* 77 (July 2006): 847–860, which suggests the power of lumping children together into arbitrary color groups (a "blue group," etc.) and which also shows interesting research results from adult categorization on children's attitudes. On childhood development of racial awareness, see Andrew Scott Baron and Mahzarin Banaji, "The Development of Implicit Attitudes," *Psychological Science* 17 (January 2006): 53–58.

26. On Jefferson's views regarding Indians, see Robert F. Berkhofer, Jr., *The White Man's Indian: Images of the American Indian from Columbus to the Present* (New York: Alfred A. Knopf, 1978), 42–44. See also generally Nancy Shoemaker, "How the Indians Got to Be Red," *American Historical Review* 102 (June 1997): 625–626 and 629–638.

27. On this confluence of savagery and race, see Berkhofer, *White Man's Indian,* 15–17; Winthrop D. Jordan, *White over Black: American Attitudes toward the Negro, 1550–1812* (Chapel Hill: University of North Carolina Press, 1968), chaps. 1–2; and the useful introduction to the early history of race in Lee D. Baker, *From Savage to Negro: Anthropology and the Construction of Race, 1896–1954* (Berkeley: University of California Press, 1998), 11–15. For examples of the ways in which blacks were character-

ized as savage and uncivilized, see Josiah Priest, *Slavery, As It Relates to the Negro, or African Race* (Albany, N.Y.: C. Van Benthuysen, 1845), 200.

28. George Turner, *Traits of Indian Character: As Generally Applicable to the Aborigines of North America* (Philadelphia: Key, Biddle and Minor, 1836), 28.

29. Lucius P. Little, *Ben Hardin: His Times and Contemporaries* (Louisville, Ky.: Courier-Journal, 1887), 6–8.

30. On Indian and white violence in Indiana during Lincoln's time, see John D. Barnhart and Dorothy L. Riker, *Indiana to 1816: The Colonial Period* (Indianapolis: Indiana Historical Society, 1971), 370–411; Andrew R. L. Cayton, *Frontier Indiana* (Bloomington: Indiana University Press, 1996), 214–224; and John D. Barnhart and Donald F. Carmony, *Indiana: From Frontier to Industrial Commonwealth* (New York: Lewis Historical, 1954), 139–140.

31. Elizabeth Crawford, Interview with William H. Herndon, September 16, 1865, *HI*, 125; John Hanks, Interview with William H. Herndon, [1865–1866], *HI*, 455; and Oliver C. Terry to Jesse W. Weik, July 1888, *HI*, 662. Quotes are from J. W. Wartmann to Jesse W. Weik, July 20, 1888, *HI*, 661.

32. On Weems's influence on Lincoln, see Donald, *Lincoln*, 31; Richard Carwardine, *Lincoln: A Life of Purpose and Power* (New York: Alfred A. Knopf, 2006), 8; William Lee Miller, *Lincoln's Virtues: An Ethical Biography* (New York: Alfred A. Knopf, 2002), 82; Dwight G. Anderson, "Quest for Immortality: A Theory of Abraham Lincoln's Political Psychology," in *The Historian's Lincoln: Pseudohistory, Psychohistory, and History*, ed. Gabor S. Boritt (Urbana: University of Illinois Press, 1996), 256–258; Gabor S. Boritt, *The Gettysburg Gospel: The Lincoln Speech That Nobody Knows* (New York: Simon & Schuster, 2006), 119; Harold Holzer, "Visualizing Lincoln: Abraham Lincoln As Student, Subject, and Patron of the Visual Arts," in *Our Lincoln: New Perspectives on Lincoln and His World*, ed. Eric Foner (New York: W. W. Norton, 2009), 80; and Bray, *Reading with Lincoln*, 23–26.

33. Mason Locke Weems, *The Life of George Washington; with Curious Anecdotes, Equally Honourable to Himself, and Exemplary to His Young Countrymen* (Philadelphia: Joseph Allen, 1833), 26, 29, 32, 43, 49.

34. Hanks, Interview with Herndon, *HI*, 36. For a succinct modern rendering of the tale, see Donald, *Lincoln*, 21.

35. A. H. Chapman, written statement, September 8, 1865, *HI*, 95.

36. Ibid., 96; also William Clagett, statement, February 22, 1866, *HI*, 220. On Billy's claim about Mordecai, see William H. Herndon, *Herndon's Lincoln: The True Story of a Great Life* (Urbana: University of Illinois Press, 2006), 19–20.

37. Lincoln to Jesse Lincoln, April 1, 1854, *CW* 2: 217; see also Lincoln, autobiography written for John Scripps, c. June 1860, *CW* 4: 61.

38. On the general circumstances of the Black Hawk War, see Kerry A. Trask, *Black Hawk: The Battle for the Heart of America* (New York: Henry Holt, 2007), and Patrick J. Jung, *The Black Hawk War of 1832* (Norman: University of Oklahoma Press, 2008). On Lincoln's involvement, see Michael S. Burlingame, *Abraham Lincoln: A Life*, 2 vols. (Baltimore, Md.: Johns Hopkins University Press, 2008), 1: 67–80.

39. Burlingame, *Abraham Lincoln*, 1: 68–75; William Miller, Interview with William

H. Herndon, c. September 1866, *HI*, 361–366; and Royal Clary, Interview with William H. Herndon, c. October 1866, *HI*, 370–372.

40. William G. Greene, Interview with William H. Herndon, May 30, 1865, *HI*, 18.

41. Thomas Dilworth, *Dilworth's Spelling Book, Improved: A New Guide to the English Tongue* (New York: John McCulloch, 1797), x; John Bunyan, *The Pilgrim's Progress: From This World to That Which Is to Come* (Boston: Massachusetts Sabbath School Society, 1833), 137–138.

42. Weems, *Life of George Washington*, 88, 211.

43. See Dennis Hanks, Interview with William H. Herndon, September 8, 1865, *HI*, 105.

44. Caleb Bingham, *The American Preceptor Improved: Being a New Selection of Lessons for Reading and Speaking, Designed for the Use of Schools* (Boston: J. H. A. Frost, 1829), 83–84.

45. On Lincoln's reading of the Bible at an early age, see Hanks, Interview with Herndon, *HI*, 37.

46. See David M. Goldberg, *The Curse of Ham: Race and Slavery in Early Judaism, Christianity, and Islam* (Princeton, N.J.: Princeton University Press, 2005), 101–105 and 108–110; Jordan, *White over Black,* chap. 1; and useful observations in James Oakes, "Natural Rights, Citizenship Rights, States' Rights, and Black Rights: Another Look at Lincoln and Race," in Foner, *Our Lincoln,* 118.

47. Lincoln, autobiography written for Scripps, CW 4: 61–62.

48. See, e.g., Browne, *Everyday Life of Abraham Lincoln,* 45.

49. Erastus R. Burba to William H. Herndon, March 31, 1866, *HI*, 240; Hanks, Interview with Herndon, *HI*, 36.

50. See Herndon, *Herndon's Lincoln,* 43n.

51. On Downs as a "disorderly preacher," see John H. Spencer, *A History of Kentucky Baptists from 1769 to 1883,* 2 vols. (Cincinnati, Ohio: J. H. Spencer, 1885), 1: 163. On Elkins, see Edgar De Witt Jones, *Lincoln and the Preachers* (New York: Harper & Row, 1948), 16–17. Legend has it that at the age of nine, Lincoln wrote his very first letter to Minister Elkins, asking him to come to Indiana to preach at his mother's funeral; Herndon believed this to be true; see *Herndon's Lincoln,* 31. See also, e.g., James Baldwin, *Abraham Lincoln: A True Life* (New York: American Book, 1904), 50; Francis Marion Van Natter, *Lincoln's Boyhood: A Chronicle of His Indiana Years* (Washington, D.C.: Public Affairs Press, 1963), 66. But an actual copy of the letter has never been found, and there is no firm documentation of the incident or of the suggestion that Lincoln and Elkins became "fast friends," as asserted by Charles Carleton Coffin, *Abraham Lincoln* (New York: Harper & Brothers, 1893), 23.

52. Warren, *Lincoln's Youth,* 117.

53. On Lincoln's early antislavery literary exposure, see Bray, *Reading with Lincoln,* 6–7, 13–15.

54. Esarey, *History of Indiana,* 307. Lincoln, autobiography written for Scripps, CW 4: 62, mentions their habit of trading along the river.

55. Alice Dunbar-Nelson, "People of Color in Louisiana, Part I," *Journal of Negro History* 1, no. 4 (October 1916): 361–366.

56. On black flatboatmen and cotton boxes, see Ulrich B. Phillips, *A History of Transportation in the Eastern Cotton Belt to 1860* (New York: Columbia University Press, 1908), 71. For examples of African Americans as cargo, see Poe, "Dots and Lines," 69, and Elizur White, *Quarterly Anti-slavery Magazine,* vol. 1 (New York: New York Anti-slavery Society, 1836), 63. An example of slaves traveling on flatboats with masters can be found in Samuel Prescott Hildreth and Ephraim Cutler, *Biographical and Historical Memoirs of the Early Pioneer Settlers of Ohio* (Cincinnati, Ohio: H. W. Derby, 1852), 374.

57. On the Sugar Coast plantations' large size and general economic function, see Mark D. Schmitz, "Economies of Scale and Farm Size in the Antebellum Sugar Sector," *Journal of Economic History* 37, no. 4 (December 1977): 959.

58. On the ancient associations of sugar with slavery, see Eric Williams, "Laissez-Faire, Sugar and Slavery," *Political Science Quarterly* 58, no. 1 (March 1943): 67–73.

59. American Anti-slavery Society, *American Slavery As It Is: Testimony of a Thousand Witnesses* (New York: American Anti-slavery Society, 1839), 38 (emphases in original); J. Caryle Sitterson, "Magnolia Plantation, 1852–1862: A Decade of a Louisiana Sugar Estate," *Mississippi Valley Historical Review* 25, no. 2 (September 1938): 199–201; Richard Follett, *The Sugar Masters: Planters and Slaves in Louisiana's Cane World, 1820–1860* (Baton Rouge: Louisiana State University Press, 2007).

60. Everett S. Brown, "Letters from Louisiana," *Mississippi Valley Historical Review* 11, no. 4 (March 1925): 579; Josiah Quincy, *Memoir of the Life of Josiah Quincy, of Massachusetts* (Boston: Cummings, Hilliard, 1825), 84.

61. Lincoln, autobiography written for Scripps, CW 4: 62.

62. These observations are based on a contemporary 1828 map of the region, available at http://usgwarchives.net/maps/louisiana/statemap/la1828.jpg.

63. On the modern Houmas plantation, see http://www.houmashouse.com/.

64. On this point, see Anna Caroline Gentry, Interview with William H. Herndon, September 17, 1865, *HI,* 131, who suggested that Lincoln and her husband had landed at "Madamoiselle Busham's plantation," 6 miles below Baton Rouge. Since there is no record of a Busham plantation in the area, I think Gentry's memory was faulty, turning "Duchesne" somehow into "Busham."

65. Lincoln, autobiography written for Scripps, CW 4: 62.

66. Ibid.; Grigsby, Richardson, Richardson, and Romine, Interview with Herndon, *HI,* 118.

67. Lincoln, autobiography written for Scripps, CW 4: 62.

68. Ibid.

Chapter 2: White Trash

1. Dennis F. Hanks, Interview with Erastus Wright, June 8, 1865, in *Herndon's Informants: Letters, Interviews and Statements about Abraham Lincoln,* ed. Douglas L. Wilson and Rodney O. Davis (Urbana: University of Illinois Press, 2007) (hereafter referred to as *HI*), 27; David Turnham, Interview with William H. Herndon, September 15, 1865, *HI,* 121. Also see Louis A. Warren, *Lincoln's Youth: Indiana Years, 1816–1830,* 2nd ed. (Indianapolis: Indiana Historical Society, 2002), 206–208, and

David H. Donald, *Lincoln* (New York: Simon & Schuster, 1995), 36. For a good general discussion of Thomas Lincoln's financial condition, see Harry E. Pratt, *The Personal Finances of Abraham Lincoln* (Springfield, Ill.: Abraham Lincoln Association, 1943), 2–5.

2. John Hanks, Interview with William H. Herndon, c. 1865–1866, *HI*, 453.

3. John Hanks, Interview with William Herndon, June 13, 1865, *HI*, 43, and Interview, c. 1865–1866, *HI*, 453–454. Also see Kenneth J. Winkle, *The Young Eagle: The Rise of Abraham Lincoln* (Dallas, Tex.: Taylor, 2001), 26.

4. Hardin Bale, Interview with William H. Herndon, May 29, 1865, *HI*, 13; Mentor Graham, Interview with William H. Herndon, May 29, 1865, *HI*, 9; and James Short to William H. Herndon, July 7, 1865, *HI*, 73. See also William G. Greene, Interview with William H. Herndon, May 30, 1865, *HI*, 18, and Herndon's assessment of Offutt in William H. Herndon, *Herndon's Lincoln: The True Story of a Great Life* (Urbana: University of Illinois Press, 2006), 63.

5. Herndon, *Herndon's Lincoln*, 62–63; James Hall to William H. Herndon, September 17, 1873, *HI*, 580. See also Denton Offutt to Abraham Lincoln, September 7, 1859, and February 11, 1861, Abraham Lincoln Papers, Library of Congress (hereafter referred to as LPLC).

6. Hanks, Interview with Herndon, *HI*, 456; J. Rowan Herndon, May 28, 1865, *HI*, 6. On the boat's cargo, see Hanks, Interview with Herndon, 44.

7. Tavern description and quotes are from Wesley Elliott, Interview with William H. Herndon, c. 1865–1866, *HI*, 447.

8. Hanks, Interview with Herndon, *HI*, 456; Lincoln, autobiography written for John Scripps, c. 1860, in *The Collected Works of Abraham Lincoln*, 8 vols. and supp., ed. Roy P. Basler (New Brunswick, N.J.: Rutgers University Press, 1953) (hereafter referred to as CW), 4: 63.

9. Hanks, Interview with Herndon, *HI*, 456–457. Apparently, they were aided by others in the area; see William G. Greene to William H. Herndon, May 29, 1865, *HI*, 11.

10. Hanks, Interview with Herndon, *HI*, 43, and Interview with Herndon, *HI*, 457.

11. Hanks, Interview with Herndon, *HI*, 457.

12. Lincoln, autobiography written for Scripps, CW 4: 64.

13. Hanks, Interview with Herndon, *HI*, 44; Lincoln, autobiography written for Scripps, CW 4: 64.

14. Lincoln, autobiography written for Scripps, CW 4: 64.

15. Hanks, Interview with Herndon, *HI*, 457.

16. For statistics on flatboat traffic in New Orleans, see James Mak and Gary M. Walton, "The Persistence of Old Technologies: The Case of Flatboats," *Journal of Economic History* 33 (1973): 444, and the description in James D. B. De Bow, *The Industrial Resources, etc., of the Southern and Western States*, 3 vols. (New York: John Street, 1852), 2: 137.

17. Emerson Gould, *Fifty Years on the Mississippi* (St. Louis, Mo.: Nixon-Jones Printing, 1889), 329–330; James S. Buckingham, *The Slave States of America*, 2 vols. (London: Fisher, Son, 1842), 1: 343.

18. Quotes in Buckingham, *Slave States*, 1: 344, 348.

19. Ibid., 457; Herndon, *Herndon's Lincoln*, 60. I should note here that there is a

similar story, told in a thirdhand account from what is allegedly Allen Gentry's story, related to his first New Orleans flatboat trip, but that story, like the Hanks story related in this chapter, is highly suspect. See the expert deconstruction of the Gentry testimony in Phillip S. Paludan, "Lincoln and Negro Slavery: I Haven't Got Time for the Pain," *Journal of the Abraham Lincoln Association* 27 (Summer 2006): 1–24.

20. Lincoln to Joshua Speed, August 24, 1855, CW 2: 320 On slave auctions' role in New Orleans, see Walter Johnson, *Soul by Soul: Life inside the Antebellum Slave Market* (Cambridge, Mass.: Harvard University Press, 1999), 1–3, 47.

21. Lincoln, autobiography written for Scripps, CW 4: 64. Lincoln's version is further supported in J. Rowan Herndon to William H. Herndon, May 28, 1865, HI, 6. Herndon noted that Lincoln and Johnston returned by boat from New Orleans; his omission of Hanks suggests that Hanks returned earlier.

22. Jan Morris, *Lincoln: A Foreigner's Quest* (New York: Da Capo Press, 2000), 22–23.

23. That is precisely the point numerous reviewers made about Morris's book; see, e.g., Michael Burlingame's review in *Historian* 64 (Fall 2001): 205 (referencing Morris's numerous factual errors and her "flippant, idiosyncratic judgments").

24. Woodrow Wilson, *Division and Reunion, 1829–1889* (New York: Longmans, Green, 1893), 216; W. E. B. DuBois, "Again Lincoln," in *Crisis* (September 1922), text available at http://teachingamericanhistory.org/library/index.asp?document=555.

25. Examples of this debate swirled largely around how one might characterize Thomas Lincoln or the Lincoln family in general. See, e.g., Lowell Hayes Harrison, *Lincoln of Kentucky* (Lexington: University Press of Kentucky, 2000), 20; Ida M. Tarbell, *The Early Life of Abraham Lincoln* (New York: S. S. McClure, 1896), 4–5; Wayne Whipple, *The Story-Life of Lincoln* (Philadelphia: John C. Winston, 1908), viii; and William E. Barton, *The Paternity of Abraham Lincoln* (New York: George E. Doran, 1920), 270.

26. Katherine Helm, *The True Story of Mary, Wife of Lincoln* (New York: Harper, 1928), 48–49.

27. See Margaret Bayard Smith, *A Winter in Washington* (New York: Bliss and White, 1824), 281.

28. Harriet Beecher Stowe, *A Key to "Uncle Tom's Cabin"* (Boston: John P. Jewett, 1853), 85. On the Southern antebellum antecedents of the term, see John Hartigan, Jr., *Odd Tribes: Toward a Cultural Analysis of White People* (Durham, N.C.: Duke University Press, 2005); see also a discussion of the term's etymology in Annalee Newitz and Matthew Wray, "What Is 'White Trash'?: Stereotypes and Economic Conditions of Poor Whites in the United States," in *Whiteness: A Critical Reader,* ed. Mike Hill (New York: New York University Press, 1995), 170.

29. John Russell Bartlett, *Dictionary of Americanisms,* 3rd ed. (Boston: Little, Brown, 1860), 332; Daniel Robinson Hundley, *Social Relations in Our Southern States* (New York: Henry B. Price, 1860), 257.

30. Charles Fenno Hoffman, *The Knickerbocker,* vol. 8 (New York: Clark and Edson, 1836), 285; Frederick Law Olmsted, *A Journey in the Seaboard Slave States* (New York: Dix and Edwards, 1856), 548; Edward A. Pollard, *Black Diamonds Gathered in*

the *Darkey Homes of the South* (New York: Pudney and Russell, 1859), 57; and Cassius M. Clay and Horace Greeley, *The Writings of Cassius Marcellus Clay* (New York: Harper & Brothers, 1848), 199.

31. See http://www.kancoll.org/books/cutler/terrhist/terrhist-p6.html; Richard H. Thornton, *An American Glossary* (Philadelphia: J. B. Lippincott, 1912), 707, dates the earliest usage of the term *puke* to 1838. It was also sometimes a term applied to all native Missourians by people from outside the state; see George E. Shankle, *American Nicknames* (Chicago: Putnam's, 1955), 431. For an excellent modern discussion of the ethnic overtones in the term, see Michael Fellman, *Inside War: The Guerrilla Conflict in Missouri during the Civil War* (Oxford: Oxford University Press, 1990), 14–16.

32. See generally Noel Ignatiev, *How the Irish Became White* (New York: Routledge, 2008), chap. 3 and 62–90; David R. Roediger, *Working towards Whiteness: How America's Immigrants Became White—The Strange Journey from Ellis Island to the Suburbs* (New York: Basic Books, 2006), esp. chap. 2; and Theodore W. Allen, *The Invention of the White Race: The Origin of Racial Oppression in America* (New York: Verso, 1997).

33. Helm, *True Story of Mary,* 103.

34. See Matthew J. Gavin's review of Edmund Kirke's *Among the Pines* in *North American Review* 95 (October 1862): 539; the "money" quote is in Hundley, *Social Relations,* 262.

35. Moncure Daniel Conway, "Then and Now in the Old Dominion," *Atlantic Monthly,* April 1862, 500; Fredrika Bremer and Mary Botham Howitt, *The Homes of the New World: Impressions of America,* 2 vols. (New York: Harper & Brothers, 1858), 1: 365.

36. Gavin, review of Edmund Kirke's *Among the Pines,* 540. The "too proud to dig" quote is in William Tait, "The White Population of Slavedom," *Tait's Edinburgh Magazine* 23 (January 1856): 614.

37. Quoted in Bartlett, *Dictionary of Americanisms,* 510; John Dixon Long, John Wesley, and Richard Watson, *Pictures of Slavery in Church and State,* 3rd ed. (Philadelphia: John Dixon Long, 1857), 354.

38. J. R. Gillmore, "The Poor Whites of the South," *Harper's New Monthly Magazine* 29 (June–November 1864): 115; William Londsdale Watkinson, William Theophilus Davison, and John Telford, *London Quarterly Review* 13 (October 1859–January 1860): 531. See also Newitz and Wray, "What Is 'White Trash'?," 171.

39. "Practical Suggestions," *Rhode Island Schoolmaster* 2 (1856–1857): 338.

40. Francis Colburn Adams, *Justice in the By-ways* (New York: Livermore and Rudd, 1856), 203; Elizabeth Wormely Latimer, *Our Cousin Veronica, or, Scenes and Adventures over the Blue Ridge* (New York: Bunce and Bros., 1855), 282.

41. Roediger, *Wages of Whiteness,* xv, 12–15. Roediger gets at something similar to this when describing how whiteness drove a wedge between poor blacks and whites who might otherwise have made common cause.

42. John B. Helm to William H. Herndon, August 1, 1865, *HI,* 82; Presley Nevil Haycraft to John B. Helm, July 19, 1865, *HI,* 86.

43. Helm to Herndon, *HI,* 82; Edgar Conkling to William H. Herndon, July 25, 1867, *HI,* 563; Richard N. Collins to William H. Herndon, August 19, 1867, *HI,*

567–568; "Anonymous" to William H. Herndon, c. 1867, *HI,* 571; Michael Marion Cassidy to Jesse W. Weik, March 10, 1887, *HI,* 608; and Judge Alfred M. Brown, Interview with Jesse W. Weik, March 23, 1887, *HI,* 612. See also Dennis F. Hanks to William H. Herndon, February 10, 1866, *HI,* 199, in which Hanks angrily rejects the validity of the rumors that Lincoln was a "Baseborn Child"; however, he also confirms that the rumors were present, if not true.

44. Nathaniel Grigsby, Silas Richardson, Nancy Richardson, and John Romine, Interview with William H. Herndon, September 14, 1865, *HI,* 116; Hanks, Interview with Herndon, *HI,* 456.

45. The "dirt floors" quote is in Helm, *True Story of Mary,* 86; Gillmore, "Poor Whites of the South," 115.

46. Gillmore, "Poor Whites of the South," 115; Greene, Interview with Herndon, *HI,* 17.

47. Henry E. Dummer, Interview with William H. Herndon, c. 1865–1866, *HI,* 442–443; Henry C. Whitney to William H. Herndon, June 23, 1887, *HI,* 617.

48. Green B. Taylor, Interview with William H. Herndon, September 16, 1865, *HI,* 130. On Lincoln's brawling, see J. Rowan Herndon to William H. Herndon, June 21, 1865, *HI,* 51; Joseph C. Richardson, Interview with William H. Herndon, September 14, 1865, *HI,* 120; and James A. Herndon, Interview with William H. Herndon, c. 1865–1866, *HI,* 460.

49. Dennis F. Hanks, Interview with William H. Herndon, June 13, 1865, *HI,* 37.

50. In this, I am in agreement with David Donald's analysis, though I suspect those rumors existed prior to the war; see Donald, *Lincoln,* 605n. There is also the matter of Lincoln's supposed confession that he was a "bastard" to Herndon, revealed in a letter to Ward Hill Lamon. Douglas Wilson skillfully analyzes this document in Wilson, *Honor's Voice: The Transformation of Abraham Lincoln* (New York: Vintage Books, 1999), 12–14; he finds the gist of it to be generally reliable, which in turn suggests Lincoln was quite aware of the rumors about his legitimacy.

51. Lincoln to Thomas Lincoln and John D. Johnston, December 24, 1848, *CW* 2: 15; see also Pratt, *Personal Finances of Abraham Lincoln,* 60–61.

52. Lincoln to Lincoln and Johnston, *CW* 2: 15–16 (emphases in original).

53. Sarah Bush Lincoln, Interview with William H. Herndon, September 8, 1865, *HI,* 107.

54. Mentor Graham to William H. Herndon, July 15, 1865, *HI,* 76; N. W. Branson to William H. Herndon, August 3, 1865, *HI,* 90; and Robert B. Rutledge to William H. Herndon, November 30, 1866, *HI,* 426.

55. Bush Lincoln, Interview with Herndon, *HI,*108.

56. Elizabeth Herndon Bell, Interview with Jesse W. Weik, August 24, 1883, *HI,* 591.

57. Nathaniel Grigsby, Interview with William H. Herndon, September 12, 1865, *HI,* 112; Turnham, Interview with Herndon, *HI,* 121. See also William Wood, Interview with William H. Herndon, September 15, 1865, *HI,* 123, who also noted that Lincoln wrote something on temperance while in Indiana, so the idea at least of forgoing drink was apparently present in Indiana.

58. Henry McHenry, Interview with William H. Herndon, May 29, 1865, *HI*, 15; James Short to William H. Herndon, July 7, 1865, *HI*, 73; and N. W. Branson to William H. Herndon, August 3, 1865, *HI*, 90.

59. On Lincoln's rejection of tobacco, see Abner Y. Ellis to William H. Herndon, January 23, 1866, *HI*, 170.

60. Menard *Axis*, February 15, 1862, in *HI*, 24.

61. Herndon, *Herndon's Lincoln*, 231; Hanks, Interview with Herndon, *HI*, 42.

62. For an excellent overview of the various psychological theories concerning Lincoln's ambition, I have relied on Michael P. Burlingame, "'The Most Ambitious Man in the World,'" in Burlingame, *Inner World of Abraham Lincoln* (Urbana: University of Illinois Press, 1997), 252–257.

63. Lincoln, Address to the Young Men's Lyceum, January 27, 1838, *CW* I: 114.

64. See, e.g., Dwight G. Anderson, *Abraham Lincoln: The Quest for Immortality* (New York: Alfred A. Knopf, 1982), and George B. Forgie, *Patricide in the House Divided: A Psychological Interpretation of Lincoln and His Age* (New York: W. W. Norton, 1979). However, see Mark Neely's cogent analysis of this school of thought in Neely, "Lincoln's Lyceum Speech and the Origins of a Modern Myth," *Lincoln Lore* no. 1776 (February 1987): 1–4, as well as the commentaries by Jean Baker, Herman Belz, Robert V. Bruce, Marcus Cunliffe, Kenneth Stampp, and Major L. Wilson in *The Historian's Lincoln: Pseudohistory, Psychohistory, and History*, ed. Gabor S. Boritt (Urbana: University of Illinois Press, 1996), pt. 3, and Joshua Shenk's observations in Shenk, *Lincoln's Melancholy: How Depression Challenged a President and Fueled His Greatness* (New York: Mariner Books, 2006), 238–239.

65. On the relationship between ambition and masculinity, see E. Anthony Rotundo, *American Manhood: Transformations in Masculinity from the Revolution to the Modern Era* (New York: Basic Books, 1994), 14–17.

Chapter 3: *The* Lebanon

1. The "splendid" quote is in George P. Clark, ed., *Into the Old Northwest: Journeys with Charles H. Titus, 1841–1846* (East Lansing: Michigan State University Press, 1994), 41. See Thomas E. Chavez, *Manual Alvarez, 1794–1856: A Biography* (Niwot: University Press of Colorado, 1990), 66; the reference to loading livestock on the *Lebanon* in St. Louis in Marc Simmons, *Murder on the Santa Fe Trail: An International Incident, 1843* (El Paso: Texas Western Press, 1987), 13; and the reference to the boat's stopover in Cincinnati in Victor Tixier, *Tixier's Travels on the Osage Prairies* (1843; repr., Norman: University of Oklahoma Press, 1940), 280.

2. I have based this description on the information available concerning the layouts of other steam vessels from the period; see Adam I. Kane, *The Western River Steamboat* (College Station: Texas A&M University Press, 2004), 88–93.

3. Joshua Speed, *Reminiscences of Abraham Lincoln and Notes of a Visit to California: Two Lectures* (Louisville, Ky.: John P. Morton, 1884), 21.

4. Lincoln to Joshua F. Speed, February 3, 1842, in *The Collected Works of Abraham Lincoln*, 8 vols. and supp., ed. Roy P. Basler (New Brunswick, N.J.: Rutgers University Press, 1953) (hereafter referred to as *CW*), I: 267, and Lincoln to Joshua F. Speed, Feb-

ruary 13, 1842, *CW* 1: 269. The best analysis of their relationship is David H. Donald, *"We Are Lincoln Men": Abraham Lincoln and His Men* (New York: Simon & Schuster, 2003), 29–64.

5. Ninian W. Edwards, Interview with William H. Herndon, September 22, 1865, *HI*, 133; Joshua F. Speed, Interview with William H. Herndon, c. 1865–1866, in *Herndon's Informants: Letters, Interviews and Statements about Abraham Lincoln,* ed. Douglas L. Wilson and Rodney O. Davis (Urbana: University of Illinois Press, 2007) (hereafter referred to as *HI*), 475. Also see Joshua F. Speed to William H. Herndon, November 30, 1866, *HI,* 430. This period of Lincoln's life and particularly the psychological dimensions of his breakdown have been the subject of numerous studies and nearly endless speculation. For a creative Freudian interpretation of the subject, see Charles B. Strozier, "Lincoln's Quest for Union: Public and Private Meanings," in *The Historian's Lincoln: Pseudohistory, Psychohistory, and History,* ed. Gabor S. Boritt (Urbana: University of Illinois Press, 1996), 224–227. The most lucid discussions I have seen are Douglas Wilson, "Abraham Lincoln and 'That Fatal First of January,'" in Wilson, *Lincoln before Washington: New Perspectives on the Illinois Years* (Urbana: University of Illinois Press, 1997), 99–132, and Wilson, *Honor's Voice: The Transformation of Abraham Lincoln* (New York: Vintage Books, 1999), 223–232. Also useful is Joshua Shenk, *Lincoln's Melancholy: How Depression Challenged a President and Fueled His Greatness* (New York: Mariner Books, 2006), chap. 3.

6. Joshua F. Speed to William H. Herndon, September 17, 1866, *HI,* 342; Catherine Clinton, *Mrs. Lincoln: A Life* (New York: HarperCollins, 2009), 55, argues that Mrs. Speed was "not particularly religious" but rather felt sorry for Lincoln because of their mutual battles with "melancholy."

7. Theodore Dwight Weld, *Slavery and the Internal Slave Trade in the United States of North America* (London: Thomas Ward, 1841), 52–53. Other accounts suggest that slaves were often kept in the hold during a steamboat voyage; see Solomon Northrup, *Twelve Years a Slave* (New York: Miller, Orton and Mulligan, 1855), 56. In one case, the steamboat *Niagara* kept slaves in a "room" on the main deck; see William W. Brown, *The American Fugitive in Europe* (Boston: John P. Jewett, 1855), 12. In all these cases, the slaves were fully accessible to the passengers on the boats.

8. For a cogent discussion of this point, see Phillip S. Paludan, "Lincoln and Negro Slavery: I Haven't Got Time for the Pain," *Journal of the Abraham Lincoln Association* 27 (Summer 2006): 2–6 and 10–14.

9. Brian Dirck, *Lincoln the Lawyer* (Urbana: University of Illinois Press, 2007), chaps. 1–2. The first African American lawyer licensed to practice law in the United States was Macon Bolling Allen, admitted to the Maine bar in 1844; see Gerald D. Jaynes, *Encyclopedia of African-American Society,* 2 vols. (New York: Sage, 2005), 1: 498.

10. William H. Herndon, *Herndon's Lincoln: The True Story of a Great Life* (Urbana: University of Illinois Press, 2006), 208.

11. Michael S. Burlingame, *Abraham Lincoln: A Life,* 2 vols. (Baltimore, Md.: Johns Hopkins University Press, 2008), 1: 128–129, offers a good sampling of contemporary accounts concerning Springfield's various drawbacks. See also Kenneth J. Winkle, *The Young Eagle: The Rise of Abraham Lincoln* (New York: Taylor, 2001), chap. 15.

12. Speed, *Reminiscences of Abraham Lincoln*, 20–21.

13. Here, I am arguing for a slightly different interpretation of the process so ably identified by Wilson in his perceptive study *Honor's Voice*. On the general relationship in this era between manhood and domesticity, see E. Anthony Rotundo, *American Manhood: Transformations in Masculinity from the Revolution to the Modern Era* (New York: Basic Books, 1994). Also see Vincent J. Bertolini, "Fireside Chastity: The Erotics of Sentimental Bachelorhood in the 1850s," in *Sentimental Men: Masculinity and the Politics of Affect in American Culture,* ed. Mary Chapman and Glenn Hendler (Berkeley: University of California Press, 1999), 19–42.

14. *Martin v. Martin,* November 1853, *Lincoln Legal Papers,* DVD-ROM database (Urbana: University of Illinois Press, 2001) (hereafter referred to as *LLP*).

15. The number is based on search string "Abraham Lincoln—attorney" under the heading "Cases involving African Americans," *LLP*: the search yielded 24 cases, compared to 3,862 cases in the *LLP* database for search string "Abraham Lincoln—attorney."

16. The cases in which Lincoln or his firm represented a black person were *Crowder v. Collier and Collier,* November 1847, *LLP; Dungey v. Spencer,* October 1855, *LLP* (I counted Lincoln's client, Dungey, as an African American; he was accused of having African American blood, and the accusers produced a deposition to this effect); *Florville v. Allin et al.,* September 1853, *LLP; Florville v. Stockdale et al.,* August 1849, *LLP*; and *Unknown v. Unknown,* June 1847, *LLP* (File ID L05636) (I counted these three cases as Lincoln having represented one client, given that in all three he represented William Florville); *People v. Hill,* June 1854, *LLP; Shelby v. Freeman and Freeman,* April 1858, *LLP; Shelby v. Shelby,* July 1841, *LLP* (I counted these two cases as a single client, since they both involved one person, Mary Shelby); and *Unknown v. Smith,* November 1845, *LLP*. I did not in this counting include *Ellis v. Blankenship v. "Negroes,"* October 1838, *LLP,* because it is unclear from the extant record exactly which parties Lincoln and Stuart represented.

17. *Hill v. Bennett and Maupin,* June 1852, *LLP; Kane v. May and Eastham,* November 1841, *LLP*.

18. *Shelby v. Freeman and Freeman,* April 1858, *LLP; Shelby v. Shelby,* March 1841, *LLP*; and *Napier v. Woolridge,* June 1845, *LLP*.

19. Sir William Blackstone, John E. Hovenden, and Archer Ryland, *Commentaries on the Laws of England,* 2 vols. (New York: W. E. Dean, 1838), 1: 91.

20. On the possible influence of Blackstone's natural law doctrine on Lincoln's ideas about slavery, see William M. Weicek, *The Sources of Antislavery Constitutionalism in America, 1760–1848* (Ithaca, N.Y.: Cornell University Press, 1977), and John Stauffer's discussion of this issue in his dual biography of Lincoln and Frederick Douglass in Stauffer, *Giants: The Parallel Lives of Frederick Douglass and Abraham Lincoln* (New York: Hachette, 2008), 98–99.

21. Gabor S. Boritt, *Lincoln and the Economics of the American Dream,* 2nd ed. (Urbana: University of Illinois Press, 1994), ix.

22. Eric Foner, *The Fiery Trial: Abraham Lincoln and American Slavery* (New York: W. W. Norton, 2010), 122. See also Foner, "Lincoln and Colonization," in *Our Lincoln:*

New Perspectives on Lincoln and His World, ed. Eric Foner (New York: W. W. Norton, 2009), 146.

23. Lincoln, Protest in the Illinois Legislature on Slavery, March 3, 1837, CW 1: 75; Lincoln, Remarks and Resolution Concerning the Abolition of Slavery in the House of Representatives, January 10, 1849, CW 2: 20–22.

24. Vance was the supposed source of a collection of anecdotes compiled by a Lincoln devotee named Adah Sutton; see Lloyd Ostendorf, ed., *Lincoln's Unknown Private Life: An Oral History by His Housekeeper Mariah Vance, 1850–1860* (Mamaroneck, N.Y.: Hastings House, 1995). I agree with those scholars who question this volume's authenticity, and I have therefore discounted its contents as unverifiable and of questionable origin. See James O. Hall's review essays on these issues in *Journal of the Abraham Lincoln Association* 19 (Winter 1998): 35. For a better, if brief, source on Vance's work in the Lincoln household, see Ostendorf, "A Monument for One of the Lincoln Maids," *Lincoln Herald* 66 (Winter 1964): 184–186.

25. Winkle, *Young Eagle,* 266. The Portuguese servant girl's quote is in Octavia Roberts, *Lincoln in Illinois* (Boston: Houghton Mifflin, 1918), 72. Roberts's source for this quote is unclear; she seems to have interviewed the servant girl when she was a very old woman.

26. See Lincoln to Salmon P. Chase, November 29, 1861, CW 5: 33, in which Lincoln refers to Johnson as "a colored boy who came from Illinois with me." Lincoln's general note of recommendation for Johnson, "To Whom It May Concern," March 7, 1861, CW 4: 278, indicates that Lincoln met Johnson, in whatever capacity, in early 1860. The "worthy man" quote is from Lincoln's recommendation letter for Johnson, October 24, 1862, CW 5: 474.

27. Jordan D. Fiore, "Mr. Lincoln's Portuguese Neighbors," *Lincoln Herald* 74 (Fall 1972): 150–152. Also see mortgage from Ritta A. da Silva, August 11, 1854, CW 2: 224–225, and promissory note drawn for Ritta A. da Silva, August 11, 1854, CW 2: 226.

28. *Sangamon Journal,* January 7, 1842. On Indians, see the *Journal* issue dated February 29, 1844, and on the Gypsies, see the issue dated March 24, 1844.

29. *Sangamon Journal,* March 18, 1842. The "sermon" reference is in the issue dated January 21, 1842; the steam mill story is in the issue dated April 22, 1842.

30. John Stauffer, *The Black Hearts of Men: Radical Abolitionists and the Transformation of Race* (Cambridge, Mass.: Harvard University Press, 2002), 7.

31. N. W. Branson to William H. Herndon, August 3, 1865, *HI,* 91; Dennis Hanks, Interview with William H. Herndon, September 8, 1865, *HI,* 105. On women being too "frivolous," see Anna Caroline Gentry, Interview with William H. Herndon, September 17, 1865, *HI,* 131. On Lincoln's shyness, see Abner Y. Ellis to William H. Herndon, January 23, 1866, *HI,* 171. On his self-consciousness around women, see Elizabeth Todd Edwards, Interview with William H. Herndon, c. 1865–1866, *HI,* 443. See also Sara Bush Lincoln, Interview with William H. Herndon, September 8, 1865, *HI,* 108.

32. The Owens quote is in Mary Owens Vineyard to William H. Herndon, May 23, 1866, *HI,* 256. On the Lincoln-Owens courtship, see Winkle, *Young Eagle,* 152–155, and Wilson, *Honor's Voice,* 129–141 and 134–137. In counting these four letters, I am

not including a letter to Mrs. Orville H. Browning, December 11, 1839, *CW* 1: 156; this letter has Lincoln among multiple authors, and it is not clear who actually wrote it.

33. Lincoln to Mary S. Owens, December 13, 1836, *CW* 1: 55 (brackets inserted by the *CW* editor, Roy P. Basler), and Lincoln to Mary S. Owens, May 7, 1837, *CW* 1: 78.

34. Lincoln to Mrs. Orville H. Browning, April 1, 1838, *CW* 1: 117 (emphases in original).

35. Lincoln to Mary Speed, September 27, 1841, *CW* 1: 260.

36. Donald, *"We Are Lincoln Men,"* 46. See also Gary Lee Williams, "James and Joshua Speed: Lincoln's Kentucky Friends" (Ph.D. diss., Duke University, 1971), 27.

37. Lincoln to Speed, *CW* 1: 260.

38. Weld, *Slavery and the Internal Slave Trade,* 52.

39. Lincoln to Speed, *CW* 1: 260.

40. On Paley's thoughts about happiness, see William Paley, *The Principles of Moral and Political Philosophy* (New York: B. and S. Collins, 1835), 24–33. On Lincoln's familiarity with Paley, see Joshua F. Speed to William H. Herndon, December 6, 1866, *HI,* 499.

41. I base this assertion on my reading of the Lincoln humor contained in P. M. Zall's useful collection *Abe Lincoln Laughing: Humorous Anecdotes from Original Sources by and about Abraham Lincoln* (Berkeley: University of California Press, 1982); this collection is the best-authenticated source for Lincoln humor. I saw little in the way of such sarcasm in Lincoln's humor here, which far more often ran toward puns and the use of ludicrous situations to illustrate points.

42. Clark, *Into the Old Northwest,* 42.

43. Jefferson Davis, Speech before the U.S. House of Representatives, April 20, 1848, in *The Papers of Jefferson Davis,* ed. Lynda Laswell Christ, James T. McIntosh, and Mary S. Dix (Baton Rouge: Louisiana State University Press, 1981), 3: 315.

44. Lincoln, Address before the Young Men's Lyceum of Springfield, Illinois, January 27, 1838, *CW* 1: 108; Lincoln, Speech on Sub-Treasury Bill, December 26, 1839, *CW* 1: 167. See also the "angel from heaven" reference in Lincoln, Reply to James Adams, September 6, 1837, *CW* 1: 99.

45. Joshua F. Speed to William H. Herndon, January 12, 1866, *HI,* 156; James H. Matheny, Interview with William H. Herndon, November 1866, *HI,* 432; Isaac Cogdal, Interview with William H. Herndon, c. 1865–1866, *HI,* 441; and Jesse W. Fell to Ward Hill Lamon, September 22, 1870, *HI,* 579–580.

46. On the pamphlet, see Matheny, Interview with Herndon, *HI,* 432; clipping from *Menard Axis,* February 15, 1862, *HI,* 24; John Hill to William H. Herndon, June 27, 1865, *HI,* 61–62.

47. Handbill Replying to Charges of Infidelity, July 31, 1846, *CW* 1: 382. The best studies of Lincoln's early life suggest that he was imbued with religious skepticism at this time; see, e.g., Wilson, *Honor's Voice,* 75–87.

48. Joshua Speed believed this to be so; see his letter to Herndon, January 12, 1866, *HI,* 156. This is the general tenor of the most recent scholarship concerning Lincoln's religious views; see, e.g., Allen C. Guelzo, *Abraham Lincoln, Redeemer President* (Grand Rapids, Mich.: Eerdman's, 1999), 152–158, and William Lee Miller, *Lincoln's Virtues:*

An Ethical Biography (New York: Alfred A. Knopf, 2002), 42–43, 83–86. Even Richard Carwardine, who places a heavy emphasis on religion and Christianity in the formation of Lincoln's political thought, acknowledges Lincoln's early skepticism; see Carwardine, *Lincoln: A Life of Purpose and Power* (New York: Alfred A. Knopf, 2006), 4, 35–36, and his essay, "Lincoln's Religion," in Foner, *Our Lincoln*, 223–248.

49. Lincoln to Owens, *CW* 1: 78.

50. William Shepard Walsh, *Handy Book of Literary Curiosities* (Philadelphia: J. B. Lippincott, 1909), 420.

51. Lincoln, Second Inaugural Address, March 4, 1865, *CW* 8: 333.

52. Lincoln, Temperance Address, February 22, 1842, *CW* 1: 272.

53. Lincoln to C. U. Schlater, January 5, 1849, *CW* 2: 20; Lincoln, Address to the Young Men's Lyceum, *CW* 1: 115. Also useful is a comparison of Lincoln's lack of sentimentality and the attitude of others who took much the opposite tack; see Brian Dirck, *Lincoln and Davis: Imagining America, 1809–1865* (Lawrence: University Press of Kansas, 2001).

54. David Davis, Interview with William H. Herndon, September 20, 1866, *HI,* 348; Edwards, Interview with Herndon, *HI,* 443; Leonard Swett to William H. Herndon, January 17, 1866, *HI,* 168 (emphasis in original); Herndon, *Herndon's Lincoln,* 349–350.

55. On the role of masking in slave life, see John W. Blassingame, *The Slave Community: Plantation Life in the Antebellum South,* 2nd ed. (Oxford: Oxford University Press, 1979), 314–315; Eugene Genovese, *Roll, Jordan, Roll: The World the Slaves Made* (New York: Vintage Books, 1976), 87–91; Stephan Talty, *Mulatto America: At the Crossroads of Black and White Culture—A Social History* (New York: Harper, 2004), 27–29; and James Walvin, *Questioning Slavery* (New York: Routledge, 1996), 132–137.

56. Ethan Allen Andrews, *Slavery and the Domestic Slave Trade in the United States* (Boston: Light and Stearns, 1836), 150.

Chapter 4: The White A and the Black B

1. Brian Dirck, *Lincoln the Lawyer* (Urbana: University of Illinois Press, 2007), 9–12.

2. On the radical attempts to reconfigure white supremacy and the nature of racial thought in America, see John Stauffer, *The Black Hearts of Men: Radical Abolitionists and the Transformation of Race* (Cambridge, Mass.: Harvard University Press, 2002), 3–8 and 18–34;

3. Quoted in William and Robert Chambers, *Chambers' Journal of Popular Literature, Science and Arts* 7 (January–June 1857): 10.

4. George Combe, *The Constitution of Man Considered in Relation to External Objects* (Boston: Marsh, Capen and Lyon, 1837), 274; Daniel Mallory, ed., *The Life and Speeches of the Hon. Henry Clay,* 2 vols. (Hartford, Conn.: Silas Andrus and Son, 1855), 2: 367.

5. Elizur Wright, "The Horrors of Saint Domingue," *Quarterly Anti-slavery Magazine* 1 (October 1835): 252. See also Douglas R. Egerton, "The Scenes Which Are Enacted in St. Domingo: The Legacy of Revolutionary Violence in Early National Vir-

ginia," in *Antislavery Violence: Sectional, Racial, and Cultural Conflict in Antebellum America,* ed. John R. McKivigan and Stanley Harrold (Knoxville: University of Tennessee Press, 1999), 42–64.

6. John C. Calhoun, Speech against the Conquest of Mexico, January 4, 1848, in *American Review* 1, no. 3 (March 1848): 221–222.

7. Lincoln, Address to the Young Men's Lyceum of Springfield, January 27, 1838, CW 1: 109–110.

8. N. H. Purple, comp., *A Compilation of the Statutes of the State of Illinois, of a General Nature in Force January 1, 1856,* 2 vols. (Chicago: Keen and Lee, 1856), 2: 776–782.

9. Speech of Thomas W. Gibson, in *Report of the Debates and Proceedings of the Convention for the Revision of the Constitution of the State of Indiana* (Indianapolis, Ind.: H. Fowler, 1850), 447. On the general and pervasive racial fears of the times, see Najia Aarim-Heriot, *Chinese Immigrants, African-Americans: Racial Anxiety in the United States, 1848–1882* (Urbana: University of Illinois Press, 2003), chaps. 1–3.

10. Quoted from the resolution on colonization, February 21, 1852, *Journal of the House of Representatives of the State of Indiana, during the Thirty-sixth Session of the General Assembly, Commencing December 1, 1852* (Indianapolis, Ind.: J. P. Chapman, 1852), 1025.

11. Quoted in "Selections: Cartwright on the Negro Constitution," *American Medical Gazette and Journal of Health* (1853): 213.

12. Benjamin Silliman, review of *Crania Americana,* in *American Journal of Science* 38 (April 1840): 341, 352.

13. Josiah Clark Nott, *Two Lectures, on the Natural History of the Negro and Caucasian Races* (Mobile, Ala.: Dade and Thompson, 1844), 16–17, 29.

14. Stephen A. Douglas, *The Spurious Kansas Memorial: Debate in the Senate of the United States on the Memorial of James H. Lane* (Washington, D.C.: Union Office, 1856), 17.

15. Lincoln, Speech in Bloomington, Illinois, September 26, 1854, CW 2: 234 (emphases in original).

16. Douglas, *Spurious Kansas Memorial,* 15; Stephen A. Douglas, *Speeches of Senator S. A. Douglas, on the Occasion of His Public Receptions by the Citizens of New Orleans, Philadelphia, and Baltimore* (Washington, D.C.: Lemuel Towers, 1859), 5.

17. William H. Herndon, *Herndon's Lincoln: The True Story of a Great Life* (Urbana: University of Illinois Press, 2006), 242; Theodore Parker and Francis Power Cobbe, eds., *The Collected Works of Theodore Parker* (London: Trubner, 1864), 8: 145; and Robert Bray, *Reading with Lincoln* (Carbondale: Southern Illinois University Press, 2010), 175–182.

18. Henry Clay Whitney, *Life on the Circuit with Lincoln* (Boston: Estes and Lauriat, 1892), 199.

19. Paul M. Zall, *Abe Lincoln Laughing: Humorous Anecdotes from Original Sources by and about Abraham Lincoln* (Berkeley: University of California Press, 1982), 136.

20. Ibid., 152.

21. Andrew Dickson White and Thomas Robinson Dawley, *Old Abe's Jokes* (New York: T. R. Dawley, 1864), 75.

22. Zall, *Abe Lincoln Laughing*, 17, 42, 133.

23. On Hampton's personality and background, see the biographical sketch in George Thornton Fleming, *History of Pittsburgh and Environs* (New York: American Historical Society, 1922), 191–192.

24. Moses Hampton to Abraham Lincoln, March 30, 1849, Abraham Lincoln Papers, Library of Congress (hereafter referred to as LPLC) (emphases in original). For his part, Lincoln asked Hampton to return the favor, requesting from him a letter recommending Lincoln for the General Land Office in Illinois; Lincoln to Moses Hampton, June 1, 1849, in *The Collected Works of Abraham Lincoln*, 8 vols. and supp., ed. Roy P. Basler (New Brunswick, N.J.: Rutgers University Press, 1953) (hereafter referred to as CW), 2: 1–2.

25. Lincoln, Fragment on Slavery, c. April 1854, CW 2: 222–223 (emphases in original).

26. See generally James G. Bilotta, *Race and the Rise of the Republican Party, 1848–1865* (New York: Libris, 1992).

27. Lincoln, Notes for a Law Lecture, c. July 1850, CW 2: 81; Herndon, *Herndon's Lincoln*, 215n.

28. Herndon, *Herndon's Lincoln*, 208.

29. Douglas quoted in Allen Johnson, *Stephen A. Douglas: A Study in American Politics* (New York: Macmillan, 1908), 394–395.

30. James W. Sheahan, *The Life of Stephen A. Douglas* (New York: Harper & Brothers, 1860), 519.

31. Lincoln, Speech in Lewistown, Illinois, August 17, 1858, CW 2: 545; Lincoln, Speech at Springfield, Illinois, October 4, 1854, CW 2: 245; Lincoln, Speech in Peoria, Illinois, October 16, 1854, CW 2: 264.

32. Lincoln, Speech in Peoria, Illinois, October 14, 1854, CW 2: 281.

33. Lincoln, First Debate with Stephen Douglas, August 21, 1858, CW 3: 2–8.

34. Ibid., 3: 12.

35. Lincoln, Second Debate with Stephen Douglas, August 27, 1858, CW 3: 56–57, 60–61, 63, 65.

36. Lincoln, Third Debate with Stephen Douglas, September 15, 1858, CW 3: 112–113; Lincoln, Fourth Debate with Stephen Douglas, September 18, 1858, CW 3: 176; Lincoln, Fifth Debate with Stephen Douglas, October 7, 1858, CW 3: 216; Lincoln, Sixth Debate with Stephen Douglas, October 15, 1858, CW 3: 296.

37. Lincoln, First Debate with Douglas, CW 3: 9; Lincoln, Third Debate with Douglas, CW 3: 105; Lincoln, Second Debate with Douglas, CW 3: 56.

38. Lincoln, First Debate with Douglas, CW 3: 16.

39. Lincoln, Fourth Debate with Douglas, CW 3: 146.

40. Lincoln, Speech in Springfield, Illinois, June 26, 1857, CW 2: 405.

41. Lincoln, Fourth Debate with Douglas, CW 3: 146. See also Lincoln, Speech in Chicago, Illinois, July 20, 1858, CW 2: 498. On Lincoln's general views concerning interracial marriage, see George M. Fredrickson, *Big Enough to Be Inconsistent: Abraham*

Lincoln Confronts Slavery and Race (Cambridge, Mass.: Harvard University Press, 2008), 66.

42. Lincoln, Speech in Peoria, Illinois, October 15, 1854, *CW* 2: 268; Lincoln, Speech in Springfield, *CW* 2: 407–408.

43. Lincoln, Speech in Beardstown, Illinois, August 12, 1858, *CW* 2: 541 (emphases in original).

44. Lincoln, First Debate with Douglas, *CW* 3: 16 (emphases in original).

45. Lincoln was more specific on this point in an earlier speech; see Lincoln, Speech in Springfield, *CW* 2: 405–406.

46. Lincoln, Fourth Debate with Stephen Douglas, September 18, 1858, ibid., 3: 146; he expressed a similar sentiment in a speech at Clinton, Illinois, July 27, 1858, ibid., 2: 526–527.

47. Lincoln, Speech in Peoria, October 15, 1854, *CW* 2: 256.

48. Ibid.

49. Lincoln, Note for Speeches, August 21, 1858, *CW* 2: 552–553.

50. Ibid., 2: 553.

Chapter 5: The Broader Difference

1. Lincoln, Speech in Springfield, Illinois, June 26, 1857, in *Collected Works of Abraham Lincoln,* 8 vols. and supp., ed. Roy P. Basler (New Brunswick, N.J.: Rutgers University Press, 1953) (hereafter referred to as *CW*), 2: 404.

2. See, e.g., Lincoln, Speech at Columbus, Ohio, September 16, 1859, *CW* 3: 405.

3. Lincoln, Speech in Peoria, Illinois, October 16, 1854, *CW* 2: 255. For examples of Lincoln's denial that he supported racial equality, see Lincoln, Speech in Peoria, Illinois, October 16, 1854, *CW* 2: 266; Lincoln, Speech at Monticello, Illinois, July 29, 1858, *CW* 2: 527; Lincoln, First Debate with Stephen Douglas, August 21, 1858, *CW* 3: 16–17; and Lincoln, Speech at Carlinville, Illinois, August 31, 1858, *CW* 3: 79.

4. Lincoln to Samuel Galloway, June 19, 1860, *CW* 4: 80.

5. Lincoln, Speech in Pittsburgh, Pennsylvania, February 15, 1861, *CW* 4: 211 (emphasis in original).

6. Charles B. Dew, *Apostles of Disunion: Southern Secession Commissioners and the Causes of the War* (Charlottesville: University of Virginia Press, 2002), 85, 98.

7. *Mercury* quoted in Emerson David Fite, *The Presidential Campaign of 1860,* 3 vols. (New York: Macmillan, 1910), 3: 210.

8. Charles Dickens, "Election Time in America," *All the Year Round: A Weekly Journal* 5 (April 18, 1861): 68.

9. A. G. Frick to Abraham Lincoln, February 14, 1861, reprinted in *Dear Mr. Lincoln: Letters to the President,* ed. Harold Holzer (Reading, Mass.: Addison-Wesley, 1993), 341.

10. Frederick Douglas, "The American Apocalypse," June 16, 1861, in *The Frederick Douglass Papers,* ser. 1, 4 vols., ed. John Y. Blassingame (New Haven, Conn.: Yale University Press, 1999), 3: 437; Garrison quoted in Henry Mayer, *All on Fire: William Lloyd Garrison and the Abolition of Slavery* (New York: St. Martin's Press, 1998), 520.

11. Francis Blackburn to Abraham Lincoln, November 24, 1860, Abraham Lincoln

Papers, Library of Congress (hereafter referred to as LPLC) (emphases in original); L. A. Calmes to Lincoln, December 10, 1860, and J. B. Long to [unknown], January 18, 1861, LPLC.

12. W. V. Barnett to Lincoln, November 30, 1860, LPLC; A. J. Hause, J. D. Wright, and W. D. Hardy to Lincoln, November 27, 1860, LPLC.

13. Lincoln, Address to Delegation of Washington, D.C., Leaders, February 27, 1861, CW 4: 246.

14. Lincoln, First Inaugural Address, March 4, 1861, CW 4: 264.

15. Ibid., 4: 267, 271.

16. A small sampling of the more recent literature that documents Lincoln's move toward emancipation includes Allen C. Guelzo's balanced and thorough *Lincoln's Emancipation Proclamation: The End of Slavery in America* (New York: Simon & Schuster, 2006); Richard Striner's largely uncritical *Father Abraham: Lincoln's Relentless Struggle to End Slavery* (Oxford: Oxford University Press, 2007), esp. 137–188; and LaWanda Cox's similarly laudatory account, *Lincoln and Black Freedom: A Study in Presidential Leadership*, 2nd ed. (Columbia: University of South Carolina Press, 1994). Phillip S. Paludan, *The Presidency of Abraham Lincoln* (Lawrence: University Press of Kansas, 1994), chaps. 7–9, stresses the legal and constitutional constraints under which Lincoln operated. William K. Klingaman, *Abraham Lincoln and the Road to Emancipation, 1861–1865* (New York: Viking Press, 2001), esp. chaps. 6–8, stresses Lincoln's moral growth and development.

17. "Omega" to Abraham Lincoln, March 16, 1861, LPLC; Lincoln, Remarks to a Delegation of Progressive Friends, June 20, 1862, CW 5: 278–279; Lincoln, Reply to Emancipation Memorial Presented by Chicago Christians, September 13, 1862, CW 5: 419–425; Petition of Citizens of Portage County, Ohio, c. 1862, LPLC.

18. Lincoln, Reply to Emancipation Memorial, CW 5: 421. On Lincoln, Taney, and emancipation, see Brian Dirck, "Abraham Lincoln, Emancipation, and the Supreme Court," in *Lincoln Emancipated: The President and the Politics of Race,* ed. Brian Dirck (DeKalb: Northern Illinois University Press, 2007), 99–116.

19. Lincoln to Alexander Stephens, December 22, 1860, CW 4: 160 (emphases in original).

20. Lincoln, Remarks to a Delegation of Progressive Friends, CW 5: 279. Along the same lines, see Lincoln, Remarks to a Delegation from the Reformed Presbyterian Synod, July 17, 1862, CW 5: 328; Lincoln to Albert G. Hodges, April 4, 1864, CW 7: 281.

21. Lincoln to Horace Greeley, March 24, 1862, CW 5: 169.

22. Lincoln, Annual Address to Congress, December 1, 1862, CW 5: 534–536. For examples of his discussion of black people directly, see Lincoln, Speech to a Massachusetts Delegation, March 13, 1862, CW 5: 158; Lincoln, Remarks to a Deputation of Western Gentlemen, August 4, 1862, CW 5: 356–357; Lincoln to Horace Greeley, August 22, 1862, CW 5: 388; Lincoln to Edwin M. Stanton, September 29, 1862, CW 5: 445; Memorandum Concerning William Johnson, December 17, 1862, CW 6: 8; Lincoln, Reply to Emancipation Memorial, CW 5: 421–422.

23. On his orders to the U.S. marshal, see http://www.thelincolnlog.org/view/1862/2.

Lincoln offered a rather disingenuous response to Marylanders complaining of his nonenforcement of fugitive slave laws in May; see Lincoln, Reply to Maryland Slaveholders, May 19, 1862, CW 5: 224. On the humane treatment of fugitives, see Edwin M. Stanton to Benjamin F. Butler, July 3, 1862, in *Private and Official Correspondence of Benjamin F. Butler,* 5 vols., ed. Benjamin F. Butler and Jessie Ames Marshall (Norwood, Mass.: Privately issued, 1917), 2: 41; Lincoln, Speech to a Massachusetts Delegation, CW 5: 158. On the African American school issue, see *New York Tribune,* June 7, 1862.

24. Guelzo, *Lincoln's Emancipation Proclamation,* 158. Recent scholarship has provided a corrective to older accounts painting these men as "contrabands"; instead, they were free African Americans known for their opposition to colonization. See Kate Masur, "The African American Delegation to Abraham Lincoln: A Reappraisal," *Civil War History* 56 (June 2010): 117–144.

25. Lincoln, Appeal to Border State Representatives, July 12, 1862, CW 5: 318.

26. Lincoln, Address on Colonization to a Deputation of Negroes, August 14, 1862, CW 5: 371.

27. Ibid., 372.

28. Ibid., 371–372.

29. Frederick Douglass, "The President and His Speeches," *Douglass' Monthly,* September 1862, text available at http://www.lib.rochester.edu/index.cfm?PAGE=4387.

30. John Niven, ed., *The Salmon P. Chase Papers,* 2 vols. (Kent, Ohio: Kent State University Press, 1993), 1: 362; Donald Yacavone, ed., *A Voice of Thunder: The Civil War Letters of George E. Stephens* (Urbana: University of Illinois Press, 1997), 306–307. A good summary of the criticisms leveled at Lincoln for this speech is in Eric Foner, *The Fiery Trial: Abraham Lincoln and American Slavery* (New York: W. W. Norton, 2010), 225.

31. Gideon Welles, "Administration of Abraham Lincoln," *Galaxy* 24 (October 1877): 438.

32. Lincoln, Eulogy on Henry Clay, July 6, 1852, CW 2: 132. Lincoln also briefly mentioned Clay and colonization in later speeches at Bath, Illinois, on August 16, 1858, CW 2: 544, and at Edwardsville, Illinois, on September 11, 1858, CW 3: 93.

33. Lincoln, Outline for Speech to American Colonization Society, c. January 4, 1855, CW 2: 298–299; Lincoln, Speech in Springfield, CW 2: 409.

34. Lincoln, Speech in Springfield, Illinois, June 6, 1857, CW 2: 409 (emphasis added); Lincoln, Eulogy on Henry Clay, CW 2: 132.

35. Lincoln, Speech in Springfield, CW 2: 409.

36. Michael S. Burlingame, *Abraham Lincoln: A Life,* 2 vols. (Baltimore, Md.: Johns Hopkins University Press, 2008), 383–396, offers a thorough and succinct assessment of Lincoln's various colonization schemes.

37. Lincoln, Annual Message to Congress, December 3, 1861, CW 5: 48.

38. Ibid.; Lincoln, Preliminary Emancipation Proclamation, September 22, 1862, CW 5: 434.

39. Lincoln, Annual Message to Congress, CW 5: 49; Lincoln, Proclamation Revoking General Hunter's Order, December 1, 1862, CW 5: 520.

40. James W. Stone to Abraham Lincoln, September 23, 1862, LPLC; U.S. Citizens to Abraham Lincoln, c. September 1862, LPLC; Tennessee Loyal Citizens to Abraham Lincoln, December 4, 1862, LPLC; George B. McClellan to Abraham Lincoln, July 7, 1862, in *The Civil War Papers of George B. McClellan: Selected Correspondence, 1860–1865*, ed. Stephen W. Sears (New York: Da Capo Press, 1992), 345.

41. Lincoln, Annual Message to Congress, December 1, 1862, CW 5: 530.

42. Ibid., 5: 537.

43. Ibid.

44. Ibid.

Chapter 6: Some Compunctions

1. William B. Campbell and Jordan Stokes to Emerson Etheridge, December 16, 1862, Abraham Lincoln Papers, Library of Congress (hereafter referred to as LPLC); Richard H. Parham to Abraham Lincoln, December 16, 1862, LPLC.

2. Walter H. Gaines and Henry S. Rowland to Abraham Lincoln, December 21, 1862, LPLC. See also J. F. Bullitt, W. E. Hughes, and C. Ripley to Joshua F. Speed, September 13, 1861, LPLC. Text of Indiana letter reprinted in William Sumner Dodge, *History of the Old Second Division, Army of the Cumberland* (Chicago: Church and Goodman, 1864), 342–343n. For overviews of Democratic Party racial rhetoric during the election, see Michael S. Burlingame, *Abraham Lincoln: A Life,* 2 vols. (Baltimore, Md.: Johns Hopkins University Press, 2008), 2: 419–423; Philip A. Klinkner and Rogers M. Smith, *The Unsteady March: The Rise and Decline of Racial Equality in America* (Chicago: University of Chicago Press, 1999), 61–62; and Patience Essah, *A House Divided: Slavery and Emancipation in Delaware, 1635–1865* (Charlottesville: University of Virginia Press, 1996), 174–176.

3. Gerry W. Cochrane and John M. Forbes, December 24, 1862, LPLC; Green Adams to Abraham Lincoln, December 31, 1862, LPLC; Thomas B. Thorpe and Benjamin F. Flanders to Salmon P. Chase, November 29, 1862, LPLC.

4. Cochrane and Forbes, LPLC; Samuel Smith Nicholas, *Conservative Essays, Legal and Political* (Philadelphia: J. B. Lippincott, 1865), 37.

5. John Allison to Abraham Lincoln, September 23, 1862, LPLC.

6. Frederick Douglass, "Oration in Memory of Abraham Lincoln," text available at http://teachingamericanhistory.org/library/index.asp?document=39.

7. Nicholas, *Conservative Essays,* 51.

8. Text of speech reprinted in *The American Annual Cyclopedia and Register of Important Events of the Year 1863* (New York: Appleton, 1864), 3: 269.

9. "Editor's Table," *Harper's Magazine,* Volume 25, June to November 1862 (New York: Harper & Brothers, 1862), 846.

10. Brooks's speech reprinted in "Delphine," *Solon, or the Rebellion of '61: A Domestic and Political Tragedy* (Chicago: S. P. Rounds, 1862), 59; Edward I. Sears, "Our President and Governors Compared to Petty Princes," *National Quarterly Review* 9 (June 1863): 175.

11. George Alfred Townsend, *Washington Inside and Outside* (Hartford, Conn.: James Betts, 1874), 715.

12. Benjamin Thomas, *Abraham Lincoln: A Biography*, 3rd ed. (1952; repr., Carbondale: Southern Illinois University Press, 2008), 456.

13. Allen C. Guelzo, *Lincoln's Emancipation Proclamation: The End of Slavery in America* (New York: Simon & Schuster, 2006), 181–183, offers a very detailed account of the day's proceedings.

14. Frederick Seward, *Reminiscences of a War-Time Statesman and Diplomat, 1830–1915* (New York: G. P. Putnam's, 1916), 3: 227; Benjamin Quarles, *Lincoln and the Negro* (New York: Oxford University Press, 1962), 139–141.

15. Lincoln, Notes for a Law Lecture, c. July 1850, in *The Collected Works of Abraham Lincoln*, 8 vols. and supp., ed. Roy P. Basler (New Brunswick, N.J.: Rutgers University Press, 1953) (hereafter referred to as *CW*), 2: 81.

16. Lincoln, Interview with Alexander W. Randall and Joseph T. Mills, August 19, 1864, *CW* 7: 507; Lincoln, Interview with delegation of Kentuckians, November 21, 1862, *CW* 5: 503; Michael Burlingame, ed., *Inside Lincoln's White House: The Complete Civil War Diary of John Hay* (Carbondale: Southern Illinois University Press, 1999), 41.

17. Lincoln to John A. Dix, January 14, 1863, *CW* 6: 56; Rufus K. Williams to Abraham Lincoln, July 8, 1864, LPLC.

18. Lincoln to John A. McClernand, January 8, 1863, *CW* 6: 49.

19. Lincoln to Stephen A. Hurlbut, July 31, 1863, *CW* 6: 358; Lincoln to Charles D. Robinson, August 17, 1864, *CW* 7: 499 (emphasis in original).

20. Francis B. Carpenter, *Six Months at the White House with Abraham Lincoln: The Story of a Picture* (New York: Hurd and Houghton, 1866), 90.

21. Lincoln, Reply to Serenade in Honor of Emancipation Proclamation, September 24, 1862, *CW* 5: 439.

22. On Lincoln's relationship with Florville, see, e.g., William Florville to Abraham Lincoln, December 27, 1863, LPLC; Kenneth J. Winkle, *The Young Eagle: The Rise of Abraham Lincoln* (New York: Taylor, 2001), 266–268; Quarles, *Lincoln and the Negro,* 26–27. On Johnson, see Burlingame, *Abraham Lincoln: A Life,* 2: 577–578, who recently uncovered the details of these transactions, and George M. Fredrickson, *Big Enough to Be Inconsistent: Abraham Lincoln Confronts Slavery and Race* (Cambridge, Mass.: Harvard University Press, 2008), 54.

23. Lincoln to James S. Wadworth, c. January 1864, *CW* 7: 101.

24. Richard Hofstadter, *The American Political Tradition and the Men Who Made It* (New York: Alfred A. Knopf, 1968), 131–132. For a perceptive critique of Hofstadter's "bill of lading" prose, see Guelzo, *Lincoln's Emancipation Proclamation,* 2–5.

25. On the Border State factors in Lincoln's thinking on emancipation, see Guelzo's incisive analysis in *Lincoln's Emancipation Proclamation,* 120–121, and Eric Foner, *The Fiery Trial: Abraham Lincoln and American Slavery* (New York: W. W. Norton, 2010), 274–275. On the concerns that the proclamation might be struck down by the Supreme Court, see Brian Dirck, "Abraham Lincoln, Emancipation, and the Supreme Court," in *Lincoln Emancipated: The President and the Politics of Race,* ed. Brian Dirck (DeKalb: Northern Illinois University Press, 2007), 99–116.

26. Lincoln to John M. Schofield, June 22, 1863, *CW* 6: 291 (emphases in original). See also Lincoln to Hurlbut, *CW* 6: 358.

27. On the apprenticeship system for Arkansas, see Burlingame, *Inside Lincoln's White House,* 68; Lincoln to McClernand, *CW* 6: 49; Lincoln to Nathaniel P. Banks, August 5, 1863, *CW* 6: 365.

28. On attendance of blackface show, see *New York Herald,* February 26, 1863; Lincoln, Interview with Alexander W. Randall and Joseph T. Mills, August 19, 1864, *CW* 7: 508.

29. Henry Villard, *Lincoln on the Eve of '61* (New York: Alfred A. Knopf, 1941), 29. The "Cuffie" quote is in James G. Randall and Richard N. Current, *Lincoln the President: Last Full Measure,* 4 vols. (Urbana: University of Illinois Press, 1955), 4: 320.

30. Michael Burlingame, ed., *Lincoln Observed: Civil War Dispatches of Noah Brooks* (Baltimore, Md.: Johns Hopkins University Press, 1998), 140.

31. See Carleton Mabee, "Sojourner Truth and President Lincoln," *New England Quarterly* 61 (December 1988): 519–529, and Nell Irvin Painter's quite critical treatment of Lincoln in her biography of Truth, *Sojourner Truth: A Life, a Symbol* (New York: W. W. Norton, 1996), 206–207.

32. Douglass, Oration in Memory of Abraham Lincoln, April 14, 1876, text available at http://teachingamericanhistory.org/library/index.asp?documentprint=39.

33. Lincoln, Speech in Peoria, Illinois, October 16, 1854, *CW* 2: 256.

34. Ambrose W. Thompson to Abraham Lincoln, March 28, 1863, LPLC.

35. See, e.g., the excellent recent study of Lincoln's postemancipation support for colonization by Phillip W. Magness and Sebastian N. Page, *Colonization after Emancipation: Lincoln and the Movement for Black Resettlement* (Columbia: University of Missouri Press, 2010).

36. Benjamin Butler, *Autobiography and Personal Reminiscences of Benjamin F. Butler* (Boston: A. M. Thayer, 1892), 902–903.

37. For good examples of scholarship critical of the Butler testimony, see Michael Vorenberg, "Abraham Lincoln and the Politics of Black Colonization," *Journal of the Abraham Lincoln Association* 14 (Summer 1993): 23–46, and Phillip S. Paludan, "Lincoln and Colonization: Policy or Propaganda?" *Journal of the Abraham Lincoln Association* 25 (Winter 2004): 23–37. Foner, *Fiery Trial,* is also skeptical, though the author seems to argue that Butler may have been truthful. Philip Magness's meticulous deconstruction of the Butler testimony in his article "Benjamin Butler's Colonization Testimony Reevaluated," *Journal of the Abraham Lincoln Association* 29 (Winter 2009): 1–27, suggests that Butler's claims are at least somewhat plausible. I would tend to agree with Magness's general point that Lincoln continued to harbor colonization plans after 1863, but I am less convinced of Butler's veracity.

38. Eric Foner, "Lincoln and Colonization," in *Our Lincoln: New Perspectives on Lincoln and His World,* ed. Eric Foner (New York: W. W. Norton, 2009), 161. See also Magness and Page, *Colonization after Emancipation,* esp. 125–130, which offers a succinct summary of what I believe are convincing arguments that Lincoln may well have believed in some form of colonization until the end of his life.

39. Burlingame, *Inside Lincoln's White House,* 217; Foner, "Lincoln and Colonization," 160.

40. On the Philadelphia incident, see Lincoln to Robert C. Schenck, February 4, 1863, *CW* 6: 90n. On the racial content of the New York City draft riots, see Iver Bernstein, *The New York City Draft Riots: Their Significance for American Society and Politics in the Age of the Civil War* (New York: Oxford University Press, 1990), 28, 53–54, and 66–72.

41. Confederate congressional deliberations reprinted in *The American Annual Cyclopedia and Register of Important Events of the Year 1862* (New York: Appleton, 1863), 2: 268. See also a good general overview of the Confederate response in Edna Greene Medford, "Imagined Promises, Bitter Realities: African Americans and the Meaning of the Emancipation Proclamation," in *The Emancipation Proclamation: Three Views,* ed. Harold Holzer, Edna Greene Medford, and Frank J. Williams (Baton Rouge: Louisiana State University Press, 2006), 24–26.

42. On the lullaby thesis, see Magness and Page, *Colonization after Emancipation,* 111–128.

43. Carpenter, *Six Months at the White House,* 77 (emphases in original).

44. Fredrickson, *Big Enough to Be Inconsistent,* 92, points out that Lincoln's Southern roots made him generally sympathetic with the white South.

45. Lincoln, Speech in Peoria, *CW* 2: 255; Lincoln, Speech at Sanitary Fair, Baltimore, Maryland, April 18, 1854, *CW* 7: 302.

46. Lincoln to John A. Andrew, February 18, 1864, *CW* 7: 191.

47. Lincoln to Albert G. Hodges, April 4, 1864, *CW* 7: 282.

48. Marcellus Mundy to Abraham Lincoln, July 28, 1864, LPLC.

49. E. M. Sothoron to Abraham Lincoln, March 7, 1864, LPLC; Lincoln to McClernand, *CW* 6: 49.

50. Lincoln to Andrew Johnson, March 26, 1863, *CW* 6: 149.

51. Lincoln to Alpheus Lewis, January 23, 1864, *CW* 7: 145.

52. See, e.g., Quarles, *Lincoln and the Negro,* 187–190.

53. Lincoln to James C. Conkling, August 26, 1863, *CW* 6: 408–409.

54. Ibid., 6: 410.

55. Lincoln, Speech at Sanitary Fair, *CW* 7: 302–303; Lincoln to Cabinet Members, May 3, 1864, *CW* 7: 328; Lincoln to Edwin M. Stanton, May 17, 1864, *CW* 7: 345. See also Lincoln, Remarks to New York Committee, May 30, 1863, *CW* 6: 239, and Lincoln's involvement with request made by a Fort Pillow victim's widow, in Lincoln to Charles Sumner, May 19, 1864, *CW* 10: 243–244.

56. Lincoln to General George Thomas, June 13, 1864, *CW* 7: 390; Lincoln to John Glenn, February 7, 1865, *CW* 7: 266. See also Lincoln to Edwin Stanton, February 7, 1865, *CW* 8: 268.

57. Lincoln, Interview with Alexander W. Randall and Joseph T. Mills, August 19, 1864, *CW* 7: 506–507.

58. Lincoln, Annual Message to Congress, December 6, 1864, *CW* 8: 151.

59. John Nicolay to John McMahon, August 6, 1864, *CW* 7: 483 (emphasis in original).

Chapter 7: Abraham Africanus the First

1. Katherine Helm, *The True Story of Mary, Wife of Lincoln* (New York: Harper, 1928), 259; Ward Hill Lamon, *Recollections of Abraham Lincoln* (1895; repr., Lincoln: University of Nebraska Press, 1994), 245–248.

2. Esther May Carter, *She Knew Lincoln* (n.p.: Esther May Carter, 1930), 7–10.

3. William Seale, *The President's House* (Washington, D.C.: White House Historical Association, 1986).

4. Ibid., 147–149.

5. It is unclear whether black staff members were directly added to the White House by Lincoln himself; when he brought William Johnson with him from Springfield, Johnson was said to have caused friction among other black staff members as an outsider whose skin was too dark. See Gabor S. Boritt, *The Gettysburg Gospel: The Lincoln Speech Nobody Knows* (New York: Simon & Schuster, 2008), 54. I am grateful to Gerald Prokopowicz for pointing this out.

6. John E. Washington, *They Knew Lincoln* (New York: Dutton, 1942), 105–108, 119–123; Elizabeth Keckley, *Behind the Scenes in the Lincoln White House: Memoirs of an African-American Mistress* (1868; repr., Mineola, N.Y.: Dover, 2006). In the text, I use *Keckly*, which has more recently been established (through the careful research of Jennifer Fleischner) as the correct spelling; see Fleischner, *Mrs. Lincoln and Mrs. Keckly: The Remarkable Story of the Friendship between a First Lady and a Former Slave* (New York: Broadway Books, 2004), 7.

7. On Lincoln's stay in Washington as a congressman, see Samuel Clagett Busey, *Personal Reminiscences and Recollections of Forty-six Years' Membership in the Medical Society of the District of Columbia* (Philadelphia: Donan, 1895), 25–27. Census data for black inhabitants of Washington, D.C., in 1860 are available at https://www.whitehousehistory.org/whha_timelines/images/whha_timeline-african-american.pdf.

8. Benjamin Quarles, *Lincoln and the Negro* (New York: Oxford University Press, 1962), 199–200. See various observations by Keckly in *Behind the Scenes,* 36, 40–41, 50–53, and 67.

9. William H. Townsend, *Lincoln and His Wife's Hometown* (Indianapolis, Ind.: Bobbs-Merrill, 1929), 80–83, suggests that Mary educated Lincoln on the subject of slavery's horrors, a train of thought echoed by Ruth Painter Randall in *Mary Lincoln: Biography of a Marriage* (Boston: Little, Brown, 1953), 30–31, but there is no direct evidence of this. Moreover, Townsend's assertion that Lincoln was already passionately interested in slavery at the time of his courtship of Mary Todd suggests that the author may well be reading Lincoln's Great Emancipator status backward.

10. Helm, *True Story of Mary,* 38–39. Catherine Clinton makes a good case for Mary's early antislavery proclivities in *Mrs. Lincoln: A Life* (New York: HarperCollins, 2009), 20–27. For an interesting and nuanced perspective that sets her views on slavery in the context of her servant relationships, see Fleischner, *Mrs. Lincoln and Mrs. Keckly,* 5. On the Todd family's antislavery leanings, see ibid., 55, and Stephen Berry, *House of Abraham* (Boston: Houghton Mifflin, 2007), 40–41. The account of Mary's meeting with Henry Clay can be found in Helm, *True Story of Mary,* 1–5.

11. Helm, *True Story of Mary,* 23. On Mary's relationship with Sally, see Fleischner, *Mrs. Lincoln and Mrs. Keckly,* 5, 20–23,30–33, 50.

12. Ibid., [CITE STILL TO COME]175; Helm, *True Story of Mary,* 103.

13. Helm, *True Story of Mary,* 19, 51, 111–112, 140–141; Fleischner, *Mrs. Lincoln and Mrs. Keckly,* 50, interprets the practical jokes Mary played on Sally differently than I do here, suggesting that these actions were a ritual "meant to restage and prove" Sally's emotional bonds with Mary. Although that is a plausible interpretation, I would still suggest that such jokes also reinforced a racial differentiation between the two women.

14. Swisshelm's comments are in Justin G. Turner, ed., *Mary Todd Lincoln: Her Life and Letters* (New York: Alfred A. Knopf, 1972), 145. On Mary's urging that Lincoln adopt emancipation, see Clinton, *Mrs. Lincoln,* 182.

15. Keckly, *Behind the Scenes,* 48–49.

16. On Dines's recollections, see Don E. and Virginia Fehrenbacher, eds., *Recollected Words of Abraham Lincoln* (Palo Alto, Calif.: Stanford University Press, 1996), 142, and Washington, *They Knew Lincoln,* 81–85.

17. Benjamin Quarles makes this point well; see Quarles, *Lincoln and the Negro,* 205–206.

18. Lincoln, Speech in Chicago, Illinois, July 10, 1858, CW 2: 501; James Oakes, *The Radical and Republican: Frederick Douglass, Abraham Lincoln, and the Triumph of Antislavery Politics* (New York: W. W. Norton, 2007), 125–126, makes the point that before the war, Lincoln saw race as a distraction and wanted it moved off the table.

19. Lincoln, Address on Colonization to a Deputation of Negroes, August 14, 1862, CW 5: 371.

20. For the routine, perfunctory nature of Lincoln's interaction with Dole (and Indian affairs in general), see, e.g., Lincoln to Caleb B. Smith, April 30, 1861, CW 4: 349; Lincoln to William P. Dole, June 11, 1861, CW 4: 403–404; Designation of William P. Dole to Present Treaty to Delaware Indians, August 7, 1861, CW 4: 476–477; and Lincoln to Edwin M. Stanton, October 9, 1862, CW 5: 455.

21. Michael Burlingame, ed., *Inside Lincoln's White House: The Complete Civil War Diary of John Hay* (Carbondale: Southern Illinois University Press, 1999), 14.

22. Lincoln, Speech to Indians, March 27, 1863, CW 6: 153n.

23. Ibid., 151–152.

24. Ibid., 152.

25. See generally Duane Schultz, *Over the Earth I Come: The Great Sioux Uprising of 1862* (New York: St. Martin's Press, 1993), and Jerry Keenan, *The Great Sioux Uprising: Rebellion on the Plains, August–September 1862* (New York: Da Capo Press, 2003).

26. Keenan, *Great Sioux Uprising,* chap. 4.

27. John Pope to Abraham Lincoln, November 24, 1862, Abraham Lincoln Papers, Library of Congress (hereafter referred to as LPLC); Stephen R. Riggs to Abraham Lincoln, November 17, 1862, LPLC (emphases in original); Thaddeus Williams to Abraham Lincoln, November 22, 1862, LPLC (emphasis in original).

28. William P. Dole to Caleb B. Smith, November 10, 1862, LPLC.

29. Lincoln to John Pope, November 10, 1862, CW 5: 493; Lincoln Henry H. Silbey, December 6, 1862, CW 5: 542–543. The president was himself unsure of his precise authority on this matter and considered designating the task of identifying the exact Indians to be pardoned to an army officer or official who was actually on the scene; see Lincoln to Joseph Holt, December 1, 1862, CW 5: 537–538.

30. Lincoln, Annual Message to Congress, December 1, 1862, CW 5: 525.

31. Speech by Representative Hough, in *Journal of the Missouri State Convention, Held in Jefferson City, June 1863* (St. Louis, Mo.: George Knapp, 1863), 229.

32. D. A. Mahoney, *The Prisoner of State* (New York: Carleton, 1863), 199–200.

33. James W. Hunnicut, *The Conspiracy Unveiled* (Philadelphia: J. B. Lippincott, 1863), 37.

34. Robert Dale Owen, *The Wrong of Slavery, the Right of Emancipation, and the Future of the African Race in the United States* (Philadelphia: J. B. Lippincott, 1864), 224.

35. Mahoney, *Prisoner of State,* 200–201.

36. William Wells Brown, *The Black Man, His Antecedents, His Genius, and His Achievements,* 2nd ed. (New York: Thomas Hamilton, 1863), 218–219.

37. Lincoln, "To Whom It May Concern," August 21, 1863, CW 6: 401.

38. Lincoln, Reply to Loyal Colored People, September 11, 1864, CW 7: 542–543.

39. *New York Times,* September 11, 1864.

40. Lincoln, Response to Evangelical Lutherans, May 13, 1862, CW 5: 212–213; Lincoln, Remarks to Committee of Reformed Presbyterian Synod, July 17, 1862, CW 5: 327; Lincoln, Remarks to Delegation of Progressive Friends, June 20, 1862, CW 5: 278–279; Abraham Lincoln to Abraham Hart, May 13, 1862, CW 5: 212.

41. *The Lincoln Catechism* (New York: J. F. Feeks, 1864), 12, 15, 40, 45. See also Charles B. Flood, *1864: Lincoln at the Gates of History* (New York: Simon & Schuster, 2009), esp. chaps. 13–14, and Sidney Kaplan, "The Miscegenation Issue in the Election of 1864," *Journal of Negro History* 34 (July 1949): 276.

42. See Flood, *1864,* chap. 9.

43. Horace Porter, *Campaigning with Grant* (New York: Century, 1907), 216–217.

44. On Lincoln's troop reviews, see William C. Davis, *Lincoln's Men: How President Lincoln Became Father to an Army and a Nation* (New York: Free Press, 2000).

45. See generally Dudley T. Cornish, *The Sable Arm: Black Troops in the Union Army, 1861–1865,* 2nd ed. (Lawrence: University Press of Kansas, 1987), and Joseph Glatthaar, *Forged in Battle: The Civil War Alliance between Black Soldiers and White Officers* (Baton Rouge: Louisiana State University Press, 2000).

46. Porter, *Campaigning with Grant,* 219–220.

47. Robert H. Wendover, *Views on the Monroe Doctrine; Vital Importance of Peace; Railroads, the Nation's Hope and Blessing; The Progressive Age; Union and Fraternity, etc. etc.* (St. Louis, Mo.: George Knapp, 1865), 30; C. Chauncey Burr, The Old Guard, *a Monthly Journal, Devoted to the Principles of 1776 and 1787* (New York: Van Evrie, Horton, 1864), 2: 168; George R. Graham, "Editors Table," *Graham's Magazine* 42 (1853): 365.

48. See, e.g., Lincoln, Second Debate with Stephen Douglas, August 27, 1858, CW 3: 55–56.

49. *Douglass' Monthly,* September 1861, text available at http://teachingamerican history.org/library/index.asp?document=1459; Oakes, *Radical and Republican,* 99, makes the interesting point that Douglass's view of the Lincoln presidency was early on influenced by his lionization of John Brown.

50. *Douglass' Monthly,* February 1863, text available at http://teachingamerican history.org/library/index.asp?document=428.

51. Oakes, *Radical and Republican,* 212.

52. Ibid., 210–213. In my account, I have drawn on Professor Oakes's excellent use of the multiple sources available concerning this meeting, but I have relied on Douglass's published recollections in his third autobiography, with all due caution concerning the passage of time and possible lapses in his memory.

53. Frederick Douglass, *Life and Times of Frederick Douglass, Written by Himself* (Hartford, Conn.: Park, 1882), 422–423.

54. Oakes, *Radical and Republican,* 215.

55. Douglass, *Life and Times,* 421.

56. Ibid., 434.

57. Ibid., 435.

58. Ibid., 436.

59. Ibid., 439.

60. Ibid., 443–444.

61. Ibid., 444–445.

62. John Stauffer, *Giants: The Parallel Lives of Frederick Douglass and Abraham Lincoln* (New York: Hachette, 2008), 24.

Conclusion

1. Adolphe de Pineton, Marquis de Chambrun, *Impressions of Lincoln and the Civil War: A Foreigner's Account* (New York: Random House, 1952), 38–40.

2. Henry Clay Whitney, *Life of Lincoln,* vol. 2, *Lincoln, the President* (New York: Baker and Taylor, 1908), 322; John Rhodehamel and Louis Taper, eds., *"Right or Wrong, God Judge Me": The Writings of John Wilkes Booth* (Urbana: University of Illinois Press, 1997), 125 (emphases in original).

3. Lincoln, Second Inaugural Address, March 4, 1865, in *The Collected Works of Abraham Lincoln,* 8 vols. and supp., ed. Roy P. Basler (New Brunswick, N.J.: Rutgers University Press) (hereafter referred to as CW), 8: 332–333.

4. Lincoln, Speech in Peoria, Illinois, October 16, 1854, CW 2: 256.

5. Numerous recent scholars have described this "growth thesis," as I would label it, concerning Lincoln and blacks during the war; see, e.g., James Oliver Horton, "Slavery during Lincoln's Lifetime," in *Lincoln and Freedom: Slavery, Emancipation, and the Thirteenth Amendment,* ed. Harold Holzer and Sara Vaughn Gabbard (Carbondale: Southern Illinois University Press, 2007), 14.

6. Lincoln, Response to a Serenade, February 1, 1865, CW 8: 254.

Bibliography

Primary Sources

Abraham Lincoln Papers. Library of Congress. Washington, D.C.

Adams, Francis Colburn. *Justice in the By-ways.* New York: Livermore and Rudd, 1856.

The American Annual Cyclopedia and Register of Important Events of the Year 1862. New York: Appleton, 1863.

The American Annual Cyclopedia and Register of Important Events of the Year 1863. New York: Appleton, 1864.

American Anti-slavery Society. *American Slavery As It Is: Testimony of a Thousand Witnesses.* New York: American Anti-slavery Society, 1839.

Andrews, Ethan Allen. *Slavery and the Domestic Slave Trade in the United States.* Boston: Light and Stearns, 1836.

Baird, Robert. *View of the Valley of the Mississippi, or the Emigrant's and Traveler's Guide to the West,* 2nd ed. Philadelphia: H. S. Tanner, 1834.

Barclay, James. *A Complete and Universal English Dictionary.* London: J. P. and C. Rivington, 1774.

Bartlett, John Russell. *Dictionary of Americanisms,* 3rd ed. Boston: Little, Brown, 1860.

Basler, Roy P., ed. *The Collected Works of Abraham Lincoln,* 8 vols. and supp. New Brunswick, N.J.: Rutgers University Press, 1953.

Bennett, Emerson. *Mike Fink, Legend of the Ohio.* Cincinnati, Ohio: J. A. and U. P. James, 1853.

Berry, Stephen. *House of Abraham.* Boston: Houghton Mifflin, 2007.

Bingham, Caleb. *The* American Preceptor *Improved: Being a New Selection of Lessons for Reading and Speaking, Designed for the Use of Schools.* Boston: J. H. A. Frost, 1829.

Blackstone, Sir William, John E. Hovenden, and Archer Ryland. *Commentaries on the Laws of England,* 2 vols. New York: W. E. Dean, 1838.

Blake, John L. *A Geographical, Chronological, and Historical Atlas, on a New and Improved Plan.* New York: Cook, 1826.

Blassingame, John Y., ed. *The Frederick Douglass Papers,* ser. 1, 4 vols. New Haven, Conn.: Yale University Press, 1999.

Bremer, Frederika, and Mary Botham Howitt. *The Homes of the New World: Impressions of America,* 2 vols. New York: Harper & Brothers, 1858.

Brown, Everett S. "Letters from Louisiana." *Mississippi Valley Historical Review* 11, no. 4 (March 1925): 579–592.

Brown, William Wells. *The American Fugitive in Europe.* Boston: John P. Jewett, 1855.

———. *The Black Man, His Antecedents, His Genius, and His Achievements,* 2nd ed. New York: Thomas Hamilton, 1863.

Buckingham, James S. *The Slave States of America,* 2 vols. London: Fisher, Son, 1842.

Bunyan, John. *The Pilgrim's Progress: From This World to That Which Is to Come.* Boston: Massachusetts Sabbath School Society, 1833.

Burlingame, Michael, ed. *Inside Lincoln's White House: The Complete Civil War Diary of John Hay.* Carbondale: Southern Illinois University Press, 1999.

———, ed. *Lincoln Observed: Civil War Dispatches of Noah Brooks.* Baltimore, Md.: Johns Hopkins University Press, 1998.

Burr, C. Chauncey. The Old Guard, *a Monthly Journal, Devoted to the Principles of 1776 and 1787.* New York: Van Evrie, Horton, 1864.

Busey, Samuel Clagett. *Personal Reminiscences and Recollections of Forty-six Years' Membership in the Medical Society of the District of Columbia.* Philadelphia: Donan, 1895.

Butler, Benjamin. *Autobiography and Personal Reminiscences of Benjamin F. Butler.* Boston: A. M. Thayer, 1892.

Butler, Benjamin F., and Jessie Ames Marshall, eds. *Private and Official Correspondence of Benjamin F. Butler,* 5 vols. Norwood, Mass.: Privately issued, 1917.

Carpenter, Francis B. *Six Months at the White House with Abraham Lincoln: The Story of a Picture.* New York: Hurd and Houghton, 1866.

Carter, Esther May. *She Knew Lincoln.* N.p.: Esther May Carter, 1930.

Chambrun, Adolphe de Pineton, Marquis de. *Impressions of Lincoln and the Civil War: A Foreigner's Account.* New York: Random House, 1952.

Christ, Lynda Laswell, James T. McIntosh, and Mary S. Dix, eds. *The Papers of Jefferson Davis.* Baton Rouge: Louisiana State University Press, 1981.

Clark, George P., ed. *Into the Old Northwest: Journeys with Charles H. Titus, 1841–1846.* East Lansing: Michigan State University Press, 1994.

Clay, Cassius M., and Horace Greeley. *The Writings of Cassius Marcellus Clay.* New York: Harper & Brothers, 1848.

Clinton, Catherine. *Mrs. Lincoln: A Life.* New York: HarperCollins, 2009.

Combe, George. *The Constitution of Man Considered in Relation to External Objects.* Boston: Marsh, Capen and Lyon, 1837.

De Bow, James D. B. *The Industrial Resources, etc., of the Southern and Western States,* 3 vols. New York: John Street, 1852.

Defoe, Daniel. *The Life and Adventures of Robinson Crusoe.* London: A. J. Valpy, 1831.

Delphine [pseud.]. *Solon, or the Rebellion of '61: A Domestic and Political Tragedy.* Chicago: S. P. Rounds, 1862.

Dilworth, Thomas. *A New Guide to the English Tongue.* London: Richard and Henry Causton, 1798.

Dodge, William Sumner. *History of the Old Second Division, Army of the Cumberland.* Chicago: Church and Goodman, 1864.

Douglas, Stephen A. *Speeches of Senator S. A. Douglas, on the Occasion of His Public Receptions by the Citizens of New Orleans, Philadelphia, and Baltimore.* Washington, D.C.: Lemuel Towers, 1859.

———. *The Spurious Kansas Memorial: Debate in the Senate of the United States on the Memorial of James H. Lane.* Washington, D.C.: Union Office, 1856.

Douglass, Frederick. *Life and Times of Frederick Douglass, Written by Himself.* Hartford, Conn.: Park, 1882.

Fehrenbacher, Don E., and Virginia Fehrenbacher, eds. *Recollected Words of Abraham Lincoln.* Palo Alto, Calif.: Stanford University Press, 1996.

Fleming, George Thornton. *History of Pittsburgh and Environs.* New York: American Historical Society, 1922.

Gould, Emerson. *Fifty Years on the Mississippi.* St. Louis, Mo.: Nixon-Jones Printing, 1889.

Helm, Katherine. *The True Story of Mary, Wife of Lincoln.* New York: Harper, 1928.

Herndon, William H. *Herndon's Lincoln: The True Story of a Great Life.* Urbana: University of Illinois Press, 2006.

Hildreth, Samuel Prescott, and Ephraim Cutler. *Biographical and Historical Memoirs of the Early Pioneer Settlers of Ohio.* Cincinnati, Ohio: H. W. Derby, 1852.

Holzer, Harold M., ed. *Dear Mr. Lincoln: Letters to the President.* Reading, Mass.: Addison-Wesley, 1993.

Howe, Henry. *Historical Collections of Ohio,* 2 vols. Norwalk, Ohio: Laning Printing, 1896.

Hundley, Daniel Robinson. *Social Relations in Our Southern States.* New York: Henry B. Price, 1860.

Hunnicut, James W. *The Conspiracy Unveiled.* Philadelphia: J. B. Lippincott, 1863.

Jay, William. *Inquiry into the Character and Tendency, of the American Colonization and Antislavery Societies,* 6th ed. New York: R. G. Williams, 1833.

Keckley, Elizabeth. *Behind the Scenes in the Lincoln White House: Memoirs of an African-American Mistress.* Mineola, N.Y.: Dover, 2006. Originally published in 1868.

Lamon, Ward Hill. *Recollections of Abraham Lincoln.* Lincoln: University of Nebraska Press, 1994. Originally published in 1895.

Latimer, Elizabeth Wormely. *Our Cousin Veronica, or, Scenes and Adventures over the Blue Ridge.* New York: Bunce and Bros., 1855.

The Lincoln Catechism. New York: J. F. Feeks, 1864.

Lincoln Legal Papers. DVD-ROM database. Urbana: University of Illinois Press, 2001.

Little, Lucius P. *Ben Hardin: His Times and Contemporaries.* Louisville, Ky.: Courier-Journal, 1887.

Long, John Dixon, John Wesley, and Richard Watson, eds. *Pictures of Slavery in Church and State,* 3rd ed. Philadelphia: John Dixon Long, 1857.

Mahoney, D. A. *The Prisoner of State.* New York: Carleton, 1863.

Mallory, Daniel, ed. *The Life and Speeches of the Hon. Henry Clay,* 2 vols. Hartford, Conn.: Silas Andrus and Son, 1855.

Nicholas, Samuel Smith. *Conservative Essays, Legal and Political.* Philadelphia: J. B. Lippincott, 1865.

Niven, John, ed. *The Salmon P. Chase Papers,* 2 vols. Kent, Ohio: Kent State University Press, 1993.

Northrup, Solomon. *Twelve Years a Slave.* New York: Miller, Orton and Mulligan, 1855.

Nott, Josiah Clark. *Two Lectures, on the Natural History of the Negro and Caucasian Races.* Mobile, Ala.: Dade and Thompson, 1844.

Olmsted, Frederick Law. *A Journey in the Seaboard Slave States.* New York: Dix and Edwards, 1856.

Owen, Robert Dale. *The Wrong of Slavery, the Right of Emancipation, and the Future of the African Race in the United States.* Philadelphia: J. B. Lippincott, 1864.

Paley, William. *The Principles of Moral and Political Philosophy.* New York: B. and S. Collins, 1835.

Parker, Theodore, and Francis Power Cobbe, eds. *The Collected Works of Theodore Parker.* London: Trubner, 1864.

Poe, Edgar Allan. "Dots and Lines, No. 11; or, Sketches of Scenes and Incidents in the West." In *The Ladies' Companion,* vol. 11. New York: William Snowden, 1839, 69–82.

Pollard, Edward A. *Black Diamonds Gathered in the Darkey Homes of the South.* New York: Pudney and Russell, 1859.

Porter, Horace. *Campaigning with Grant.* New York: Century, 1907.

Priest, Josiah. *Slavery, As It Relates to the Negro, or African Race.* Albany, N.Y.: C. Van Benthuysen, 1845.

Purple, N. H., comp. *A Compilation of the Statutes of the State of Illinois, of a General Nature in Force January 1, 1856,* 2 vols. Chicago: Keen and Lee, 1856.

Quincy, Josiah. *Memoir of the Life of Josiah Quincy, of Massachusetts.* Boston: Cummings, Hilliard, 1825.

Randall, Ruth Painter. *Mary Lincoln: Biography of a Marriage.* Boston: Little, Brown, 1953.

Rhodehamel, John, and Louis Taper, eds. *"Right or Wrong, God Judge Me": The Writings of John Wilkes Booth.* Urbana: University of Illinois Press, 1997.

Roberts, Octavia. *Lincoln in Illinois.* Boston: Houghton Mifflin, 1918.

Sears, Edward I. "Our President and Governors Compared to Petty Princes." *National Quarterly Review* 9 (June 1863): 175–190.

Sears, Stephen W., ed. *The Civil War Papers of George B. McClellan: Selected Corre-spondence, 1860–1865*. New York: Da Capo Press, 1992.

Seward, Frederick. *Reminiscences of a War-Time Statesman and Diplomat, 1830–1915*. New York: G. P. Putnam's, 1916.

Sheahan, James W. *The Life of Stephen A. Douglas*. New York: Harper & Brothers, 1860.

Smith, Margaret Bayard. *A Winter in Washington*. New York: Bliss and White, 1824.

Speed, Joshua. *Reminiscences of Abraham Lincoln and Notes of a Visit to California: Two Lectures*. Louisville, Ky.: John P. Morton, 1884.

Spencer, John H. *A History of Kentucky Baptists from 1769 to 1883*, 2 vols. Cincinnati, Ohio: J. H. Spencer, 1885.

Stowe, Harriet Beecher. *A Key to "Uncle Tom's Cabin."* Boston: John P. Jewett, 1853.

Tixier, Victor. *Tixier's Travels on the Osage Prairies*. Norman: University of Oklahoma Press, 1940. Originally published in 1843.

Townsend, George Alfred. *Washington Inside and Outside*. Hartford, Conn.: James Betts, 1874.

Townsend, William H. *Lincoln and His Wife's Hometown*. Indianapolis, Ind.: Bobbs-Merrill, 1929.

Turner, George. *Traits of Indian Character: As Generally Applicable to the Aborigines of North America*. Philadelphia: Key, Biddle and Minor, 1836.

Turner, Justin G., ed. *Mary Todd Lincoln: Her Life and Letters*. New York: Alfred A. Knopf, 1972.

Villard, Henry. *Lincoln on the Eve of '61*. New York: Alfred A. Knopf, 1941.

Walsh, William Shepard. *Handy Book of Literary Curiosities*. Philadelphia: J. B. Lippincott, 1909.

Weems, Mason Locke. *The Life of George Washington; with Curious Anecdotes, Equally Honourable to Himself, and Exemplary to His Young Countrymen*. Philadelphia: Joseph Allen, 1833.

Weld, Theodore Dwight. *Slavery and the Internal Slave Trade in the United States of North America*. London: Thomas Ward, 1841.

Welles, Gideon. "Administration of Abraham Lincoln." *Galaxy* 24 (October 1877): 438–464.

Wendover, Robert H. *Views on the Monroe Doctrine; Vital Importance of Peace; Rail-roads, the Nation's Hope and Blessing; the Progressive Age; Union and Fraternity, etc. etc.* St. Louis, Mo.: George Knapp, 1865.

White, Andrew Dickson, and Thomas Robinson Dawley. *Old Abe's Jokes*. New York: T. R. Dawley, 1864.

White, Elizur. *Quarterly Anti-slavery Magazine*, vol. 1 New York: New York Anti-slavery Society, 1836.

Whitney, Henry Clay. *Life of Lincoln: Lincoln, the President*, 2 vols. New York: Baker and Taylor, 1908.

———. *Life on the Circuit with Lincoln*. Boston: Estes and Lauriat, 1892.

Wilson, Douglas L., and Rodney O. Davis, eds. *Herndon's Informants: Letters, Inter-*

views and Statements about Abraham Lincoln. Urbana: University of Illinois Press, 2007.

Yacavone, Donald, ed. *A Voice of Thunder: The Civil War Letters of George E. Stephens.* Urbana: University of Illinois Press, 1997.

Secondary Sources

Aarim-Heriot, Najia. *Chinese Immigrants, African-Americans, Racial Anxiety in the United States, 1848–1882.* Urbana: University of Illinois Press, 2003.

Allen, Michael. *Western Rivermen, 1763–1861: Ohio and Mississippi Boatmen and the Myth of the Alligator Horse.* Baton Rouge: Louisiana State University Press, 1994.

Allen, Theodore W. *The Invention of the White Race: The Origin of Racial Oppression in America.* New York: Verso, 1997.

Allport, Gordon W. *The Nature of Prejudice,* 25th ed. New York: Basic Books, 1979.

Anderson, Dwight G. *Abraham Lincoln: The Quest for Immortality.* New York: Alfred A. Knopf, 1982.

Baker, Lee D. *From Savage to Negro: Anthropology and the Construction of Race, 1896–1954.* Berkeley: University of California Press, 1998.

Bakken, Dawn E. "A Young Hoosier's Adventures on the Mississippi River." *Indiana Magazine of History* 102 (March 2006): 1–7.

Baldwin, James. *Abraham Lincoln: A True Life.* New York: American Book, 1904.

Barnhart, John D., and Donald F. Carmony. *Indiana: From Frontier to Industrial Commonwealth.* New York: Lewis Historical, 1954.

Barnhart, John D., and Dorothy L. Riker. *Indiana to 1816: The Colonial Period.* Indianapolis: Indiana Historical Society, 1971.

Baron, Andrew Scott, and Mahzarin Banaji. "The Development of Implicit Attitudes." *Psychological Science* 17 (January 2006): 53–58.

Barton, William E. *The Paternity of Abraham Lincoln.* New York: George E. Doran, 1920.

Berkhofer, Robert F., Jr. *The White Man's Indian: Images of the American Indian from Columbus to the Present.* New York: Alfred A. Knopf, 1978.

Bernstein, Iver. *The New York City Draft Riots: Their Significance for American Society and Politics in the Age of the Civil War.* New York: Oxford University Press, 1990.

Bilotta, James G. *Race and the Rise of the Republican Party, 1848–1865.* New York: Libris, 1992.

Blassingame, John W. *The Slave Community: Plantation Life in the Antebellum South,* 2nd ed. Oxford: Oxford University Press, 1979.

Blight, David W. *Frederick Douglass and Abraham Lincoln: A Relationship in Language, Politics, and Memory.* Milwaukee, Wis.: Marquette University Press, 2001.

Boritt, Gabor S. *The Gettysburg Gospel: The Lincoln Speech That Nobody Knows.* New York: Simon & Schuster, 2006.

———, ed. *The Historian's Lincoln: Pseudohistory, Psychohistory, and History.* Urbana: University of Illinois Press, 1996.

———. *Lincoln and the Economics of the American Dream,* 2nd ed. Urbana: University of Illinois Press, 1994.

Bray, Robert. *Reading with Lincoln.* Carbondale: Southern Illinois University Press, 2010.

Browne, Francis Fisher. *The Everyday Life of Abraham Lincoln.* Lincoln: University of Nebraska Press, 1995. Originally published in 1887.

Burlingame, Michael S. *Abraham Lincoln: A Life,* 2 vols. Baltimore, Md.: Johns Hopkins University Press, 2008.

———. *The Inner World of Abraham Lincoln.* Urbana: University of Illinois Press, 1997.

Carwardine, Richard. *Lincoln: A Life of Purpose and Power.* New York: Alfred A. Knopf, 2006.

Cayton, Andrew R. L. *Frontier Indiana.* Bloomington: Indiana University Press, 1996.

Chapman, Mary, and Glenn Hendler, eds. *Sentimental Men: Masculinity and the Politics of Affect in American Culture.* Berkeley: University of California Press, 1999.

Chavez, Thomas E. *Manual Alvarez, 1794–1856: A Biography.* Niwot: University Press of Colorado, 1990.

Clinton, Catherine. *Mrs. Lincoln: A Life.* New York: HarperCollins, 2009.

Coffin, Charles Carleton. *Abraham Lincoln.* New York: Harper & Brothers, 1893.

Colaiaco, James A. *Frederick Douglass and the Fourth of July Oration.* New York: Palgrave Macmillan, 2006.

Cornish, Dudley T. *The Sable Arm: Black Troops in the Union Army, 1861–1865,* 2nd ed. Lawrence: University Press of Kansas, 1987.

Cox, LaWanda. *Lincoln and Black Freedom: A Study in Presidential Leadership,* 2nd ed. Columbia: University of South Carolina Press, 1994.

Dasgupta, Nilanjana. "Automatic Preference for White Americans: Eliminating the Familiarity Explanation." *Journal of Experimental Social Psychology* 36 (2000): 316–328.

Davis, William C. *Lincoln's Men: How President Lincoln Became Father to an Army and a Nation.* New York: Free Press, 2000.

Dew, Charles P. *Apostles of Disunion: Southern Secession Commissioners and the Causes of the War.* Charlottesville: University of Virginia Press, 2002.

Dirck, Brian. *Lincoln and Davis: Imagining America, 1809–1865.* Lawrence: University Press of Kansas, 2001.

———, ed. *Lincoln Emancipated: The President and the Politics of Race.* DeKalb: Northern Illinois University Press, 2007.

———. *Lincoln the Lawyer.* Urbana: University of Illinois Press, 2007.

Donald, David H. *Lincoln.* New York: Simon & Schuster, 1995.

———. *"We Are Lincoln Men": Abraham Lincoln and His Men.* New York: Simon & Schuster, 2003.

Dunbar, Seymour. *A History of Travel in America.* Indianapolis, Ind.: Bobbs-Merrill, 1915.

Dunbar-Nelson, Alice. "People of Color in Louisiana, Part I." *Journal of Negro History* 1, no. 4 (October 1916): 361–366.

Esarey, Logan. *History of Indiana from the Exploration to 1922,* 3 vols. Dayton, Ohio: Dayton Historical, 1922.

Essah, Patience. *A House Divided: Slavery and Emancipation in Delaware, 1635–1865.* Charlottesville: University of Virginia Press, 1996.

Evans, Nelson W. "The First Steamboat on the Ohio." *Ohio History* 16 (July 1907): 310–315.

Fellman, Michael. *Inside War: The Guerrilla Conflict in Missouri during the Civil War.* Oxford: Oxford University Press, 1990.

Fiore, Jordan D. "Mr. Lincoln's Portuguese Neighbors." *Lincoln Herald* 74 (Fall 1972): 150–152.

Fite, Emerson David. *The Presidential Campaign of 1860,* 3 vols. New York: Macmillan, 1910.

Fleischner, Jennifer. *Mrs. Lincoln and Mrs. Keckly: The Remarkable Story of the Friendship between a First Lady and a Former Slave.* New York: Broadway Books, 2004.

Flood, Charles B. *1864: Lincoln at the Gates of History.* New York: Simon & Schuster, 2009.

Follett, Richard. *The Sugar Masters: Planters and Slaves in Louisiana's Cane World, 1820–1860.* Baton Rouge: Louisiana State University Press, 2007.

Foner, Eric. *The Fiery Trial: Abraham Lincoln and American Slavery.* New York: W. W. Norton, 2010.

———, ed. *Our Lincoln: New Perspectives on Lincoln and His World.* New York: W. W. Norton, 2009.

Forgie, George P. *Patricide in the House Divided: A Psychological Interpretation of Lincoln and His Age.* New York: W. W. Norton, 1979.

Fredrickson, George M. *Big Enough to Be Inconsistent: Abraham Lincoln Confronts Slavery and Race.* Cambridge, Mass.: Harvard University Press, 2008.

Genovese, Eugene. *Roll, Jordan, Roll: The World the Slaves Made.* New York: Vintage Books, 1976.

Glatthaar, Joseph. *Forged in Battle: The Civil War Alliance between Black Soldiers and White Officers.* Baton Rouge: Louisiana State University Press, 2000.

Goldberg, David M. *The Curse of Ham: Race and Slavery in Early Judaism, Christianity, and Islam.* Princeton, N.J.: Princeton University Press, 2005.

Guelzo, Allen C. *Abraham Lincoln, Redeemer President.* Grand Rapids, Mich.: Eerdman's, 1999.

———. *Lincoln's Emancipation Proclamation: The End of Slavery in America.* New York: Simon & Schuster, 2006.

Haites, Erik F., James Mak, and Gary M. Walton. *Western River Transportation: The Era of Early Internal Development, 1810–1860.* Baltimore, Md.: Johns Hopkins University Press, 1974.

Harrison, Lowell Hayes. *Lincoln of Kentucky.* Lexington: University Press of Kentucky, 2000.

Hartigan, John, Jr. *Odd Tribes: Toward a Cultural Analysis of White People.* Durham, N.C.: Duke University Press, 2005.

Hill, Mike, ed. *Whiteness: A Critical Reader.* New York: New York University Press, 1995.

Hofstadter, Richard. *The American Political Tradition and the Men Who Made It.* New York: Alfred A. Knopf, 1968.

Holzer, Harold, and Sara Vaughn Gabbard, eds. *Lincoln and Freedom: Slavery, Emanci-*

pation, and the Thirteenth Amendment. Carbondale: Southern Illinois University Press, 2007.

Holzer, Harold, Edna Greene Medford, and Frank J. Williams. The Emancipation Proclamation: Three Views. Baton Rouge: Louisiana State University Press, 2006.

Ignatiev, Noel. How the Irish Became White. New York: Routledge, 2008.

Jacobson, Matthew F. Whiteness of a Different Color: European Immigrants and the Alchemy of Race. Cambridge, Mass.: Harvard University Press, 1999.

Jaynes, Gerald D. Encyclopedia of African-American Society, 2 vols. New York: Sage, 2005.

Johnson, Allen. Stephen A. Douglas: A Study in American Politics. New York: Macmillan, 1908.

Johnson, Emory R., Thurman William Van Metre, Grover G. Huebner, and D. S. Hanchett. History of Foreign and Domestic Commerce in the United States, 2nd ed. Washington, D.C.: Carnegie, 1922.

Johnson, Walter. Soul by Soul: Life inside the Antebellum Slave Market. Cambridge, Mass.: Harvard University Press, 1999.

Jones, Edgar De Witt. Lincoln and the Preachers. New York: Harper & Row, 1948.

Jordan, Winthrop D. White over Black: American Attitudes toward the Negro, 1550–1812. Chapel Hill: University of North Carolina Press, 1968.

Jung, Patrick J. The Black Hawk War of 1832. Norman: University of Oklahoma Press, 2008.

Kane, Adam I. The Western River Steamboat. College Station: Texas A&M University Press, 2004.

Kaplan, Sidney. "The Miscegenation Issue in the Election of 1864." Journal of Negro History 34 (July 1949): 276–288.

Keenan, Jerry. The Great Sioux Uprising: Rebellion on the Plains, August–September 1862. New York: Da Capo Press, 2003.

Klingaman, William K. Abraham Lincoln and the Road to Emancipation, 1861–1865. New York: Viking Press, 2001.

Klinkner, Philip A., and Rogers M. Smith. The Unsteady March: The Rise and Decline of Racial Equality in America. Chicago: University of Chicago Press, 1999.

Kolchin, Peter. "Whiteness Studies: The New History of Race in America." Journal of American History 89 (June 2002): 154–173.

Leffel, John C. History of Posey County, Indiana. Chicago: Standard, 1913.

Lucas, Marion B. A History of Blacks in Kentucky: From Slavery to Segregation, 1760–1891. Lexington: Kentucky Historical Society, 2003.

Mabee, Carleton. "Sojourner Truth and President Lincoln." New England Quarterly 61 (December 1988): 519–529.

Magness, Phillip W. "Benjamin Butler's Colonization Testimony Reevaluated." Journal of the Abraham Lincoln Association 29 (Summer 2009): 1–27.

Magness, Phillip W., and Sebastian N. Page. Colonization after Emancipation: Lincoln and the Movement for Black Resettlement. Columbia: University of Missouri Press, 2010.

Mak, James, and Gary M. Walton. "The Persistence of Old Technologies: The Case of Flatboats." *Journal of Economic History* 33 (March 1973): 444–451.

Masur, Kate. "The African American Delegation to Abraham Lincoln: A Reappraisal." *Civil War History* 56 (June 2010): 117–144.

Mayer, Henry. *All on Fire: William Lloyd Garrison and the Abolition of Slavery.* New York: St. Martin's Press, 1998.

McKivigan, John R., and Stanley Harrold, eds. *Antislavery Violence: Sectional, Racial, and Cultural Conflict in Antebellum America.* Knoxville: University of Tennessee Press, 1999.

McMurtry, R. Gerald. "The Lincoln Migration from Kentucky to Indiana." *Indiana Magazine of History* 33 (December 1937): 385–421.

Miller, William Lee. *Lincoln's Virtues: An Ethical Biography.* New York: Alfred A. Knopf, 2002.

Morris, Jan. *Lincoln: A Foreigner's Quest.* New York: Da Capo Press, 2000.

Neely, Mark E. "Lincoln's Lyceum Speech and the Origins of a Modern Myth." *Lincoln Lore* no. 1776 (February 1987): 1–4.

Oakes, James. *The Radical and Republican: Frederick Douglass, Abraham Lincoln, and the Triumph of Antislavery Politics.* New York: W. W. Norton, 2007.

Ostendorf, Lloyd. *Lincoln's Unknown Private Life: An Oral History by His House-keeper Mariah Vance, 1850–1860.* Mamaroneck, N.Y.: Hastings House, 1995.

———. "A Monument for One of the Lincoln Maids." *Lincoln Herald* 66 (Winter 1964): 184–186.

Painter, Nell Irvin. *The History of White People.* New York: W. W. Norton, 2010.

———. *Sojourner Truth: A Life, a Symbol.* New York: W. W. Norton, 1996.

Paludan, Phillip S. "Lincoln and Colonization: Policy or Propaganda?" *Journal of the Abraham Lincoln Association* 25 (Winter 2004): 23–37.

———. "Lincoln and Negro Slavery: I Haven't Got Time for the Pain." *Journal of the Abraham Lincoln Association* 27 (Summer 2006): 1–24.

———. *The Presidency of Abraham Lincoln.* Lawrence: University Press of Kansas, 1994.

Patterson, Meagan, and Rebecca S. Bigler. "Preschool Children's Attention to Environmental Messages about Groups: Social Categorization and the Origins of Intergroup Bias." *Child Development* 77 (July 2006): 847–860.

Phillips, Ulrich B. *A History of Transportation in the Eastern Cotton Belt to 1860.* New York: Columbia University Press, 1908.

Pratt, Harry E. *The Personal Finances of Abraham Lincoln.* Springfield, Ill.: Abraham Lincoln Association, 1943.

Quarles, Benjamin. *Lincoln and the Negro.* New York: Oxford University Press, 1962.

Randall, James G., and Richard N. Current. *Lincoln the President: Last Full Measure,* 4 vols. Urbana: University of Illinois, 1955.

Roediger, David R. *The Wages of Whiteness: Race and the Making of the American Working Class,* 2nd ed. New York: Verso, 2007.

———. *Working towards Whiteness: How America's Immigrants Became White—The Strange Journey from Ellis Island to the Suburbs.* New York: Basic Books, 2006.

Rotundo, E. Anthony. *American Manhood: Transformations in Masculinity from the Revolution to the Modern Era.* New York: Basic Books, 1994.

Savage, Kirk. *Standing Soldiers, Kneeling Slaves: Race, War and Monument in Nineteenth-Century America.* Princeton, N.J.: Princeton University Press, 1997.

Schmitz, Mark D. "Economies of Scale and Farm Size in the Antebellum Sugar Sector." *Journal of Economic History* 37, no. 4 (December 1977): 959–980.

Schultz, Duane. *Over the Earth I Come: The Great Sioux Uprising of 1862.* New York: St. Martin's Press, 1993.

Seale, William. *The President's House.* Washington, D.C.: White House Historical Association, 1986.

Sears, Richard D. *The Kentucky Abolitionists in the Midst of Slavery, 1854–1864: Exiles for Freedom.* New York: Edwin Mellen Press, 1993.

Shankle, George E. *American Nicknames.* Chicago: Putnam's, 1955.

Shenk, Joshua L. *Lincoln's Melancholy: How Depression Challenged a President and Fueled His Greatness.* New York: Mariner Books, 2006.

Shoemaker, Nancy. "How the Indians Got to Be Red." *American Historical Review* 102 (June 1997): 625–644.

Simmons, Marc. *Murder on the Santa Fe Trail: An International Incident, 1843.* El Paso: Texas Western Press, 1987.

Sitterson, J. Caryle. "Magnolia Plantation, 1852–1862: A Decade of a Louisiana Sugar Estate." *Mississippi Valley Historical Review* 25, no. 2 (September 1938): 199–211.

Stauffer, John. *The Black Hearts of Men: Radical Abolitionists and the Transformation of Race.* Cambridge, Mass.: Harvard University Press, 2002.

———. *Giants: The Parallel Lives of Frederick Douglass and Abraham Lincoln.* New York: Hachette, 2008.

Striner, Richard. *Father Abraham: Lincoln's Relentless Struggle to End Slavery.* Oxford: Oxford University Press, 2007.

Talty, Stephan. *Mulatto America: At the Crossroads of Black and White Culture—A Social History.* New York: Harper, 2004.

Tarbell, Ida M. *The Early Life of Abraham Lincoln.* New York: S. S. McClure, 1896.

Thomas, Benjamin. *Abraham Lincoln: A Biography,* 3rd ed. Carbondale: Southern Illinois University Press, 2008. Originally published in 1952.

Thornton, Richard H. *An American Glossary.* Philadelphia: J. B. Lippincott, 1912.

Trask, Kerry A. *Black Hawk: The Battle for the Heart of America.* New York: Henry Holt, 2007.

Van Natter, Francis Marion. *Lincoln's Boyhood: A Chronicle of His Indiana Years.* Washington, D.C.: Public Affairs Press, 1963.

Vorenberg, Michael. "Abraham Lincoln and the Politics of Black Colonization." *Journal of the Abraham Lincoln Association* 14 (Summer 1993): 23–46.

Walvin, James. *Questioning Slavery.* New York: Routledge, 1996.

Warren, Louis A. *Lincoln's Youth: Indiana Years, 1816–1830,* 2nd ed. Indianapolis: Indiana Historical Society, 2002.

Washington, John E. *They Knew Lincoln.* New York: Dutton, 1942.

Weicek, William M. *The Sources of Antislavery Constitutionalism in America, 1760–1848*. Ithaca, N.Y.: Cornell University Press, 1977.

Whipple, Wayne. *The Story-Life of Lincoln*. Philadelphia: John C. Winston, 1908.

Williams, Eric. "Laissez-Faire, Sugar and Slavery." *Political Science Quarterly* 58, no. 1 (March 1943): 67–82.

Williams, Gary Lee. "James and Joshua Speed: Lincoln's Kentucky Friends." Ph.D. diss., Duke University, 1971.

Wilson, Douglas L. *Honor's Voice: The Transformation of Abraham Lincoln*. New York: Vintage Books, 1999.

———. *Lincoln before Washington: New Perspectives on the Illinois Years*. Urbana: University of Illinois Press, 1997.

Wilson, Woodrow. *Division and Reunion, 1829–1889*. New York: Longmans, Green, 1893.

Winkle, Kenneth J. *The Young Eagle: The Rise of Abraham Lincoln*. New York: Taylor, 2001.

Zall, Paul M. *Abe Lincoln Laughing: Humorous Anecdotes from Original Sources by and about Abraham Lincoln*. Berkeley: University of California Press, 1982.

Index

and slavery in the South, 86
and slavery in Washington, D.C., 51
and slaves aboard the *Lebanon,*
    45–46, 53–62, 95
Southern roots, 36, 87
and Southerners, 64, 76–77, 86–87,
    90, 129–132, 134
as a state legislator, 47, 50–51
and Stephen Douglas, 72–73, 75–84
Temperance Address, 52, 60
temperance of, 41
and white racism, 63–64, 74–75,
    82–83, 86, 89, 97–100, 103–107,
    115–116, 122–129, 131,
    135–136, 141–142, 158–159
and white trash stereotypes, 36–43,
    123
and women, 53, 159
Lincoln, Abraham (grandfather), 14
Lincoln Catechism, 150
Lincoln, Josiah (uncle), 14
Lincoln, Mary (wife)
    mentioned, 31, 33, 45, 51–52, 61,
        75, 119, 138
    racial attitude of, 139–140
Lincoln, Mordecai (uncle), 14–15
Lincoln, Nancy Hanks (mother), 25, 36
Lincoln, Robert (son), 137
Lincoln, Sara Bush (stepmother), 41
Lincoln, Thomas (father)
    mentioned, 5, 7, 14, 17, 18, 25
    relationship with Abraham Lincoln,
        38–39, 41
    as white trash, 32, 38–40
Long, J. B., 90
Louisiana
    race in, 20–21
    reconstruction in, 124, 131

Magness, Phillip, 128
Mammy Sally, 139
Martin, Mary, 48–49

Martin, Samuel, 48–49
May, William, 49
McClellan, George B., 103
McClernand, John, 131
McMahon, John, 135–136
Mexicans, fear of race mixing with, 66
Minnesota, Sioux uprising in, 144–146
Miscegenation. *See* Amalgamation,
    racial
Mississippi River, 5, 7, 20–24, 26–28,
    35, 44
Missouri
    emancipation in, 124, 146
    ethnic stereotyping of "pukes" in,
        30, 34
Mitchell, Cornelia, 138
Morel, Lucas, 2
Morris, Jan, 30–31
Morton, Samuel George, 68

Napier, Elias, 49
Napier v. Woolridge (1845), 49
Native Americans
    and African Americans, 12, 142
    in Kentucky, 8
    and Lincoln, 14–16, 48–49,
        142–146
    and Lincoln's law practice, 48–49
    as savage, 11–15, 19–20, 52, 66,
        143, 146
    Sioux Uprising (1862), 144–146
    and white trash stereotypes, 34–35
Nelson (slave), 31
New Guide to the English Tongue, 10
New Orleans, Louisiana, 9, 26, 28–29
New Salem, Illinois, 27, 37, 39, 41–42,
    47
New Ulm, Minnesota, 144
New York City draft riots, 128
Nicolay, John, 135–136
Northwest Ordinance (1787), 8
Nott, Josiah, 68, 70

Washington, D.C.
  mentioned, 31, 50, 51, 90, 94,
    96, 122, 135
  racial environment of, 138–
    139
Washington, George, 1, 13–14, 16,
  42
Washington Society of Colored
  People, 52
Washington Temperance Society,
  52, 60
Webster, Noah, 10
Webster's Dictionary, 10, 16
Weems, Mason Locke ("Parson"),
  13–14, 40
Weld, Theodore Dwight, 64
Welles, Gideon, 99–100
Whig Party, 73

Whiteness
  anxieties associated with, 30, 65–69,
    88–89, 94, 99, 127, 146–147
  and childhood, 11–12
  and citizenship, 10
  historical studies of, 2
  and language, 10–11
  and the law, 50
  as neutral racial identity, 3–4, 50,
    115, 135–136
  and the Other, 11, 63, 70, 141–142,
    148, 159
  and scientific racism, 68–69
  white trash stereotypes, 30–39
Wickliffe, Charles, 117
Williams, Thaddeus, 145
Wilson, Woodrow, 30–31
Woolridge, Clairborne, 49